WITHDRAWN

W0081995

THE UNIVERSITY OF TEXAS AT AUSTIN
THE GENERAL LIBRARIES
PERRY-CASTAÑEDA LIBRARY

DATE DUE	DATE RETURNED
JUL 1 4 1989 PCL	RET'D JUN 2 1 1989 PCL
MAR 1 8 1991 PCL	RET'D RET'D FEB 0 1 1994 PCL PCL
FEB 2 8 1994 PCL	

JU

EXCELLENCE <u> </u> IN SCHOOL
MEDIA
PROGRAMS

EXCELLENCE

IN SCHOOL MEDIA PROGRAMS

Thomas J. Galvin
Margaret Mary Kimmel
Brenda H. White, editors

American Library Association
Chicago 1980

Library of Congress Cataloging in Publication Data

Main entry under title:

Excellence in school media programs.

"Bibliography of Elizabeth T. Fast": p.
Includes bibliographical references.

1. School libraries—Addresses, essays, lectures. 2. Instructional materials centers—Addresses, essays, lectures. 3. Fast, Elizabeth T., 1931-1977—Addresses, essays, lectures. I. Fast, Elizabeth T., 1931-1977. II. Galvin, Thomas J.   III. Kimmel, Margaret Mary. IV. White, Brenda.   Z675.S3E94   027.8   79-26944

ISBN 0-8389-3239-8

Copyright © 1980 by the American Library Association

All rights reserved. No part of this publication may be reproduced in any form without permission in writing from the publisher, except by a reviewer who may quote brief passages in a review.

Printed in the United States of America

CONTENTS

To the memory of Elizabeth T. Fast:

> There be childer and there be childer in
> this world, but ye'd have to go the
> length and breadth of it to find the likes
> of this one. She had a way of her own and
> she had it entirely.
>
> —from an Irish folktale

PREFACE

The occasion of this book is the celebration of a tragically short but richly productive professional life. When Elizabeth T. Fast died in 1977, the American Association of School Librarians wished to create a living memorial to her as one of its most distinguished members. We have been honored to serve as editors of this collection consisting of articles both by Betty Fast herself and by others in the school media field. All the contributors hope that this book will be at once worthy of the memory of the woman we seek to honor, as well as useful to her colleagues, current and future, in the school library-media community.

Many individuals helped to make this book possible. Our sincerest thanks go to those leaders in the school library-media world who contributed the original papers that make up the greater part of this volume. Special appreciation is due the officers and members of the Board of Directors of AASL; the AASL Ad Hoc Committee to Recommend an Appropriate Memorial to Betty Fast; the AASL Publications Advisory Committee; the anonymous donor whose gift to AASL provided for secretarial, travel, research and other costs of manuscript preparation; Nicholas Fast, Bernice Yesner, and Leona Kanter, who faciliated the compilation of the bibliography; Karen Schirra, who prepared the final manuscript; and Jane Ries, who handled numerous details of correspondence, record keeping, and project management.

Finally, we acknowledge with deep appreciation the personal commitment to the project of Donald E. Stewart, Associate Executive Director for Publishing Services, and Alice Fite, Executive Secretary of the American Association of School Librarians of the American Library Association. Without their interest, assistance, and support, this book would not exist.

THOMAS J. GALVIN
MARGARET M. KIMMEL
BRENDA H. WHITE

INTRODUCTION

by THOMAS J. GALVIN

This book is about several things—children, schools, learning, libraries, reading, viewing, and listening. But it is chiefly about the life and enduring legacy of an extraordinary woman—Elizabeth T. Fast.

Betty Fast died on June 16, 1977, at age forty-six. But what is important is not when she died, or even how long she lived, but *how* she lived. How she lived her professional life as a librarian is what this book commemorates. It was planned and prepared as a tribute to the idea of excellence in library media services to children and youth, because Betty Fast's career was the embodiment of an unswerving commitment to excellence.

That career is summarized in the bibliography of her writings and the affectionate biographical remembrance by a close friend and professional colleague that completes the opening section of this volume. Interspersed throughout the rest of the book are selections from her published writings. These have been chosen in part because they provide a natural structure for the four major themes—the child, the school media center, the community, the future—around which this collection of essays is organized, but principally because of their enduring value to those who serve the library and media needs of the young. One major objective of this book has been to assure that at least a portion of the written record of Betty Fast's thinking about key professional issues and concerns is preserved in an easily accessible form for both practicing and prospective library-media professionals.

The nine selections from Betty Fast's many contributions to the literature of librarianship incorporated in this volume reveal something of the unusually broad range of her professional interests. They also capture a small portion of the product of an extraordinarily active and inquiring mind. Little in the world of ideas escaped her attention, and nothing even remotely relevant to her central professional concern—children and media—was alien to her interest. She read widely, and she had the rare capacity to see relationships that most of the rest of us would have been likely to overlook. Of more importance, she had the true librarian's gift for sharing what she read, saw, and heard in a way that stimulated others to investigate and explore new ideas through reading, viewing, and listening.

Perhaps most characteristic are the seven "Mediacentric" columns that she contributed to the *Wilson Library Bulletin* between January, 1976, and October, 1977. She originated that feature, which proved the perfect vehicle for placing her ideas before the school library-media community. The "Mediacentric" columns deal with topics that are immediate, relevant, and practical, but the treatments are neither prosaic nor pedestrian. The approach is inevitably fresh, penetrating, and positive. She had the editorialist's talent to focus intensively on a specific issue or concept, and to expand an idea within strict limitations of space. Her thought patterns were telegraphic rather than monographic, so that her prose generated a kind of contagious enthusiasm that matched her personality. What is most extraordinary about these columns is that they were all produced during the last sixteen months of a courageous five-year battle against the cancer that finally ended her life two months after the April, 1977, talk at Kent State University that appeared as her last written contribution to her profession, published alongside her obituary, in *WLB*.

But Betty Fast's bibliography is neither an adequate summary nor even a partial measure of her contribution to her profession. Her influence extended far beyond the written word to touch the minds and lives of those of us among her contemporaries who had the good fortune to know her. The eighteen original essays by nineteen authors prepared especially for this book collectively reveal something of that other, larger dimension of her career. Almost without exception, they reflect a substantial explicit or implicit debt to her thinking on professional issues.

A general comment about the nineteen contributors is in order here. All of their essays were written for this book at the invitation of the editors. Contributors were selected on the basis of their stature in the school and children's fields, because of the quality of their previous contributions to the professional literature, and because of their personal associations with Betty Fast. Each was free to select his or her own subject, within the broad context of a very general, four-part thematic outline. Each author was asked to address a topic that he or she knew best and felt most strongly about. As a consequence, the papers deliberately reflect a range of styles, from the personal to the dispassionate, from research studies to essays of opinion. What unifies them, in my view, is not merely or even primarily their relationship to the thought or the writings of Betty Fast, but their direct relevance to that central passion for excellence in library-media services to children that was the ráison d'être of her career as a librarian.

It is appropriate that the first of the book's four major sections is entitled "The Child" for, as Betty Fast consistently reminded us, the child is central to the whole library-media enterprise. Lillian Gerhardt's opening paper challenges some traditional stereotypes that have resulted in library-media collections for children that fall short of the ideal of excellence. Clara Jackson's paper reviews the interactions between children and media resources as these are revealed in the literature. Margaret Mary Kimmel examines the persistent, complex, and critical issue of the child's right to know. Virginia Crowe considers the role of the child not as consumer, but as producer and creator of media.

Just as Betty Fast's career as a librarian began with a concern for children and progressed to a recognition of the importance of the school-media program to the development of children, so the second part of this book comprises five papers that focus on critical aspects of the school-media center. Blanche Woolls offers a practical, workable approach to that most pressing current problem—the demand for accountability. Alice Fite sketches out the evolution of the contemporary model of excellence against which the elementary school-media program must be measured. Recognizing that the building-level school-media program cannot operate successfully in isolation, Richard L. Darling provides an essential perspective on quality from the standpoint of the district level. In a thought-provoking essay, Evelyn H. Daniel considers the school-media specialist as an autonomous, self-evaluating professional fulfilling the role and responsibilities of "media manager." Cosette N. Kies returns to the theme of accountability and evaluation from the most important vantage point of all, that of the ultimate user. She writes, in words Betty Fast would have applauded, "It is *student* use and understanding of the school-media center that justify the existence of school-media centers."

The third section of the book places the school-media center and its program in the larger context of the community served by the school and the media specialist. Following Betty Fast's eloquent plea for an adherence to standards of excellence in times of fiscal adversity, a Connecticut colleague, D. Philip Baker, examines current and likely future patterns of expanding community-based learning in their impact on schools and library-media services. Kay E. Vandergrift's paper considers field experience as the essential bridge between principle and application in the community setting for the prospective school-media specialist. Patricia B. Pond examines the present and potential impact of school library-media professionals in the larger context of their national associations, an aspect of the professional role to which Betty Fast gave a generous share of her time, energy, and talent. Phyllis Land exemplifies the manner in which individual schools will increasingly need to overcome the illusion of self-sufficiency through linkages with emerging state, regional, and national resource-sharing networks.

The final portion of this collection of essays looks beyond the current scene to opportunities the future may hold for those school media specialists who, like Betty Fast, have the capacity and the courage to convert optimsitic hopes and dreams into realities. Morton Schindel describes how the woman to whose memory this book is dedicated contributed to his own acknowledged role as a shaper of the future in film. Given Betty Fast's personal commitment to continued learning both for herself and others, this volume would have been incomplete without Bernard S. Schlessinger's and Patricia Jensen's thoughtful consideration of the special needs and concerns of school-media professionals in continuing education. Jane Anne Hannigan examines controversial issues in the pre-service education of school library-media specialists in the graduate library school setting, in terms of the competencies needed in responding to institutional and social change. The political arena, a milieu in which Betty Fast flourished, is the subject of Thomas Hart's paper on accreditation and legislative programs. The volume concludes with a deeply personal reflection by Peggy A. Sullivan on the significance of Betty Fast's service to the local, state, and national committees.

Despite its broad scope, this volume could not begin to encompass the range of Betty Fast's professional interests or even of her contributions to the school library-media field. As Clara Stanton Jones, then president of the American Library Association, wrote at the time of her death, "Betty's life demonstrated love in control, with courage triumphant." If the many individuals who helped to make this book have collectively managed to capture even a portion of those unique qualities that were central to the character of the woman whose life is celebrated here, then it will have been well worth the making.

BIOGRAPHY OF BETTY FAST

by BERNICE YESNER

Elizabeth Astrid Trygstad was born on Sunday, February 8, 1931, on Long Island, New York, and quickly proved the prophecy "a child that's born on the Sabbath Day is fair and wise and good and gay." She was the first of the three children of Dr. Ethel Hirsch Trygstad, a pediatrician, and Dr. Reidar Trygstad, a practitioner of general medicine. Betty's younger sister, Paula, became a pediatrician and her brother, Carl, is an associate professor at U.C.L.A. specializing in pediatric neurology. It is clear that a strong interest in the welfare and development of children was nurtured in the Trygstad home, but Betty chose the fields of librarianship and education, rather than medicine, in which to further her ideas for service to young people.

Betty attended the local public schools and graduated from Bay Shore High in 1948. The school yearbook has many pictures of Betty at 16 and 17 showing her active in many groups—from basketball to orchestra. Capture of first prize in the American Legion Oratorical Contest and "Best Speaker" with the debating team presaged her future as a lecturer. She was on the staff of both the yearbook and the school newspaper, becoming associate editor of the latter in her junior year and editor-in-chief as a senior. The faculty advisor referred to her as the best editor he ever had. Here were the beginnings of the rich outpouring of her writings which ran the gamut from irate letters to the editor of the local newspaper to a regular column in the *Wilson Library Bulletin*. In the yearbook roster of the class of 1948, Betty's picture shows the same grin and the direct look at the camera that remained unchanged through subsequent years. "We shall always remember Elizabeth Trygstad as the brilliant blond bombshell who amazes all of us with her ability to do anything, any time."

Betty and Nicholas Fast were "going together" before she left for Radcliffe, and they were married in 1950 while she was still a "Cliffie" and Nick was at M.I.T. In her junior year, Betty was elected to Phi Beta Kappa and in 1952 she was graduated *cum laude* with a B.A. as an English major. A month later, her son Stephen Reidar Fast was born.

In 1953 the family moved to Groton, Connecticut, where Nick became an engineer with Electric Boat. Five years later, there were three additional Fast sons: James Wilbur, Carl Douglas, and Kenneth Russell. Betty was deeply involved with her family and in community affairs. She was very active in the Cub Scouts and served as team manager for the Little League. She was chairman of the National Freedom Agenda Committee for Groton in 1955–56, and also served as chairman of the Citizens' Study Group on the Bright and Gifted Child that same year. Betty was also a member of the board of directors of the Groton League of Women Voters from 1954–59, becoming president in 1956.

Betty's interest in libraries developed around the need for a public library in Groton. Serving on the board of trustees from 1958 to 1964, she helped plan for the Groton Town Library's first building. Her work as publicity director for the library board generated an incredible variety of press releases that were collected in scrapbooks. The American Library Association recognized this campaign, which was a 1960 winner of a John Cotton Dana Award.

In September of 1957, Steve Fast entered kindergarten, Jimmy and Carl were toddlers, and Betty was expecting her fourth baby in November. On the first day of school, the principal asked Betty if she would help start a centralized school library. She accepted this new challenge and attacked the problems with her characteristic energy, determination, and political acumen. In the fall of 1959, Betty asked the superintendent of the Groton Schools to appoint a School Library Advisory Committee. The committee, with Betty as chair, issued its first report in January, 1960, and has continued to function through the years, changing its name in 1969 to the School Media Advisory Committee. In 1961–62 it won a Better Homes and Gardens Action-in-Education Award for a noteworthy community project.

When the Advisory Committee was first formed, only the high school had a professional librarian. The next professional personnel were requested at the junior high level. In the 1962–63 budget there was money for an elementary school librarian and Betty accepted the post—a move that eventually led to her being named director of educational media.

The litany of the procedures that led to the opening of media centers in all the Groton Elementary Schools is an exciting list of classic moves in mobilizing community interest and channeling that aroused enthusiasm. Betty's understanding of human behavior, her inspiring leadership, and her gift for communication produced an army of volunteers and encouraged dozens of women to return to college and become certified media specialists. A still larger number visited the processing center and the Butler Demonstration School Library. She shared her materials and her experiences and she gave suggestions, recommendations, and warning to educators and volunteers alike. For these women, as well as hundreds of others, however, it was the enthusiasm and genuineness of the sharing that made Betty so immediately a part of their lives.

In 1965, the cataloging of nonprint media began and the media program for the Groton Schools went into effect. The following year, Groton was selected as a finalist in the Encyclopaedia Britannica School Library Awards. Betty had become increasingly involved with the local and state P.T.A. and also with the Mental Health Association of Southeastern Connecticut and the Citizens Mental Health Planning Council of the same area, serving first on the board of directors, then as vice-president and, finally, as president in 1970–72. In 1965, Betty Fast was chosen as an alternate to the White House Fellows Program. She was an active participant in the School Library Association and library organizations on the state, regional, and national levels. She ran workshops, planned programs, chaired panels, contributed to journals, and got her M.L.S. from the University of Rhode Island in 1968.

Betty herself stated that the 1968–69 school year saw the zenith of volunteer participation in the Groton School Media Program, but the needs of the program and its personnel were changing. Typically, Betty had anticipated this and was immersed in training teachers as well as the children especially in the use of the newer media. In her studies for her administrator's certificate, Betty had learned to use television and in the next few years she worked diligently for the advancement of cable TV. Of all her talents, the most outstanding was her teaching. It was a true gift and she turned in virtuoso performances in the classroom. For Betty, teaching was more than the ability to drop the proper names and statistics at the right time or place, to write grant proposals and curriculum outlines, or to know how to scan publications from HEW. From the in-service classes she began for the volunteers in the early 1960s through the classes for graduate students at the University of Connecticut that she taught until only a few weeks before her death in 1977, she polished and honed the instructional techniques that she had developed and refined to the point where they were works of art.

Her interest in teaching led Betty to continue with her own studies. By 1974 she was a Ph.D. candidate at the University of Connecticut, Department of Curriculum and Supervision. The Council on Library Resources granted her a fellowship in 1972–73 to study possible cooperation between universities, library schools, and public schools, especially for mid-career people. This was the first CLR fellowship ever given to a part-time candidate. Much of the work for this grant was carried on with the faculty at Simmons College School of Library Science, where Betty catered to exotic tastes by bringing a different homemade pie each time she came. Visits of the "Pie Lady" were celebrations.

Involvement with the American Library Association and with the development of the profession nationally was an early priority of Betty's. From her work with the public library as a trustee, Betty was aware of the need for public support for any successful program. She saw ALA as an important part of professional activities and became a member even before finishing her M.L.S. In 1969 she was elected counselor-at-large and in 1970 began work with the ad hoc Committee on New Directions (ACONDA/ANACONDA).

School libraries were her first interest, and work with the Association of School Librarians (AASL) spurred her interest in other ALA divisions. As a member and then chair of the Encyclopaedia Britannica School Library Awards Committee, for instance, Betty had an opportunity to see the scope of school library development across the country. She served on a joint committee (with AECT) to develop guidelines for school media programs, but realized the importance of association-wide visibility for people who were interested in service to youth. Membership in CSD (now ALSC) resulted in election to the Newbery/Caldecott Committee in 1973–74—and a special series of discussions about new books with the children in Groton schools. Her participation in the Library Administration Division took on a variety of roles and resulted in her election as president-elect for 1977.

Perhaps the most public part of Betty Fast's activities was as a member of Council. The New Directions Committee led to participation in COPES, including chair of that important committee. In 1975 Betty was elected to the Executive Board, a responsibility she took very seriously.

Betty's battle with cancer began in 1972. As with both her professional and personal activities, she managed this aspect of her life with all the energy she could devote to it. Her sense of humor kept her going and her enthusiasm for living carried a spirit that infected all around her. The telephone (which she referred to as "the next best thing to being there") kept her in constant touch with friends and associates across the country. She even used the phone to help her participate in or chair those few meetings she was unable to attend. She had always been respectful of time, but now she made each hour pay dividends. The five years she had cancer were productive, energetic, fruitful years. At her death in 1977, Betty was a member of five Divisions and two Round Tables in ALA, a member of the Executive Board, and president-elect of one division.

Betty Fast was a remarkably energetic woman whose influence in the profession of librarianship was far-reaching. She was given the Grolier Foundation Award in 1977 in recognition of her outstanding contributions to the stimulation and guidance of reading of children and young people. The citation read, "A succession of librarians and teachers have been inspired to carry out her goals. . . . Elizabeth T. Fast's continued success as an administrator, teacher, lecturer, and as a person exemplifies outstanding librarianship."

BIBLIOGRAPHY

By Elizabeth T. Fast

Asia, A Guide to Books for Children. New York: The Asia Society, 1966. (One of nine compilers of this annotated bibliography.)

"Blueprint for Action: Program Development in Preparation for New Facilities." *School Media Quarterly* 2, 3 (Spring 1974): 194–99.

"Cable TV: Developing Video Awareness through Public Library and School Media Programs." *Cable Television and Media* (CAVEA Bulletin No. 27), 31–34. Connecticut Audiovisual Education Association, 1974.

"Cable Television Fact Sheet." Prepared for Connecticut School Library Association—Connecticut Audiovisual Education Association Meeting, October 25, 1974.

"Cooperative Projects of Graduate Library Schools and Public School Systems: A Report to the Council on Library Resources." 1973 (ED–093–335).

"Enjoy Your Stay at ALA." *American Library Association Bulletin* 57, 5 (May 1963): 413, 440.

"Flash." *Connecticut Parent-Teacher,* 32 (January 1963): 4.

"The Gifted Child—Changing Community Attitudes." *Radcliffe Quarterly* 16 (November 1957): 15–17.

Handbook for Library Volunteers. Groton, Conn.: Groton Public Schools, 1964. (Reprinted by Campbell and Hall, Boston.)

"In-Service Staff Development as a Logical Part of Performance Evaluation." *School Media Quarterly* 3, 1 (Fall 1974): 35–41.

"The Knapp Film Project—Something More Than a Movie." *School Librarian* 15, 1 (October 1965): 53–57.

———— and Yesner, Bernice. "Connecticut's Elementary School Library Project." *Scholastic Teacher* 14 (February 17, 1967): 14–15.

"Librarian and Students—Multimedia Team." *Instructor* 75 (November 1965) : 75, 80–81+.

"Librarianship: Fascinating Career." *Connecticut Parent-Teacher* 32 (March 1963): 10.

"A Library Is an Instructional Resource Center." *Connecticut Parent-Teacher* 33 (December 1963-January 1964) : 5.

"Media: The Language of the Young." *Top of the News* 33, 1 (Fall 1976) : 50–63.

"The Media Program Is an Integral Part of the Reading Program." Groton, Conn.: Groton Public Schools, March, 1974, (ED–098–931).

"Media Selection for the Learner." *The Individual Learner: A Challenge for Educational Technology.* (CAVEA Bulletin No. 25), 37–40. Connecticut Audiovisual Education Association, 1972.

"The Media Supervisor Does Make a Difference." *Media Professionals: District and School.* (Bulletin No. 1), 5–8. Connecticut Educational Media Association.

"NLW and You." *School Libraries* 19, 3 (Spring 1970): 26–27.

"Read: The Fifth Freedom . . . Enjoy It; National Library Week, April 21–27." *Connecticut Parent-Teacher* 32 (April 1963): 11.

"Reading Is the Key—National Library Week, 1964." *Connecticut Parent-Teacher* 33 (March 1964): 6.

"Results of a Survey of School Library Media Supervisors' Preferences in Continuing Education." *School Libraries* 19, 1 (Fall 1969): 59–60; 19, 3 (Spring 1970): 47–48.

"School Libraries and Media Centers." In *ALA Yearbook, 1977,* pp. 291–96. Chicago: American Library Association, 1977.

"Standards of Excellence in Hard Times: A Rational Defense of Media Programs Based on *Media Programs: District and School.*" *School Media Quarterly* 4, 2 (Winter 1976) : 121–25.

"Students in Libraries—Crisis or Opportunity." *Connecticut Parent-Teacher* 33 (October 1963): 4.

"System-wide Program: Centralized Cataloging." *Audiovisual Media in Connecticut Schools* (CAVEA Bulletin No. 26), 14–15. 1973.

"Take a Giant Step." *Connecticut Parent-Teacher* 32 (January 1963) : 4.

"Teachers and Librarians: Stage Managers for the Learning Process." *Childhood Education* 43 (October 1966) : 73–75.

LETTERS

[Letter in reply to M. Bloss.] "Collections Beyond School." *Library Journal* 101, 17 (October 1, 1976): 1984.

[Letter: comment by V. Levenson.] *Wilson Library Bulletin* 50, 2 (October 1, 1975): 127.

COPES Clarification [letter in reply to "Annual Conference: Business as Usual in New York."] *American Libraries* 6, 1 (January 1975): 4.

[Letter in reply to L. N. Gerhardt and others.] "Correction." *Library Journal* 99, 20 (November 15, 1974): 2993–94; *School Library Journal* 21, 3 (November 1974): 3–4.

REVIEWS

"The Elementary School Library Collection: A Guide to Books and Other Media." Edited by Mary V. Gaver. 5th ed. *School Libraries* 20 (Fall 1970): 62–64.

"The Lively Art of Picure Books." *Film News* 21 (August 1965): 14–15.

Scholastic Teacher. October, 1966–January, 1970.

"The Role of the School Media Center and the School Media Specialist." Groton, Conn.: Groton Public Schools, April, 1974 (ED–098–930).

SCHOOL LIBRARIES COLUMNS

"Spotlight on the Supervisors Section." 19, 1 (Fall 1969): 59–60.

"Spotlight on the Supervisors Section" and "Questionnaire about Continuing Education for School Library-Media Supervisors." 18, 4 (Summer 1969): 49–51, 53.

"Supervisors News Notes." 18, 1 (Fall 1968) 67–68.

"The Supervisors Section." 19, 2 (Winter, 1970): 59–60; 19, 3 (Spring, 1970): 47–48; 19, 4 (Summer 1970): 56–58.

WILSON LIBRARY BULLETIN COLUMNS

"The Case for Multipurpose Media: Bibliography." 50 (April 1976): 634–35.

"Looking at the Balanced Collection." 50 (January 1976): 370–71.

"Mediacentric: Media and the Handicapped Child." 52 (October 1977): 133–35.

"On Learning How to Learn." 51 (December 1976): 310–11.

"Overdue—The Media Specialist as an Agent for Change." 49 (May 1975): 636–37.

"Polish Up Your Backhand." 51 (March 1977): 572–73.

"Publisher's Catalogs: Puffery or Resource?" 51 (October 1976): 178–79.

"Why Susie Can't Use the Library." 51 (May 1977): 732–33.

About Elizabeth T. Fast

"An AASL Tribute to Elizabeth Fast." *School Media Quarterly* 6, 1 (Fall 1977): 20.

"Betty Fast: 1931–1977; An Irreplaceable 'Advocate' for Libraries." *American Libraries* 8 (July 1977): 369.

"Elizabeth T. Fast Received the 1975 Rheta A. Clark Award of Merit for Outstanding Librarianship and Devotion to the Profession." *School Library Journal* 22 (December 1975): 18.

Galvin, T. J. "Elizabeth T. Fast: A Tribute." *School Library Journal* 24 (September 1977): 15.

Library Journal 52, 1 (September 1977): 1553.

New York Times, June 19, 1977, p. 28.

"1977 ALA Awards Winners: Grollier Foundation Award." *American Libraries* 8 (October 1977): 495; *Library Journal* 102 (August 1977): 1567; *Wilson Library Bulletin* 52, 1 (September 1977): 44.

Wilson Library Bulletin 52, 1 (September 1977): 41.

THE CHILD

*This column [beginning on the facing page] comprises
excerpts of a speech given by Betty Fast at the 19th School
Media Workshop at Kent State University, April 29, 1977.
On June 16th Betty Fast died. She was a school media
specialist for the Groton, Conn., PS, member of the ALA
Executive Board, and originator of WLB's "Mediacentric"
column. Involved in many other professional activities, she
received the 1977 Grolier Foundation Award. Following
is the tribute that Clara Jones gave on behalf of the
ExecBd at the first ALA Membership meeting in Detroit
on June 19th:*

Those of us serving with Betty Fast on the Executive Board
are grateful for the privilege of close association with her.
Betty was a very special person to *all* who knew her. In her
relatively brief span of life, she fulfilled herself—her
potential—to an unusual degree. It was a pleasure to
observe the depth and clarity of her mind and her ability
to articulate her thoughts. She was motivated by high
principle, and her interests, attitude, and judgment
transcended pettiness and selfishness. She was sensitive and
perceptive in her feelings for people she knew and for
humanity in the aggregate. Betty's life demonstrated love
in control, with courage triumphant.

From
Wilson Library Bulletin

by BETTY FAST

MEDIA AND THE
HANDICAPPED CHILD

My friends who teach the emotionally disturbed tell me that they are called emotionally disturbed teachers. I am a handicapped media specialist at the moment; except for some involved logistics, there are a lot of advantages to looking at the world through someone else's eyes. You understand a little bit more about the handicapped because you are one.

Fifteen years ago, when I started working for the Groton schools, I was hired to be the first elementary school librarian and to set up libraries in our 12 schools. In one the principal asked me to work with three classes of retarded children and their teachers. We worked very closely, and I had a wonderful time with the kids.

Although I didn't know much about them, I thought, well, they're children. And that, it turned out, was the most important thing of all. The real message is that even though special ed children have special needs and problems, essentially, they are children. They have the same needs as

Wilson Library Bulletin 52, 2 (October 1977): 133–35.

everyone else for love and affection, for positive experiences, for self-development, and for people to accept them.

Because we didn't have real media programs when I started working with my classes of retarded children, I turned to my good friends at Weston Woods and asked to borrow some of their sound filmstrips. I found that *The Red Carpet, The Story About Ping,* and *Make Way for Ducklings*—resources we tend to use just with normal pupils—worked beautifully with these children. They responded to and remembered the stories, particularly the ones they had seen in the filmstrips.

Another thing I found is that a visual approach with the retarded isn't all that vital, and that the old-fashioned eye-to-eye contact in storytelling can be very effective. Improvisational drama also works well. Special ed children have a grand time acting out stories related to their abilities, and videotaping their efforts has been extremely fruitful. That's a way for children to see themselves and gain self-understanding; today, children don't think something's real unless they see it on television—and that includes themselves.

When a child has lost the use of one of his or her senses, he or she will usually focus on others. This is ideal for us as media specialists because we have access to materials that can concentrate on the strong sense. For instance, a blind child who develops a keen comprehension through hearing is able to pick up many things. A deaf child responds well to visual materials and to concrete objects.

All realia is very important in special education. Although we do have some materials, unfortunately, many companies have not looked at the special education market to any great extent, and much is still lacking. We also need resources so that children with special needs can produce their own materials. Production *has* to be one of the strong arms of our media programs with such children.

We really have to work to match the strengths of the media to the weaknesses of the children. This is one way we can help teachers create a strong learning environment that will enable them to help children perceive more. It's actually instructional development on an individual basis, and the more work of this sort we can do with the special ed instructor and regular classroom teacher with mainstreamed pupils, the better.

I would hope that as mainstreaming comes in, it is not used as an excuse for spending less money on special education. I see a real danger in that principals, superintendents, and boards of education may say, "Well, it's cheaper to put them in the regular classroom," and not do enough to help them function in the new situation, help the teacher in the classroom work with them, or help the other children in the class.

Unless mainstreaming is done with a real effort to provide the best education for all the children, it's going to be a very big problem, and I think it's up to us as media specialists to become child advocates. We may have a conflict of interest between our loyalty to the school and our loyalty to the children. The conflict arises because we know that the principal doesn't have enough money to do things the way he or she would like to, yet the children are there, and what is going to be done for them?

The big three

I think that we're going to have three places for children in a mainstreaming situation: the regular classroom (with the ultimate goal of having them function there), the resource room with a special education teacher (the opposite end of the spectrum), and then the media center, which can be a type of resource room for these children, an intermediate room where they can get up and walk around. They need not be interacting with other children, but can be working independently, something that we can help with, too, as extra resource persons.

I don't think mainstreaming can work at all without a strong media program. Children need to have access to a variety of materials and machines. There's something very calming about putting on a pair of earphones over a child's ears to eliminate some of the noise he or she can't take, literally and figuratively, and also to focus a limited concentration.

If mainstreaming is going to work at all, it has to start early. By the time the child gets to junior high school, if he or she has been in a special education class during elementary school, it's not a good time to make a transition to a mainstreaming situation. When the child is identified as being a special ed candidate, mainstreaming should start almost immediately. Then the professional media specialist can work with both the classroom and special ed teachers.

We've got to try to get written into funding proposals, provisions that include the media specialist as an important member of the team working with the special child. If there is separate funding for this type of education, some of it should go to pay part of the media specialist's salary. We have to be free to work with all children, but the special child in particular needs a strong media program.

We should also be looking around for ways to fund model programs of media utilization for special education children. Fifteen percent of the money under Title IV-C for innovative and exemplary programs is set aside for special ed programs, and in Connecticut at least, where I'm a member of the Title IV advisory council, I'm not seeing very many such model projects crossing our committee table. So get hold of the guidelines in your state, and think of ways in which you could apply. Never give up; there is money around if you will look for it.

From the practical to Patty's story

If you do have classes of special education children in your school, be an innovator; start mainstreaming the media program by integrating the children with regular classes for storytelling or special projects. Oftentimes this will mean taking only one or two children from a special ed class and mixing them in with the children closest to their own age-level with whom they can sustain activity.

It may mean talking to the children in the regular class ahead of time, or after a few times saying to them, "Look, you've got to turn the other cheek to these children; these new friends of yours have some problems. Will you help me in helping them and make them welcome as part of your class for this media center experience?" It's amazing how big children can be when you expect them to be.

Also, help the special ed children learn to operate independently in your center, so they can come to visit you when you have another class there and work successfully on their own—really the ultimate test. Can they do that without disrupting the class you're working with? They can if you have some simple but flexible rules—and you have to be very flexible with these children.

I'd like to conclude my remarks by telling you about one of the special education children that I came to know and love: Patty, a student I worked with last year. She was in the sixth grade, although she read on a primer level and was so disruptive that even in a two-person group she couldn't function. I spent most of the year getting to know Patty, talking to Patty, and listening to Patty. The principal and I decided to try letting her tutor in a third-grade classroom to help her reading. I said to her: "Patty, how would you like to help some of the third graders make a slide-tape presentation on their social studies program? You can help them the way I've been helping you."

She did that extremely well, and we moved on to one of the I-Can-Read books about the Revolution, which the class was studying for the Bicentennial. I recorded it and gave Patty a cassette recorder to take home with the book. She practiced the story, until she could read it to the class without the tape recorder—a very proud moment for Patty. As the year went along we became quite good friends, and I was just extremely impressed with the change in Patty's attitude.

In the media center we see a different side of children. We have a role to play, I think, in special education programs and a leadership role to play in mainstreaming programs. I know that you'll find ways in which you can make a really solid contribution. If you think of the children as children first and special second, you won't have any problems at all with them, because they are very lovable kids.

WHY SUSIE CAN'T
USE THE LIBRARY

With the creation of a new round table in the American Library Association devoted to library skills instruction, no doubt the debate about the purpose, methods, and value of this type of teaching will be reactivated. Opinions on the subject range from the belief that learning how to learn is predicated on library skills to the viewpoint that teaching people how to locate library resources gives them a false sense of proficiency in reference work.

Many school library media specialists spend an inordinate amount of time on teaching library skills, updated to include competency in the use and production of AV materials, yet public and academic librarians claim that students are unable to use libraries without help.

Is it possible that John Holt's theory on children's reading, suggesting that the overemphasis on formal instruction in skills actually prevents students from becoming readers, applies to the teaching of library skills? Is there a sequence of library and media skills, or have we arbitrarily in-

Wilson Library Bulletin 51, 9 (May 1977): 732–33.

vented lists of needed proficiencies for the convenience of the teacher rather than the learner? Perhaps we need less instruction—not more.

An examination of recently drafted library curricula showed such "improvements" as using behavioral objectives, testing for mastery with criterion-referenced instruments, adding lessons in the operation of audio-visual equipment, tying skill sequences to reading level rather than grade level, and using a variety of media to teach the skills. Frances Henne's observation, made in 1966, that "library skills are means to other educational ends and not ends in themselves"[1] appears to be ignored as we rush to demonstrate that 90 percent of the fifth-graders can identify author cards in the card catalog or that 85 percent of the ninth-graders can produce a transparency for the overhead projector. Unless library and media skills are solidly integrated with classroom instruction and independent study, we will never be able to move from the skills level to the *real* goal, which is using information obtained through a synthesis of knowledge and creative expression of ideas.

One dilemma of library skills instruction is its concentration on superficial objectives that can be readily mastered and as quickly forgotten. We teach students about the card catalog by explaining the different types of cards in a set and the various categories of the Dewey Decimal System, instead of explaining the concept of the catalog as a locational device that can be used successfully, regardless of one's knowledge of its organization.

Like a horse and carriage?

Although most educators (librarians included) profess a belief in the value of integrating skills instruction with classroom instruction, the enormous amount of staff time required to do this successfully has led to the compromise of teaching library skills in isolation. The inadequacy of this alternative should be obvious as we see the large number of people who fail to learn from this type of teaching. In the long run we may save time by adapting the concepts of Patricia Knapp's Montieth College project of integrated instruction to all levels of education.[2] Shunting the responsibility for teaching library skills onto the classroom teacher doesn't really work, either. Since most teachers don't understand the way in which knowledge is organized in libraries, they are unable to help students understand.

There is, also, a tendency to concentrate on the use of a limited number of tools to locate answers, instead of teaching students to refine their questions, identify the kind of information they need, and enlarge their list of possible sources. In other words we should show students how to become intelligent searchers able to carry on a meaningful dialogue in a reference interview, rather than try to train them to locate a single, all-purpose source for their answer.

Another dilemma in library-skills instruction is the conflict between the idea of individualizing instruction and the use of programmed and audio-visual materials for this kind of teaching. Conceivably, a computerized program with elaborate branching could be geared to the individual student's need, and if the instructional program were dovetailed with classroom activities, the library media center could produce simple AV lessons to teach skills in the context of the information search involved in the assignment.

However, audiovisual materials, whether commercial or "homegrown," typically describe a different situation from the one on hand. Even though they are used by only one person at a time, programmed and AV materials that teach library skills are, in reality, a form of large-group instructions. Frances Henne pinpointed this dilemma when she stated that "ironically enough, the use of programmed aids and of audiovisual materials in conjunction with library instruction often contributes to the perpetuation of arbitrary, non-integrated instruction."

We should demand that the content of self-instructional materials be more accurate and should also be tougher in our evaluation of these media. Some examples: How many skills programs begin by teaching that all books have three catalog cards: author, title, and subject? Or a filmstrip teaching the arrangement of books on the shelf shows misshelved books without commenting on the error. Although very few elementary schools use Cutter numbers, an AV set for this level illustrates call numbers with Cutter designation, without any explanation of this teachnique.

Wide world of learning

It is hoped that the movement to reexamine library skills instruction will look at the total universe instead of concentrating on teaching the use of specific tools. Rather than trying to prepare library media specialists to plan and teach a program in the use of library media center materials and equipment, we may need to aim at the larger goal of expanding the role of the library media center in learning. We may be trying to solve the problem at the wrong end of the learning spectrum by incorporating skills instruction at the college level, when the real need is for more professional staff in elementary schools, so that children can absorb skills individually as their needs and interests dictate. We may discover that the most successful way to help students best use resources is to abandon skills instruction programs and press for enough professional staff at all levels to permit individual guidance in locating, analyzing, and appreciating the wide variety of media available for each search situation.

REFERENCES

1. Frances Henne, "Learning to Learn in School Libraries," *School Libraries* (May 1966).
2. Patricia Knapp, *Montieth College Experiment*. Metuchen, N.J.: Scarecrow, 1966.

ON LEARNING
HOW TO LEARN

Is the school media center of today really different from the library study hall of the past? Do today's carrels symbolize independent learning, or are they just a new way to enforce the old rule of silence? Have we merely modified mass instruction by designing a few lessons using colorful transparencies and an overhead projector? Are we providing the right media for the right learner at the right time, or are nonprint media still regarded as second-class citizens? Before we rush out to reform classroom objectives and procedures, perhaps we media specialists should inspect our own centers.

We're quick to spot fuzzy thinking in a teacher's lesson plans and trained to apply first aid to develop more precise objectives, methods, and evaluation procedures for student learning. This expertise allowed us to move from the position of suppliers of materials to co-designers of instruction. When we look at the objectives we set for our own media pro-

Wilson Library Bulletin 51, 4 (December 1976): 310–11.

grams, however, we often find that we are still thinking in terms of input rather than student learning. We may have progressed from the goal of adding a certain number of books to our collections to the goal of increasing student and teacher use of our new machines, but we need to examine what learning is taking place as the machine is used. We are reluctant to move from the service function to our professed role as an integral part of the school's total program.

What would happen if we took the philosophy of education seriously and concentrated on helping each student learn how to learn? At a conference on "Futurism and School Media Development" at Western Michigan University in August 1974, Henry Brickell commented on *Media Programs: District and School* by telling his audience of media professionals: ". . . The common goal of the school is, of course, to provide lifelong learning skills, learning how to learn and all that stuff. . . . It's the one that's natural for you guys because that's the skill that you can fairly easily, we presume, produce. It's a natural one for you, and it doesn't require you to show that [the child] learned more arithmetic or something else that you might not be working on."[1] Do we realize that this implies a lot more than teaching a class to use the card catalog or the *Readers' Guide* because this is the time they are "supposed" to master this skill? Do we encourage teachers and administrators to make use of the media center for independent study?

How to be truly educated

A prerequisite for learning how to learn is the motivation or desire to learn. California's *RISE Report* (Report of the California Commission for Reform of Intermediate and Secondary Education) defines the number-one characteristic of the educated adult in these terms: "The educated person should have a thirst for knowledge. He/she should be motivated to keep on learning throughout a lifetime. In a changing society, this means that people must learn *how to learn* because new knowledge is being constantly created by the current of change."[2]

In addition to independent learning as part of the curriculum of the school, the media center program can go beyond this to deal with the concerns of students. We may even change the image of the school as a waste of time, a picture held by the majority of 30-year-olds in a recent study as a follow-up to Project Talent. In reporting this study, the *ASCD*

News Exchange revealed that "when the 30-year-olds looked back at their high school experience, they found it irrelevant to their later lives." One of the experts who analyzed the interviews, Robert Gagne, said, "The evidence of these interviews suggests that a high school education as a whole serves no very useful purpose."[3] Why can't the media program work on this immense gap?

Student, direct thyself

Learning how to learn involves learning how one learns. Media centers, with their wide range of available options, are a natural for this process. The main reasons for providing information in formats other than the printed page are that some people learn better from other methods than from reading. Each student has to discover which format works best with which information, for his or her individual needs at a particular time.

Learning how to learn presupposes a sense of self-directedness that may be easier to attain in the media center than in the classroom. Independent study is much more than an individual search for the answers to questions posed by the teacher or the textbook. Students must develop the responsibility for using time, space, and materials wisely. Independent study takes place as the toddler explores the world; in schools preoccupied with the back-to-the-basics movement, it may be only in the media center that the freedom required for the development of self-directedness exists. The paradox is that an essential part of this freedom may disappear when we try to measure or evaluate the effectiveness of the media program for accountability advocates.

Learning how to learn enables students to connect themselves with the ideas, thoughts, and interpretations of the great writers, artists, and dramatists of the ages, as well as with more transistory information to meet today's immediate needs. Sharing the imagination of C. S. Lewis, Ernest Pintoff, or Maurice Sendak; sensing the vitality of Dmitri Shostakovich, Marc Chagall, or Piri Thomas; feeling the concerns of Sylvia Plath, Ingmar Bergman, or Charles Dickens—all are possible through media. Media specialists help students to make these connections, and whether they result in interfaces, encounters, or circulation statistics, they are ways to broaden one's learning.

While it is true that libraries have always inspired a few students to become life-long independent learners, we cannot be content with an occasional random success today. The future will require almost everyone to possess this talent for self-directed learning. In identifying this part of the school program as our turf and adopting this goal as a top priority for our media programs, we may serve as a model for curriculum change at the same time that we guarantee our right to survival as an essential and irreplaceable part of the educational process.

REFERENCES

1. Henry Brickell, "An Afternoon Discussion with Dr. Henry Brickell," *Futurism and School Media Development*. Proceedings of a Higher Education Institute held Aug. 10–17, 1974, ed. by Marilyn L. Miller and Alida L. Geppert, School of Librarianship, Western Michigan University, March 1975, p.131.

2. *The RISE Report,* Report of the California Commission for Reform of Intermediate and Secondary Education, presented to Wilson Riles, California Superintendent of Public Instruction, 1975, p.1.

3. *ASCD News Exchange,* 18, 2: 1 (May 1976).

BIAS, PREJUDICE AND THE GROWING "-ISM" SCHISM

by LILLIAN N. GERHARDT

Librarians serving children are so regularly exhorted to lay aside their biases and prejudices and avoid the selection of any form of material that employs a stereotype that I have been repeatedly driven to dictionaries to make sure that these words are not solely associated with racism, sexism, or indifference toward ethnic sensibilities. The lexicographers lag. "Bias," in their books, still means an "unexplained predilection" for "someone or something." "Prejudice" still means "an automatic prejudgment against." And, the suffix "-ism" implies an automatic adherence to a belief. Stripped of the latter-day connotations with which they now come freighted in library selection circles, these words are important to an understanding of how library service began in this country, how it has gone forward and continues.

Popular library service began in the United States in a swirl of bias and prejudice. The bias was toward the preservation of the good, the true, and the beautiful as it was understood by the citizenry of the late nineteenth century. The public library movement gathered momentum because of a generally shared prejudice against the extant commercial sources of leisure pleasure (saloons, pool halls, etc.) and the objectionable nature of what was most clearly available in entertainment on the stage and in print—melodramas that made villainy attractive, novels of silly or subliminally salacious romance or adventure. The shared conviction that led to the rapid establishment of so many public libraries after the Civil War was a bias—an unexplained predilection for the idea that public libraries would provide an attractive alternative for the productive use of leisure that would eventually dry up the saloons and shut out the pool halls.

Begun and impelled by these idealistic urges (biases), fueled by the unexamined prejudgment that pool halls and road shows and dime novels were the path to perdition for a native untutored class and masses of new immigrants (prejudices), the first public libraries formulated collection goals that promulgated high literary standards, acceptable moral content, and accuracy of information as selection criteria. This selection philosophy is still in wide use, particularly in library collections for the young.

It is interesting to turn back to the letters that Caroline M. Hewins, the country's pioneer children's librarian, wrote to the editors of the Hartford, Connecticut, newspapers. In the 1870s she began to tell the world about the section of books especially selected for boys and girls that she had begun in her library. Hewins would occasionally write to the newspapers in words that still quiver with outrage, railing against the sort of blood-and-thunder novels the papers serialized, warning of the bad effects these might have on the minds and morals of young readers, and promising the benefits to their mental and moral development that would follow on steady reading in well-written books. The terms she employed, the heat of her denunciations of the lowest levels of popular fiction, and her zealotry in promoting the values in good reading during childhood are interchangeable with the current criticisms of blood-and-thunder TV shows and their deleterious effects on children today.

The thread that runs so true from the beginnings of library collections for children is this shared bias for guidance of young readers by adults to excellence in writing that promotes accepted or developmental values and shared prejudices against the most popular, least expensive forms of entertainment. This philosophy, accepted and adhered to, has left us without rich and accessible collections that encompass and illuminate the variety of books, films, records, or radio scripts that were an important aspect of child life in successive generations. These beginnings submerged the preservation function of librarianship in favor of an education role for children by librarians that has been detrimental to scholarship and the profession, while it has contributed mightily to the quality, variety, and scope of childhood education through reading.

"Contributed mightily" may seem an excessive claim, but I think that sales records of publishers can show that public and school librarians have been, and continue to be, a chief force behind what gets published as quality trade books for children. From the inception of departmentalized publishing for children in this country, "the institutional market" (the public library and school sales) has accounted for 75 percent and more of all children's book sales each year. Enthusiastic purchase support by this market predicates more publishing of what appears to please; library market resistance has resulted in diminished or abandoned production of certain lines of books. The apparent biases and prejudices of librarians can be traced through sales records as well as through contemporary reviews and acquisition records.

A thumbnail history of the "-isms" that have emerged as influential in children's book sales goes like this:

1915–1930 — Emphasis on patriotism, Americanization, and heroic aspects of American history, especially the Westward movement.

1930–1940 — Emphasis on family life and the interdependence of peoples (tribal groups, nations).

1940–1945 — A spate of children's books supporting the Allies in W.W. II—patriotism and jingoism.

1945–1950 — Children's books supporting "one world" approaches to the management of the affairs of nations—internationalism.

1950–1960 — A steady increase in books promoting "brotherhood," and a near total disappearance of children's books about former allies Russia and China—anticommunism.

1960–1970 — Increasing purchase resistance to new and blacklist children's books with clear biases and prejudices involving racial and sexist discrimination; the promotion of pacificism.

1970– — It's hard to see the forest for the trees, but from where I sit I've seen an abrupt decline in historic fiction and juvenile biography and a rapid increase in formula fiction purporting to reflect the social problems of our time— divorce, illegitimacy, child abuse, physical and mental handicaps, etc., and a positive boom for books prompting the retention of ethnic identification and the equality of women—pluralism, anti-sexism.

Writing down such a list forces the recognition that the topics and the moral content of children's books shift with the generally shared concerns and beliefs of the adult population. The biases and prejudices so briefly outlined above as significant to the children's books published and sold successfully in the last six decades leads to the inescapable conclusion that our library selection for the young has never been value-free. This has left public and school librarians out of sync with the development of popular library collections provided for adults. The 1950s marked the end of a widely shared belief among adult services librarians that their selection goals involved active or restrictive reader guidance toward levels of literary excellence and the elevation of the country's moral climate. We in library service to children are left increasingly isolated from colleagues in the other age level service specialities and are often subjected by them to charges of blatant censorship, the cowardice implicit in self-censorship, and the failure to support the principles of intellectual freedom and free access as pronounced and interpreted by the American Library Association's Committee on Intellectual Freedom.

External groups charge us with base motivation in preserving children's books published in the past that employ stock characters now perceived as victims of majority indifference or malice, and failure to reject new books that depict the races, the sexes, and the various hyphenated-American groups in less than heroic terms. We are charged with a bias toward an old morality and a prejudice against sexual content by colleagues as well as by individuals and groups both inside and outside library service. The thread that has run so true in our service is frayed and raveling. Successive waves of bias and prejudice and the acceptance or rejection of "-isms" have one negative element in common: they are unreasoned, untested, and seldom subjected to close examination or analysis. "Bias" and "prejudice" are now such emotionally charged terms that they are used as accusations rather than descriptors of part of the judgment process, subject to self-identification, self-analysis, and self-control.

The illogic of it all is what makes library collection development for children as fascinating as it is frustrating. It is a totally unreasonable situation that public and school librarians face in their selection practices today. On the one hand, we have the full weight of the American Library Association coming down on the side of representation of all points of view and full access to all sorts of information as the only worthwhile approach to collection building. On the other, we have a general agreement by the public and by many librarians that children require guidance in the development of personal taste and personal values. We have both within and without library service angry groups calling for the eradication in children's library collections of all negative stereotypes of the races, the sexes, or the national or ethnic groups residing in this country. These same groups generally support the idea of a free press. We expend collectively over 75 percent of all the money to be made in juvenile publishing while being told that it is not our responsibility to boycott the trivial or the tasteless or prevent access to any sort of information or persuasion, however objectionable we believe it may be as reading or viewing fare for children.

In practice, the contradictions go something like this: a picture book is turned down because a mother is consistently depicted doing her housework in an apron while her daughters are shown following the lead of their brothers and father. The reason for rejection? The book is a subtle but powerful reinforcement of limited roles for girls and women, and therefore detrimental to the development of boys and girls who may read the books, probably from no other source but their public library or school. In a book for 9- and 10-year-olds, the hero employs one profanity and one obscenity in dialogue; he is the role model figure. It is purchased over the objections of some librarians in the selection group because the majority refuse to see it as a subtle but powerful reinforcement of declining language standards, or as a promotion of immoral or irreligious behavior, and therefore detrimental to the development of boys and girls who may read the book, probably through no other source than their public or school library. Can these inconsistent selection standards be happily practiced at one and the same time? You bet! It is an internal inconsistency that is tearing our turf apart—a bias toward the idea of equality of the sexes, a current prejudice against the application of moral judgments on any aspect of human behavior, and an example of librarians to children demonstrating selection inconsistency and easy disregard for the literary standards we claim transcend most other considerations.

How to achieve a united front and a better understanding of the responsible use of purchasing power by librarians working with children? I suggest three possibilities unlikely to be swiftly taken up, but nevertheless all immediately possible.

It is drearily and wearisomely usual to settle the responsibility for the solution of all that goes wrong in library service on the library schools and on the American Library Association. These groups are central to the possibilities I shall suggest, but for once I will not begin with them, but in the area I have inhabited for so long.

As the chief editor of School Library Journal (SLJ), I believe that I share some guilt with other editors of the library and review periodical press for failing to identify early-on the "-isms" we are in a position to spot, identify, and subject to rigorous criticism. For one example, I point to the fact that a growing demand for "hi/interest-lo/vocabulary" books has not been accompanied by a full analysis of this growing school and public library selection-support bulge—not in *SLJ* and not in any other library magazine. As is usual with the emergence of library purchase support of an "-ism," declared selection priorities are set aside, standards of acceptability (aesthetic or developmental) are set aside or are invented on the run, and selection mistakes are quietly weeded out for discard after the fact of investment. I suppose this current surge of purchase is responsive to a general idea of the value of being able to read anything at any reading level and could be called "egalitarianism" for young readers. The failure to criticize and analyze the phenomenon could also be called—rightly or wrongly—the refusal to attack current education standards exacted of public schools in equipping a literate populace.

If I had it to do all over again, I would as a library magazine editor have been swifter to the pen on the irrationalities and antiintellectualism imbedded in reevaluating children's library collections guided solely by a zealous recognition of racist and sexist content in books written and published and purchased in the past. These proposals are coupled with demands that new historical fiction reflect the sensibilities of the present on the subjects of race and sex roles. The possibility of providing concurrent criticism of the shifting biases and prejudices that emerge in library materials selection lies before every library periodical and review agency. We find the supporters of every new "-ism" because they are ready with support and volunteer their appreciations. Developing concurrent criticism is much harder and far less likely to come in over the transom.

But where is this criticism to come from? No library publication now affords resident critics without other tasks to perform.

It seems to me that there are two sources of such ready criticism—or there ought to be. Our major city and county public libraries, especially those that include both public and school purchasing for children, have been running selection/examination discussions for years. These usually have in-service training as one of their stated purposes—but training toward what? Review skills are honed year after year, but the next level could move toward criticism of great practical value to librarians. The next level might include a set topic for individuals or a committee to provide at least once a year a thorough analysis—literary, political, psychological—of the forces that produced the biases, prejudices, and values to which readers, librarians, publishers, and writers have responded in some selection area of new fiction and information for children.

The extant book-by-book, film-by-film selection review approach begins in library schools where, granted, the study of children's library materials must rapidly advance from introduction to evaluation methods in under two years. History is scanted and so are acquisition procedures. The second can be learned on the job; the first is an essential—the missing essential—in the development of critics rather than reviewers. An introduction to the general responses and educational goals of the ages and stages of youngsters gets almost as much instruction time as the introduction to various types of materials. The imbalance of emphasis is continued in what passes for the continuing education of librarians to children in programs offered by their associations that are, across the country, heavily weighted toward popular author/publisher presentations unaccompanied by critiques of the nature of their popularity, their place in the scale of collection purpose, or literary excellence, and the role their work plays in reader development.

This heavy drift to the immediate, without reference or connection to a continuum of selective collection purpose, makes no sense to library collection development for children. Determined, enthusiastic exploitation of promotional resources at the command of library organizations by the suppliers leaves librarians to children swimming with the tidal flow of bias and prejudice, rather than setting a course that helps steer collections and readers through them. The possibility that library leaders in every state can exert more purposive influence over instructional content in library schools and over the content of organizational programming lies easily at hand, but requires more of an appetite for boat-rocking than county coordinators, major public library children's work supervisors, and school district librarians have generally been willing to undertake individually or together.

Which leads me finally to the possibility of some clearer leadership from the American Library Association. At the moment, the three divisions that harbor the librarians serving children and youth march to such different drums in regard to selection priorities and considerations that it is little wonder that each has failed to influence the perceptions of the rest of ALA's members or retain their full support for selective purchasing and value concerns with the content of library materials for the young. The standard-setting prerogatives of the American Association of School Librarians has given it influence over the course content of schools preparing future school librarians. The perennial failure of this division, however, to protest the doctrines on free access to and collection of all viewpoints on every current social problem that are embedded in *The Bill of Rights* has left a gap in the understanding and eroded the support of other library professionals for what priority purposes and which social concerns are involved in school library work, from elementary through junior and senior high school.

The Association for Library Service to Children (ALSC) and the Young Adult Services Division (YASD) are, by their charges from ALA, prevented from standard setting for their libraries but are by no means prevented from pace-setting policy statements, of which both have produced far too few on the subject of materials selection—a chief function of both of these divisions. Of late, ALSC's directors have responded to a membership-indicated willingness to deemphasize awards selection and beef-up membership concerns for model library programs for children employing materials at a variety of excellence checkpoints. YASD has provided leadership with a policy adopted by ALA endorsing the responsibility of libraries for the provision of unrestricted information on sex education, but has backed off from providing guidelines on selection criteria by which to judge acceptable levels of good taste or the identification of moral and social values in the presentation of such material through schools and public libraries.

All three divisions are rent with internal dissension on questions of what is right or appropriate for purchase with public funds for public and school libraries serving children and youth. The bias toward the promotion of library materials supporting the equality of races, sexes, and ethnic groups is shared. The criteria for reevaluating, discarding, and/or retaining materials that fail to promote such ideals have not been given policy statement support. The widely shared prejudice against explicit sex and profanity or obscenity in library materials for the use of minors is both upheld in discussion and condemned as censorship with no general agreement on these questions in sight. The bias toward literacy and aesthetic standards of selection are still declared in ALSC, but take second or third place in the stated concerns of YASD—after popularity and the identification of user needs and expressed interests. The ALA act is very much un-together. The third possibility for providing a united front on the levels below which public and school librarians need not go in selecting library materials for children and young people lies within the power of these units of ALA.

It was in ALA work that I met and annually talked with Betty Fast over a period of fifteen years. Almost the last of our conversations centered on the fact that censorship accusations arise within ALA meeting corridors. These heated discussions reflect the inconsistencies of a national organization that has disjointed and strangely contradictory commitments to the social responsibility of the library profession.

The "-ism" schisms in library materials selection for children are fissures that have become cracks in a surface that has held firm for a century, undoubtedly because good people of good sense have been and continue to be drawn to library work with children. We need to marshall all that good sense to provide some agreed-upon answers—suitable to and worthy of the complexity of our times—answers for the no longer simple question Caroline M. Hewins once sent out in a postcard survey to the leading librarians of the late nineteenth century: "What are you doing in your library for boys and girls?"

IN CONCERT
WITH CHILDREN

by CLARA O. JACKSON

I know of nothing more important, more difficult, and more purely loving than the nurture of children—be it as a parent, as a teacher, or as an artist wishing to serve them well. Children are the ways that the world begins again and again. If you fasten upon that concept of their promise, you will have trouble finding anything more awesome, anything more extraordinarily exhilarating, than the opportunity and obligation to further a child into his or her own freedom.

—June Jordan, *Wilson Library Bulletin* 162

In this paper honoring Betty Fast, the writer wishes to place her years of library media service in Groton (1962–77) within the context of the quotation above. Despite the conflicting forces that seeped into the 1970s, these represented fifteen fruitful years for Betty and the profession she personified so well.

The beginning of her professional work was associated with peaking interest and activity about children: their nature and growth, their total needs, their human well being, their "rights," and their education. Through its several parts, the Elementary and Secondary Education Act left tremendous impact within schools, while the Great Society programs stimulated a flood of activity including research touching young children. Tied to ESEA was the introduction of child-oriented media centers. Yet as the 70s progressed, accumulated problems became more conspicuous because of changing societal priorities, growing inflation, and threats of austerity. At the same time mainstreaming—with its multiple implications for media centers—became mandated. As part of the machinery of supportive services to education, library media programs reflected both the promises and the uncertainties of these years.

Though Harriet Long characterized the twentieth century as "the century of the child," children have fared sometimes for the better but often for the worse during the century's advancing decades. But between 1962 and the early 1970s what happened to refocus on children, their status and needs, included more studied and sympathetic approaches to their learning potential. Many aspects of children's growth and functioning were explored in numerous ways by people with a variety of approaches, understandings, and concerns about children as children.

Whose voices were raised on behalf of children? Anticipating the 60s, the late Muriel Ward (sister of artist Lynd), who was a nursery school teacher in Fort Lee, New Jersey, expressed her philosophy in a little volume, *Young Minds Need Something to Grow On*. Its heart was her "directive": "to stop, look and listen to children, to become aware of what is and can be meaningful to them, then to help them to explore it on their level, through their eyes."[2] She was especially interested in "related learning, dovetailed, crisscrossed, and bound around with the child's continuous needing, seeking, discovering, achieving."

The 60s and early 70s saw the fruition of such attitudes reflected in extensive work relating to the enlarged understanding of children and their development. Bernard Spodek[3] profiles much of the significant work of the past few decades. Publications flowed from many sources, notably the Association for Early Childhood Education International (through its magazine and other publications), Bank Street College of Education (especially through the work of Barbara Biber in children's learning, Courtney Cazden in language, and Dorothy H. Cohen in several important areas, including television), as well as the National Association for the Education of Young Children (NAEYC).

Many individuals have contributed illuminating and imaginative work, including Sylvia Ashton-Warner, whose *Teacher* (Bantam, 1971) opened the eyes of many readers to the originality of children and the curious bits of information and interests they bring to school, as well as to the sources of learning within themselves. Muriel Beadle's *Child's Mind* (Doubleday, 1970); Louise M. Berman's *Feeling, Valuing and the Art of Growing* (Association for Supervision and Curriculum Development, 1977); the work of Stella Chess and her husband Alexander Thomas (e.g., *Your Child Is a Person,* Viking, 1965); Eleanor Duckworth's work in children's intellectual development; N. W. Hart and his colleagues, who studied young children's use of oral English; Margaret Mead's continual emphasis on the humanness of children; the popularizations of Piaget's work on children's thinking; and Rita M. Warren's *Caring: Supporting Children's Growth* (NAEYC, 1977)—are only a few. The Head Start and Follow Through projects also left their trail of influences— many of which flowed into library-related publications like Diane Farrell's "Library and Information Needs of Young Children"[4] and ALA's *Start Early for an Early Start* (1976). These and others like them touched the behavior and attitudes of adults working with children and often modified their encounters with children. Betty Fast harbored many of these attitudes.

In contrast to the accumulated literature on child development, studies related to the culture of childhood are scanty. The late Mary Ellen Goodman's *The Culture of Childhood: Child's Eye Views of Society and Culture* (Teachers College Press, 1970) is one such. In the chapter covering "Self and Others . . ." Goodman asserts: "The people around a child, as they react to him, in effect hold up before him a mirror in which he sees himself. Moreover they constitute a social network in which he locates himself and establishes an identity."[5] One of the bridges Betty Fast offered to children with whom she worked was the opportunity to develop the child's positive self-image, using media such as videotape. Especially for children entering school, this kind of acceptance helped open many doorways to activity and learning.

Child-oriented educational options

Writings on education during the fifteen years under review present a crazy but wonderfully dramatic quilt of discoveries, experiments, and happenings with children. Contributing to this mélange was a lively company of thinkers and doers. The longtime editor of *Highlights,* Walter Barbe, stressed the need to build on the strengths of children, gifted and otherwise. Jerome Bruner was able to develop and introduce a fascinating curriculum, "Man: A Course of Study" (MACOS)—useful apart from its sexist appellation. This curriculum used the scientific method of inquiry accompanied by an unusual treasury of supporting materials. MACOS subsequently was banned in many school systems while Bruner himself transferred his life to Great Britain. Where it was retained, however, watching children respond to the rich variety of these materials while adding their own remains an unforgettable experience.

Robert Coles's several volumes on minority children gave us a fascinating record of their life and language. In *The Lives of Children* (Random House, 1969), George Dennison described the rich human experience that is possible even in a storefront classroom, while Joseph Feather-stone's *Schools Where Children Learn* (Liveright, 1971) offered glimpses of children functioning more independently in classrooms influenced by significant child-focused primary educational changes in Britain. Nat Hentoff is a watchdog of current educational developments as they affect children, often reacting to racism and oppressiveness found in New York City's schools, in particular. With a rare brand of humor, James Herndon grapples with making "school work for your kids" in his *How to Survive Your Native Land* (Simon & Schuster, 1971). In *How Children Learn,* John Holt reminded readers: "First that vivid, vital, pleasurable experiences are the easiest to remember, and secondly, that memory works best when unforced, that it is not a mule that can be made to walk by beating it."[1]

In the film-review segment, "Schools as Mirrors," gathered by Mariann P. Winick in *Childhood Education* (October, 1976, pp. 51–54), several significant films showing educational change are described. *Every Kid a Learner* (1974) and *What Is Teaching? What Is Learning?* (1971) are among those cited.

In his gripping *36 Children* (New American Library, 1967), ever-resourceful Herbert Kohl pictured experiences that linger in the mind because of his determination to confront students with challenging information and situations and involve them in both. His personal store-house of resources and his multiple approaches to his students are utterly inspirational. Roger Landrum and Philip Lopate represent members of the Teachers and Writers Collaborative, through which they worked with New York City school children, concentrating on stimulating them to write about themselves and their lives and making publishing facilities available to them. In a slightly different way, Nancy Larrick's several volumes of selected poetry represent the exposure and outlets she has been able to provide for children through her campus-linked workshops. Richard Lewis's compilations have brought children of the world closer together through their selected writings about many feelings, moods, and subjects to which other children can respond.

Charles and Arlene Silberman have recorded their impressions of classroom situations in schools across the country, while Lillian Weber, after long years in nursery school administration, was able to transplant some of the open education she recorded in *The English Infant School and Informal Education* (Prentice-Hall, 1971) to the corridors of New York City schools for children to learn through play and other experiences. Affording them greater continuity of influences from kindergarten to the grades, she also exposed children to a greater variety of materials. Much of the activity noted above incorporated the spirit of Neil Postman's and Charles Weingartner's *Teaching as a Subversive Activity* (Delacorte Press, 1966), since so many of the implications do touch and often alter the lives of children and have the power to shake lethargy and effect change, overturning the dismal inevitability of Jonathan Kozol's *Death at an Early Age* (Houghton Mifflin, 1967).

Allied with these published contributions were the many exploratory activities of educational groups far too numerous to mention here—though some special ones merit attention. Among them were the experiments with ungraded schools, including the first ungraded high school in Melbourne, Florida. The work of the Educational Development Center of Newton, Massachusetts, has been significant for the materials, publications, and viewpoints it has promoted, all sustaining interest in children. Schools in many corners of the country, from Akron to Palo Alto, tried out free and alternative education. In New York City the Touchstone Center continues to function as a base to engage children in imaginative activities. Under the direction of Richard Lewis, the center exists to foster the creativity its founder believes all children possess. In a brochure written for the center he explains: "We try to encourage youngsters to express their own moods and ideas in any number of ways that come naturally to them." He regards teaching as "a constant process of relating yourself to another person, so it's always experimental and always changing."

Also to be considered are the significant contributions of museums in various parts of the country, from Pittsfield, Massachusetts, and the Boston Children's Museum, to Anacostia outside Washington, D.C., to the Smithsonian group in Washington, D.C., and New York's Museum of Natural History and its Museum of New York City, where touching has long been encouraged. These have brought more of the world and its inhabitants to children's consciousness, registering both the excitement of the city and the wares of the world, touched with artistry that is so important to children.

To transfer these viewpoints to the child and the school, the writer has used a few excerpts from Edward Blishen's *The School That I'd Like* (Penguin, 1969), in which students express the wish to govern themselves, "break down the walls of the school," "admit the wider world." One thirteen-year-old envisioned a friendly school where familiarity and cooperation reigned, with ambitions and big ideas for the future. In the September, 1978, issue of *Teacher* is the article, "If I Ran the School . . ." by Ann Cox and Susan Wilson, in which a group of children respond candidly to a questionnaire stimulated by the reactions of fourth-grader Miriam Davis to Mary Lystad's book, *Jennifer Takes Over P.S. 94.* Incorporated in "What Miriam Thinks" is the following excerpt: "For reading, I would choose one or two books to test children's ability by checking the words at the back. Then I would let them choose their own books—not just readers—but books that interested them, including comic books once in a while, if it would help them read."[6] Betty Fast's "libraries" in Groton were such reservoirs.

Links to child-focused reading

During the stretch of years covered, the literature surrounding reading expanded (as evidenced in *The Journal of Reading, Reading World,* and countless other sources). In addition, debates about reading approaches and problems involving reading instruction mounted. In his chapter on "Teaching Children about Reading: An Overview," George F. Canney sidestepped the bulk of controversial issues in the field. Instead he chose to stress teacher-student roles in learning to read, general instructional approaches to reading, and librarians' involvement in children's learning to read. He proposed seven suggested experiences a librarian can introduce:

1. The freedom to be an individual reading a book of one's own choice, rather than an assigned basal reader;
2. The chance to explore topics of personal interest—rather than being faced with the task of selecting a book from a library limited in titles by lists that dictate what nine-year-old girls like to read;
3. The opportunity to select a book that is "too easy" because of wanting to be reassured that one does know something—despite the bad day in reading "that book that's too hard";
4. The experience of taking a book that has been read before and enjoyed because it feels good to know that this book is "yours";
5. The license to choose a book that is difficult because it has one intriguing picture that stimulates the imagination;
6. The power to ask for advice about books to read that might be fun, but to know that one need not be compelled to accept that advice; and
7. The experience of being treated like other students—as an intelligent, responsible, significant individual capable of making decisions.[7]

In conclusion, he expressed the hope that "perhaps librarians can share more directly and consciously in the experience of helping children to discover the value and joy of reading."[8] Thus Betty Fast was able to sustain with her resolute yet casual manner.

Despite children's exposure to Sesame Street and the Electric Company, the reading materials that they confront when they are formally introduced to reading seldom reach the level of sophistication or animation of these programs. While textbooks remain the most customarily used basal sources for student exposure, their contents have become far more attractive as they draw to a greater extent from popular trade books for children. But when children can choose trade books, interest invariably mounts. The impact of "Right to Read" projects, community efforts in support of Reading is FUNdamental, and the growing movement for common reading time throughout the school that carries various local names must also be considered. Child-centered material, such as that contained in *Student-Centered Language and Reading, K–13* (Houghton Mifflin, 1976), assembled by James Moffett and Betty Jane Wagner, can season the materials available.

Harking backward to Anne Carroll Moore's *My Roads to Childhood* (The Horn Book, 1961), one can still endorse her statement that "reading is an art. It cannot be measured by graphs or statistics. The glow of enthusiasm a boy or girl brings to the first reading of a book—whether old or new—to which he feels spiritual kinship—is an infinitely precious thing to be cherished and respected on its own terms."[9]

The wealth and variety of reading materials is nearly staggering. When one examines three of the collections published this year, *Children's Media Market Place* (Gaylord Professional Publications, 1978), which "covers every area of children's media," *Twentieth Century Children's Writers* (St. Martin's Press, 1978), with its detailed introductions to a host of creative writers of children's books on both sides of the Atlantic, and *The Cool Web: The Pattern of Children's Reading* (Atheneum, 1978), one is struck anew by both the mass and maze of materials to which children can be exposed. Add to those the current edition of the *Elementary School Collection* (Bro-Dart, 1977), with its mix of media, and the possibilities expand further. As the child's right to know in an increasingly complicated world looms ever larger, opportunities to respond multiply. For Betty Fast the process of such choice involved a kind of alchemy which the children in Groton's schools must have experienced as they sampled various types of materials and added their own creations.

Library media center developments, 1962–1977

In her speculation about "School Library Service: 1970,"[10] Mildred L. Batchelder, then chief of ALA's School and Children's Library Division, forecast that the school library would have a "stimulating and exciting future." Although Batchelder anticipated some of the developments of the period 1962–77, she couldn't possibly visualize the tremendous changes that would emerge, together with the widened range of activity. In *Our Library* (John Day, c1939, 1942), Phyllis Fenner presented situations in which everyone in the school was at home in the library, its "hearthside," radiating human warmth.

The *Experimenting Together* series of bulletins which ALA published from 1938–1945, covering successively "The Librarian and the Teacher of English," ". . . the Teacher of Science," ". . . the Teacher of Music," and ". . . the Teacher of Home Economics," was to be drawn from real experiences in schools in different parts of the country. One of the objectives was "to show the activities of pupils, teachers and librarians unite creatively in exploring fields of knowledge." The initial bulletin, "The Librarian and the Teacher of English," was developed by Frieda Heller and Lou LaBrant, colleagues at the Ohio State University School, where they worked on problem solving, encouraged the wide use of media, and supported student efforts, initiative, and creative expression.

Lucille Fargo's *The Library in the School* was published by ALA in four editions between 1930 and 1947. Several statements from the third edition (1939) remain appropriate: "But the librarian initiates in her own right, peering intimately into the crannies of the pupil's mind, searching out likes and dislikes, enthusiasms and inhibitions, and prescribing the choice potion suited to each particular case or group. . . ."[11] Or: "It is these little chats over the desk, the quick response to the challenge of a pupil's interest, the ever-ready store of titles and authors and the spirit of give-and-take characterizing the working library that mark the culminating point of the library's place in the stimulation of reading among pupils." The fourth edition registers many changes, which this statement reveals in its reference to the library as "a communications center in which were assembled and through which were routed to teachers and pupils the many and varied materials of learning, printed and audio-visual, now in use in schools. . . ."[12]

Still it is the volume *Youth, Communications and Libraries: Papers Presented before the Library Institute at the University of Chicago, August 11–16, 1947* (ALA, 1949) that heralded many of the changes to come in library media services to children and young people. New frontiers were indicated among the goals expressed: "having each librarian a materials specialist and each library a materials center." This concept was later formalized by the American Association of School Librarians and in 1960 was followed by the significant publication *Standards for School Library Programs*. This clearly stated definition of the role of the school library and its desirable contents and activities has been a major instrument in the development of quality school library programs. Promoted by the School Library Development Project, many practical approaches were made available to those seeking planning guidance. In 1961, Columbia University School of Library Science hosted a key workshop, "The Library as a Materials Center." The same year saw the publication of Jean E. Lowrie's *Elementary School Libraries* (Scarecrow), with its glimpses of children's activities in ten school systems in Georgia, Illinois, Maryland, Michigan, New York, North Carolina, Tennessee, and Texas.

What were some key developments that contributed to the extension of media centers for children in the 1960s and 1970s? The Encyclopaedia Britannica-sponsored School Library Awards Program was influential. Introduced in 1963, the program drew national participation. By 1969 some 600 school systems had responded. In 1967, when the Cleveland Public Schools won the award on behalf of their well-conceived expanding elementary school libraries, the writer had the pleasure of supporting the application after visiting many of the new centers and sharing in children's delight with tasting and testing their use. In successive issues of *Patterns of Development* (published by Encyclopaedia Britannica), Mary Gaver was able to analyze the course of these countrywide happenings more closely. In 1973, the awards were renamed the School Library Media Awards and continue to arouse interest, excitement, and curiosity about new approaches. It is invariably rewarding to trace and sample student involvement in the winning entries. Also, the occasional films released in conjunction with the awards afford excellent bases for comparison and stimulation.

Also influential during both the 60s and 70s was the significant work of the Educational Facilities Laboratories, funded by the Ford Foundation. Its spread of activities was evident in journal articles, pamphlets, books, and films, and was reflected in the contents of many important conferences of the period which often involved school administrators at many levels. R. E. Ellsworth and Hobart Wagner coauthored its *The School Library,* which attracted a wide audience of readers and helped deepen the updated concept of the library as a materials center. The contemporary setting, current concepts and terminology, and the expectations for and involvement of students were rich and exciting to ponder. Likewise their films, *Room to Learn* (describing the Early Learning Center in Stamford, Connecticut) and *A Child Went Forth* (on inner city and ghetto schools) helped visualize possibilities worth sharing and possibly emulating.

Between 1963 and 1967 the Knapp School Libraries Project offered demonstrations at several school levels to help activate and personify the

1960 *Standards,* to promote improved understanding and use of library resources on the part of teachers and administrators, to guide and encourage citizens from "as many communities as possible in the development of their own library programs," and to increase interest and support for school library development among educators (including library school members) and citizens generally. The project's final report, *Realization . . . ,* edited by its director, Peggy Sullivan (ALA, 1968), incorporates a veritable repository of documentary information about the eight project schools and the librarians involved during the various stages of their planned activities.

The school projects offered unusual opportunities to visit the libraries. This writer enjoyed unforgettable experiences in observing the setting and aspects of the program of the Central Park Road School, which was assembled in combined classrooms, the Mt. Royal School, with its suite of rooms, and the handsomely redeveloped Oak Park and River Forest High School. The latter can be seen in the film *At the Center* (released several years later by the School Library Manpower Project). In each school the involvement of the students and their contact with the library media personnel, as well as their individual and group exploration and utilization of media, was memorable. Despite the variety of the settings (from the simple to the affluent), and the differences in level of functioning, the concentration on student media competencies and the exposure to many-faceted programs was evident. The project's film, *And Something More,* features librarian Sarah Innes in the Sedgwick School in Charlotte, North Carolina. The title carries "layered" meanings which can be drawn from viewing the film; it touched the writer especially because her daughter had found Norton Juster's *The Phantom Tollbooth* a favorite book—only to discover that it was not carried in many libraries. Yet the use of this book as a vehicle for the children's dramatization in the film eventually led librarians to reevaluate it. In many instances, the book was subsequently purchased while adults responsible for the review learned a little more about children's choices.

Midway into the 60s yet another Encyclopaedia Britannica-sponsored project involved children with media and continues to have some repercussions today. Project Discovery ran its formal course from 1964 to 1967 and was planned to "re-examine the data of the project and its long-term effects on media utilization."[13] Designed to test the effect of "maximum availability" of instructional materials "on curriculum, on pupil achievement, creativity and motivation and on teaching methods and techniques," the project was carried out in four sites: Mercer Elementary School in Shaker Heights, Ohio; Thomas Edison Elementary School in Daly City, California; Scott Montgomery Elementary School in Washington, D.C.; and Terrell School District in Terrell, Texas. Two films picture a cross section of meaningful activities drawn from these sites: *Project Discovery* and *Let Them Learn*. Both feature the participation of children and their chain of activities, with sequences that remain in the mind's eye long afterward.

The publication of media standards that opened and closed the 60s and then moved into the mid 70s are dealt with in terms of both educational and philosophical outlook and impact in Lillian L. Shapiro's *Serving Youth: Communication and Commitment in the High School Library* (Bowker, 1975). It is ironic to note that while the framework for media center functioning has been so remarkably clarified at both the building and district levels, the jarring economic developments of the 70s have eroded much that has been projected and already attempted as desirable, and caused readjustments that reduce both activity and support professionals.

Among the by-products of the publication of succeeding compilations of *Standards* have been the books with suggestions for developing school media programs and operating media centers, very much along recognizably "how to" approaches. Many of these are listed in Appendix 1, "Organizing and Running the Library/Media Center" in Mary Meacham's *Information Sources in Children's Literature* (Greenwood, 1978).

Some student-oriented media centers

School library/media literature abounds in examples of media centers that have emerged in various places. One excellent source for such articles is the *Wisconsin Library Bulletin,* which often describes the facility physically and highlights student activities—usually with illustrations. In Lillian Shapiro's volume there is a series of examples representing "successful media programs in secondary schools." In the concluding paragraph of this section of her book, Shapiro emphasizes:

> Wherever a library staff, sometimes consisting of one, are promoting the idea that the library media center is an essential laboratory in the learning process, opening the eyes, ears, and minds of students to the world of humankind's thoughts and deeds, delivering information as promptly and effectively as possible for that school, and working cooperatively with all those involved in the program of the school—that library media program is commendable and praiseworthy, indeed, are the works of that staff.[14]

In much the same spirit, the January, 1975, issue of *Wilson Library Bulletin* focused on school library/media centers—articles "selected from more than 200 submissions. Speaking for themselves, these vignettes show that the profession is not only alive and well, it's lively, questioning, multi-faceted, vital, dedicated, facing difficult problems, and working very hard. . . ."[15] The issue incorporated professions at work, preparation, getting to the student, "teaching the teachers," "reaching the principal," and included an independent school experience—followed by a "random cross section of life in school libraries/media centers"—to which Betty Fast contributed. Later her "Mediacentric" feature provided her with a base to share with colleagues in the field experiences, ideas, and approaches to problems she encountered.

In 1976 a set of statements was issued from the National Reading Center, then in Washington, D.C., in partial support for the National Right to Read effort. Prepared by Blanche Korngold of Harvard University, statement number eight was devoted to the school library. In it she wrote: "The most important thing about the school library is its program: the exploring, listening, looking, reading, relating and *thinking* that it makes possible for each student," emphasizing further the individual effort to learn. She refers to the school librarian as a "mind-stretcher."

The year 1977 brought the publication of John T. Gillespie's *A Model School District Media Program: Montgomery County as a Case Study* (ALA). In studying the framewofk of this system, much can be learned about a well-conceived and coordinated program—with elements that continue to mark this system as perhaps topnotch in the country. Number 10 of the performance criteria, for instance, seeks to "establish relationships with colleagues, students, parents and the community which reflect the recognition of and respect for every individual."

It is interesting to balance Gillespie's effort with D. Philip Baker's compilation, *School and Public Library Media Programs for Children and Young Adults* (Gaylord, 1977). From the many programs described, several stand out because of their special character: Spring Street School in Atlanta, Georgia; Amelia Street School, Richmond, Virginia, where "each child is an individual, with talents, needs, problems and experiences peculiar to him, and although he may be lacking in mental, physical and emotional capacities, and development, his similarities to normal children are greater than his differences."[16] Considered one of the most creative media programs of the state, the Peach Tree Elementary School of Norcross, Georgia, boasts thematic learning stations, a recessed pit area for puppet plays and stories, and a comics corner. In the Sea Girt Elementary School in Sea Girt, New Jersey, the "living literature program" is balanced with a poets-in-the-classroom program. Also worth noting is the Dixie High School of St. George, Utah, with its annual film festival.

Baker observes that "wherever possible . . . conveying information from person to person is best done by programs that stress the humanizing capacity of media." He projects:

> The future of media programs for children is everywhere, not just in media centers or public library children's rooms. Essential to our ability to manage this future well will be the recognition that every child is really a media specialist. The ability to perceive, to be stimulated by, to learn from, and to adapt to, is present in every child, from birth. . . .[17]

Author Steven Kroll sums up the relationship between materials, the media specialist, and the child:

> The media specialist like the teacher has to be a friendly, responsive person—a person responsive to children, a person who is in some way in touch with his or her own childhood, just as writers for children. . . . In short a librarian, a teacher, a media specialist, must in some way be touched with wonder. And that wonder, if it is there, will communicate itself to the children. . . .[18]

And the children will know. As Frances Clarke Sayers observed: "In the end, book by book, and child by child, it is the gleam in the eye that is the most effective means of communication."[19]

Betty Fast had that gleam.

REFERENCES

1. John Holt, *How Children Learn* (New York: Pitman Publications, 1967), p. ix.

2. Muriel Ward, *Young Minds Need Something to Grow On* (Evanston, Ill.: Row, Peterson, 1957), p. 86.

3. Bernard Spodek, "Education and Children's Ways of Knowing," in *Children's Services of Public Libraries* (23rd Allerton Park Institute), ed. Selma K. Richardson (Urbana-Champaign, Ill: University of Illinois Graduate School of Library Science, 1978), pp. 9–22.

4. Diane Farrell, "Library and Information Needs of Young Children," in Conference on the Needs of Occupational, Ethnic, and Other Groups in the United States, *Library and Information Service Needs of the Nation* (Washington, D.C.: Government Printing Office, 1974), pp. 143–54.

5. Mary Ellen Goodman, *The Culture of Childhood: Child's Eye Views of Society and Culture* (Columbia University, N.Y.: Teachers College Press, 1970), p. 46.

6. Ann Cox and Susan Wilson, "If I Ran the School . . . ," *Teacher,* 96:79 (September 1978).

7. George F. Canney, "Teaching Children about Reading: An Overview," in

Children's Services of Public Libraries, ed. Selma Richardson (Champaign, Ill.: University of Illinois, 1978), pp. 23–34.

8. Ibid., p. 33.

9. Anne Carroll Moore, *My Roads to Childhood* (Boston: The Horn Book, 1961), p. 339.

10. Mildred L. Batchelder, "School Library Service: 1970," in *The Library of Tomorrow: A Symposium* (Chicago: ALA, 1939), pp. 133–41.

11. Lucille Fargo, *The Library in the School* (Chicago: ALA, 1939), p. 67.

12. Lucille Fargo, *The Library in the School* (Chicago: ALA, 1947), p. vii.

13. *Guidelines to Media Utilization: Lessons from Project Discovery,* Research Report 64 (Bloomington, Ind.: Agency for Instructional Television, July 1978).

14. Lillian Shapiro, *Serving Youth: Communication and Commitment in the High School Library* (New York: Bowker, 1975), pp. 21–27.

15. *Wilson Library Bulletin* 49, 5 (January, 1975) 360.

16. D. Philip Baker, *School and Public Library Media Programs for Children and Young Adults* (Syracuse, N.Y.: Gaylord Professional Publications, 1977), p. 308.

17. Ibid., p. 359.

18. Steven Kroll, *Opening the World: Motivation in the Use of Library/Media Materials* (Baltimore: Maryland State Department of Education, 1978), p. 5.

19. In *Youth, Communication and Libraries: Papers Presented before the Library Institute at the University of Chicago, August 11–16, 1947,* ed. by Frances Henne, Alice Brooks, Ruth Ersted (Chicago: ALA, 1949), p. 132.

CHILDREN'S RIGHTS, PARENTS' RIGHTS— A LIBRARIAN'S DILEMMA

by MARGARET MARY KIMMEL

Some people refer to children as the resource of a nation, tomorrow's promise, the hope of civilization. Others label children as juvenile delinquents, welfare recipients, tax burdens, or wards of the state. Still other groups think only in terms of noisy-Robert, Sarah-who-sings, or Matthew-of-blond-curls, an angelic smile and the soul of a fiend. However that perception is shaped—whether by parent or family, by court or social institution, or merely by an interested observer—it is adults who do the defining, limiting, and evaluating. This relationship between child and adult has its roots in ancient tradition as well as in twentieth-century family life style. Definitions of children, who they are, their rights and obligations, and their relationship to the rest of the community are complicated by social, economic, even political considerations. Few would deny, however, the necessity of caring for the young.

The notion that children have rights before the law is a relatively modern phenomenon and one that needs a good deal of exploration—whether by interested observers or militant advocates. The purpose of this paper, then, is to briefly review the status of children and the law and to look at the child and the family in interaction with other social institutions. As representatives of such a social institution providing a wide range of information services, librarians must specifically examine some questions relating children and their families to the information environment that we provide for them. It is important to stress the relationship of children in their family setting. Children do not exist in a vacuum, and it is their relationship to others in a community that must be clarified for us, for within that relationship lies crucial questions defining the scope of our services.

The definition of the term "children" may be viewed as a legal classification describing individuals under twenty-one or eighteen. Legal terminology suggests that "infancy" or "minority" persons have a special status that determines their rights and duties before the law and dramatizes their powerless position. This legal definition suggests some of the vagaries between children and the law, however, for the status of a minor may differ from state to state, even from crime to crime within the same jurisdiction. In some areas, for instance, individuals under eighteen or twenty-one may be tried in criminal court for such serious crimes as homicide, but in other instances are relegated to the juvenile court where their fate is decided for them.

Most historians agree that before the nineteenth century children were viewed as the property of their parents or guardians and had little or no rights at all, only the obligation to serve and be respectful. The few cases brought before the English Chancery Court laid the groundwork for the concept of *parens patriae,* the intervention of another authority when the guardian abused his power to chastise a child. By 1817, when the poet Shelley was denied custody of his children on the grounds of his behavior and his beliefs, the intervention of the state was a more accepted practice by society as a whole. Since we have inherited so much from English common law, this concept of the right of the state to intervene is an important one to note. There are some exceptions to this, especially in the American experimentation with adoption, common law marriages, and in the relative relaxation of laws pertaining to illegitimacy.[1]

The social historian, Phillippe Aires, claims that Rousseau and Locke essentially invented the concept of childhood.[2] Before Locke, children were accepted as small adults and were given little or no special treatment. Viewed as economic assets, they were valued for their contribution to the welfare of the family. While some dispute Aires's theory, few deny that in the nineteenth century the industrial revolution, urbanization, and growing efforts at education and emancipation provided the background and impetus for the concern for children. The exploited social situations and grim physical conditions of youth on the streets, in slavery, in mills, or cotton fields were cause for reform.

Two strains of legislation are observable from these early efforts. One may be defined as structural reform, the other as a deviancy-control approach. In the first approach to legislation, the efforts at expansion of the educational system and development of child-labor laws may be seen as dominating efforts. In promoting a classless society where democratic process demanded literacy as a priority, reformers found themselves faced with the task of forcing sometimes unwilling youth and parents into the classroom and sometimes unwilling taxpayers to assume the burden of educating all young people. As early as 1647, the Massachusetts General Court enacted a law that required the establishment of different types of schools when a town grew to a certain size. Although the towns assumed that parents would teach their young the basics of reading and writing, it was obviously necessary to support the establishment of schools for those families who could not or would not provide such learning. The phrases "for the sake of the children" or "in the best interests of the child" typify early efforts to clarify society's right to intervene between children and their legal guardians.

The second theme became apparent in the latter half of the nineteenth century as a part of the expansion of social services and a movement to save the deserving poor. Part of this effort was directed toward children, promoting an individualistic approach to reform, rather than a structural one. Those most closely involved in this so-called child-rescue movement were often women who claimed that they could best provide the "firm authority and human warmth" which the abandoned, the orphaned, and the wayward seemed to lack. These "child savers" (a term used by Anthony Platt in his book by the same name) attempted to defend the values of traditional family life and to emphasize the necessity for the proper socialization of children. The role of women in this effort was obvious since, as these nineteenth century reformers contended, "women were more genteel than men, better equipped to protect the innocence of children and more capable of regulating their education and recreation."[3]

The efforts of these women reformers were significant in maintaining the prestige of middle-class women in a society that was rapidly changing, but these efforts also provided legitimate career opportunities for women. The strength of the movement to save the "deserving poor" was enhanced by a workable, stable administrative system in which caretakers assumed the role of professionals and sought community sanction for their work. The volunteer was replaced by an individual who became part of a structural organization with institutional loyalties, whose efforts on behalf of the client vied with keeping "statistics which would justify their continued existence and warrant increases in personnel and budget."[4] The new role of the social worker, for instance, combined elements of an old role as defender of family life with that of a new one—social servant. Work with social agencies was not only "fitting" for women but, additionally, it was an instrument of emancipation that allowed women to leave their homes yet remain in a socially acceptable situation.

In terms of child protection standards, then, a subtle but profound change began to occur. The individualistic approach to save the deserving child shifted general community responsibility to governmental agencies. The juvenile court was deemed the appropriate instrument of intervention—enforcing policy and interrupting patterns of daily living—and children came to have separate and special status. The system defined conformity as the dominant principle of reform.

In the last ten to fifteen years, social conditions have again forced a reconsideration of the status of children and their place in the community. Civil rights activism and the women's movement have forced a reevaluation and reconsideration of many segments of society whose interests have been overlooked. The so-called children's rights movement is only one aspect of the growing concern about the case of children before the law. John Holt, in his *Escape from Childhood,* for example, suggests that children must have the same rights and responsibilities as adults. This theme is echoed by Richard Farson, who claims that children are forced into an "unnatural state" by adults who attempt to curtail their growth and impose restrictions.

Marian Wright Edleman, on the other hand, declares that much of the children's liberation talk is "just hogwash." The Children's Defense Fund, established in 1973, is a national, nonprofit, public charity that seeks to provide systematic advocacy for children. There are some instances where children should have adult rights, Edleman contends, and it must be determined which instances those are and which children need them. She continues, "But children are not adults. They need protection and nurturing. . . . My five-year-old should not be liberated and my four-year-old is not capable of managing his own money. The institutional disregard of children is pervasive and destructive, but I question whether the liberationists are raising the issue in the most helpful way."[5]

These two arguments exemplify the approaches that summarize the position taken by leaders in the field. One is to extend all adult legal rights to children in areas of jurisdictional disputes, health and welfare cases, education, discipline, work or legal immunity. The other approach insists that children have special interests and needs that should be recognized as rights under law.

There is an absence of fair, workable, realistic standards for limiting parental discretion and guiding state intervention. There is also a failure to evaluate a child's independent interests, allowing competent children to speak for themselves.

It is necessary to pause a moment and consider the term "right" in itself. The *Oxford English Dictionary* describes a legal right as an enforceable claim to the possession of property or authority or to the enjoyment of privileges or immunities. One must make a distinction, then, between legal rights and political or moral demands that have not been formally recognized by the law and have the status of needs or interests, not rights.

The extension of adult legal rights to children is a complex question, but it may be the most significant challenge to confront the movement to reform the child's place before the law. Such reform might involve, for instance, extending certain adult criminal rights to children even when those children are not in the adult court system. For example, trial by jury is not permitted in today's juvenile courts. It would involve the possibility for children to request medical care without parental consent, or might provide the child with legal representation in any situation where his or her interests are involved.

One of the most complicated aspects is also one urgently in need of reform, that of juvenile court proceedings involving those cases that apply strictly to children because they are children. These so-called status offenses label children "Persons In Need of Supervision" (or PINS). Because of their status alone, children may be detained for truancy or running away from home, disobedience of "reasonable" orders at home or school, or "improper" sexual behavior. They may also be held in protective care for being found in a railway or truck terminal, keeping late hours, or using profane language. For such offenses, the "custodial care" provided by the juvenile court often means jail or police lockups. In New York State, for instance, the Carnegie Commission estimates that in 1971 100,000 young people were in jail. Forty-three percent of them were status offenders. Furthermore, it has been noted that there are more girls than boys declared status offenders, and that children in this category are more often held for longer periods than others.[6]

In some cases, rights have been granted to children in exactly the form provided for adults. In cases involving voting, for instance, the age limits have been lowered to eighteen, and all rights and privileges have been granted to young people. In other instances, however, legislation is interpreted or tailored to the perceived characteristics of children. A case in point is *In Re Gault* (1967). Gault provides for due process guarantees, specifically:

1. Notice to both parent and child in time to prepare a defense, including a "sufficient statement of charge";
2. Right to counsel (and provision of counsel if necessary);
3. Right to remain silent—"privilege against self-incrimination"; and
4. Right to confrontation and cross-examination of witnesses.[7]

Implementation of *Gault,* however, finds lawyers still applying more stringent standards of interpretation to children, not because the courts have constrained them to do so, but because their clients are children. Although adult clients might be advised how to avoid punishment, lawyers are reluctant to help children "beat the rap." It has been suggested that the participation of lawyers in juvenile court is likely to make the system more orderly and efficient, but not substantially more fair or benevolent.

The second approach to children before the law accepts the assumption that children have some special and unique interests and needs above and beyond legal rights now granted to them. But these claims, drawn from natural law and moral philosophy, are based on needs not yet considered legal rights for anyone in our system. How can one group or agency enforce the right of a child to grow up in a world free of war? Or who is to define and enforce the right to be wanted? Or who is to define and enforce the child's right to learn? to information?

It is here that the dilemma of the librarian becomes apparent. Library service to children has traditionally been a part of a movement to save the child, to protect and defend the individual and the family as an institution. Child protection has traditionally encompassed the tasks of both salvation and reeducation, as though the child lives in sin and must be redeemed. Together with the older law of parent and child laid down over seven centuries, these two themes form the modern legal framework for the definition and implementation of permissible standards of behavior by and toward children.

But like other social institutions, we must now ask whether children are to be treated as status offenders, restricted from service and materials simply because they are children. Or do children deserve all the privileges and service given to other segments of the population—interlibrary loan and access to a total collection?

There are some very difficult questions involved in either approach that need our concern, study, and definition. For many years, the service to children in public and school libraries has subscribed to the education theory that one learns best by doing. "Have you looked it up in the card catalog?" is not unfamiliar to anyone setting foot in a library, but for children we have devised games, quizzes, and hunts to introduce various sources and help the young help themselves. Librarians and educators have sought to provide the answers and devise methods for children to find out just what we want them to know.

A recent controversial title, *Freddy's Book,* suggests a number of approaches to information-seeking patterns that a child might employ. Without debating the merits of the book, it is interesting to note that when Freddy's search for information takes him to the public library (after the failure of his mother and his friends at school to clarify his question), Freddy is once more stymied because the librarian deems his request inappropriate.

On the other hand, there is an equally tough set of questions evolving from a stand that suggests "all information for all children all the time." For one thing, children are faced with a knowledge/technology explosion as vast as the one that overwhelms adults. Children, too, need a filter, a manager of information, and relatively few of them can afford the services of Xerox Corporation, whose series of commercials offered to select, organize, and disseminate information.

At the same time, the recognition of the worth of good writing, illustration, artistically developed film, sound recordings of quality and integrity are value judgments that librarians make every day and automatically pass on to the clients served, adult or child.

These value judgments must be recognized as such and defenses for or against such disparate titles as *Dr. Dolittle* or the Nancy Drew series must accept both the responsibility of such judgments and the limitations imposed. The difficulty of defining access, selection, and guidance is magnified by community factors, by the relatively undefined nature of the relationship between social institutions and parental intervention. Does a parental request for the book *Show Me* supersede thoughtful, evaluative professional judgment that rejected a title labeled by one reviewer as "a mixture of 'corn' and 'porn' "? Are librarians obliged to respond to community demand to add a favorite, well-loved book, *Little Black Sambo?*

These questions about the rights of children are not new ones. Kate Douglas Wiggin in 1899 asked:

> Who owns the child? If a parent owns him—mind, body, and soul—we must adopt one line of argument; if, as a human being, he owns himself, we must adopt another. In my thought, the parent is simply a divinely appointed guardian, who acts for his child until he attains what we call the age of discretion—that highly uncertain period which arrives very late in life with some persons, and not at all with others.[8]

Three quarters of a century later, we still ponder these problems.

The Carnegie Commission on Children states bluntly that there are no affirmative rights in common or constitutional law for the minimum essentials needed for children and their families to survive, to grow, to flourish. Standing alone, the law cannot provide all requirements of a healthy, happy child. Love and nurturing are the foundations most of us expect beyond any legal mandate. It can be the source of some controls, some opportunities, but the library, like other social institutions, must face the questions now. The Chilean poet Mistral declares:

> Many things can wait. The child cannot. Right now his hip bones are being formed, his blood is being made, his senses are being developed. To him we cannot say tomorrow. His name is today.

REFERENCES

1. Margaret K. Rosenheim, "The Child and the Law," in *200 Years of Children,* edited by Edith Grotberg (Washington, D.C.: U. S. Department of Health, Education, and Welfare: Office of Human Development, Office of Child Development, 1977), pp. 423–86.

2. Phillippe Aires, *Centuries of Childhood: A Social History of Family Life* (New York: Random House, 1965).

3. Anthony Platt, *The Child Savers,* rev. ed. (Chicago: University of Chicago Press, 1977).

4. Ibid., p. 78.

5. Margie Casady, "Society's Pushed-Out Children," *Psychology Today* 58 (June 1975).

6. Kenneth Keniston and the Carnegie Council on Children, *All Our Children: The American Family Under Pressure* (New York: Harcourt Brace Jovanovich, 1977), p. 195.

7. Hillary Rodman, "Children under the Law," *Harvard Educational Review* 43, 4: 56 (November 1973).

8. Kate Douglas Wiggin, *Children's Rights* (Boston: Houghton Mifflin, 1899), pp. 4–5.

BIBLIOGRAPHY

Adams, Paul, et. al. *Children's Rights.* New York: Praeger Publishers, 1971.

Aires, Phillippe. *Centuries of Childhood: A Social History of Family Life.* New York: Random House, 1965.

Casady, Margie. "Society's Pushed-Out Children." *Psychology Today* (June 1975) 57–65.

Edleman, Marian Wright. "In Defense of Children's Rights." *Yale Alumni Magazine and Journal* (February, 1978) 14–16.

Farson, Richard. *Birthrights.* New York: Macmillan, 1974.

Gottlieb, David. *Children's Liberation.* Englewood Cliffs, N.J.: Prentice-Hall, 1973.

Gross, Beatrice, and Gross, Ronald, eds. *The Children's Rights Movement.* Garden City, N.Y.: Anchor Press, 1977.

Holt, John. *Escape from Childhood.* New York: Dutton, 1974.

Keniston, Kenneth, and the Carnegie Council on Children. *All Our Children: The American Family under Pressure.* New York: Harcourt-Brace Jovanovich, 1977.

Lubove, Roy. *The Professional Altruist.* New York: Atheneum, 1975.

Platt, Anthony. "Maternal Justice," pp. 75–100, in *The Child Savers.* Rev. ed. Chicago: University of Chicago Press, 1977.

Rodman, Hillary. "Children under the Law." *Harvard Educational Review* 43, 4 (November 1973) 487–514.

Rosenheim, Margaret K. "The Child and the Law." In *200 Years of Children.* Edited by Edith Grotberg. Washington, D.C.: U.S. Department of Health, Education and Welfare: Office of Human Development, Office of Child Development, 1977.

Senn, Milton. *Speaking Out for America's Children.* New Haven: Yale University Press, 1977.

Wiggin, Kate Douglas. *Children's Rights: A Book of Nursery Logic.* Boston: Houghton Mifflin, 1899.

CHILDREN AS MEDIA PRODUCERS

by VIRGINIA M. CROWE

The media specialist in the modern school library media center has a complex task with a multiplicity of responsibilities. One has only to examine the competency statements of colleges and universities with programs for the preparation of media specialists to recognize that the media specialist must be many things to many people. In the not-too-distant past the "media specialist" was a teacher who had a free period and didn't mind using that time to hand out materials, set up a 16mm projector, or show a filmstrip. Radical changes have taken place, changes that now require that the media specialist acquire a whole range of competencies related to design principles, communication and learning theory, curriculum development, organization, and administration of the media center.

The list of needed competencies identified by the Knapp School Library Manpower Project[1] is extensive and sometimes staggering to the beginning school library media specialist. It is evident from the variety of subjects in Betty Fast's publications that she has acquired and practiced the whole gamut of skills and competencies of the media specialist in the modern school library media center. But for Betty Fast, as for every truly successful library media specialist, the major focus is on the children who use the center.

Hundreds of articles and books and thousands of words have been published on the programs and activities of the school library media center in today's educational scene. The jargon of the media field is well known and widely used. Everyone in the teaching profession is aware of the impact of the "new" media. We don't even call a library by that simple term anymore. The concept has been changed to include the newer information formats such as television, films, and audiotapes.

This change has not been for the sake of change alone, but is founded on sound educational research. Children do learn from nonprint materials, sometimes more effectively than from the traditional print format. No one can deny the impact of such television programs as *Sesame Street* or the excellent films produced by Weston Woods and other leading film producers.

The most recent standards for school libraries, *Media Programs: District and School*,[2] prepared jointly by the American Library Association and the Association for Educational Communications and Technology, recognize the importance of nonprint educational materials in the educational process. No longer is the printed word the supreme authority. Filmstrips, slides, records, tapes, and numerous other forms of media occupy the time and attention of teachers, librarians, and students.

The problems of cataloging, storage, and retrieval have gained monumental importance in the minds of librarians and in the literature of the field. The selection, evaluation, reviewing, and utilization of media receives increasingly greater emphasis as we wrestle with the flood of materials, trying to select the best, the most appropriate, at the right price. The available money never seems to go as far as it should and the concerns of budgeting become ever more frustrating.

Betty Fast offered sound advice for a solution to the problem when she stated that "if program priorities are firmly anchored to the needs and interests of the users (both students and teachers), our programs will be more resistant to budget cuts."[3] Librarians become so entangled in the thickets of administrative crises that they fail to see that they must always focus on the users, and that the entire system will suffer if they forget the needs of the children. Betty Fast saw this clearly and advocated planning techniques to make wise use of available resources.

Production of materials for instructional use is recommended by the *Standards* as necessary to meet user needs. The media center should contain the materials and equipment necessary to prepare visuals, make audiotapes, produce videotapes, slides, and 8mm films.[4] The *Standards* further state that "insofar as maturity levels permit, all facilities, equipment, supplies, and professional and technical assistance are available for student use." Teachers and library media specialists frequently overlook this recommendation and consider the facilities, etc., as being available only to the professional staff who "will take better care of expensive equipment." Or perhaps they feel that students will simply waste materials or will not use their time wisely. Administrators may not encourage student use of production facilities because of negative feelings about student competence.

The recommendation in the *Standards* is important and should be heeded by library media staff and by teachers. Students must have positive experiences with media in order to become critical consumers of various types of formats. The student encounters media in nearly all activities, both in the school and in the home, and should be able to select and manipulate media to achieve worthwhile goals. If his or her only response to media is a passive one, he or she can never really use media in an effective way.

A passive response to media means that the child will view media formats as more entertaining than instructional, and therefore will be less critical and less likely to analyze media content or technology. This passive role carries on into adulthood and encourages the production of mediocre programs for a noncritical audience.

When should the child begin to produce media? In high school, junior high school, or elementary school? The sooner the better, and the primary grades are a good place to start. The young child needs to begin experiencing media as an integral part of the curriculum and to recognize its importance in the instructional process. The teacher and the media specialist, working together, must plan experiences in media production that are meaningful to the child and are on a level that the child can successfully complete.

Professional personnel tend to think of only the more complex media formats, such as television and films, and ignore the simpler formats, such as flannel boards and manipulative materials. Their sophistication and higher level of training causes them to forget that, to the child, producing his or her own flannel board figures and story is a feat worthy of accomplishment. It's only a few short steps (and years) until that same child may be running a VTR and producing a television show. The techniques of working with materials to produce a story vary in the degree of complexity, but the basics of production are learned in the very earliest experiences; therefore, those experiences should be properly guided and skillfully managed.

Will producing media cause children to become more creative? This concept might involve a rather difficult research task to prove or disprove, but the media specialist who allows children to experiment with a variety of materials is certainly fostering the creative processes. Betty Fast encouraged creative imagination on the part of the media specialist when she said that we should "envision a myriad of uses for a particular item" and that we should not allow our ideas about equipment to become stereotyped.[5]

Imaginative uses of media extend the limits of a particular format. Allow the child to use materials or equipment in a nontraditional manner. Encourage a group of children to think of different ways to use a filmstrip or a tape. Try not to be locked in by the obvious. Commercial producers of media have frequently provided the steps to follow in utilizing their product, but that does not mean that the media specialist is bound to follow those steps; even if that is the easiest path to take, it is seldom the most creative.

We should look beyond the intended use of a film or a tape and utilize it in a nontraditional approach, perhaps combined with a locally produced sound track or visuals. The only limits of a more effective utilization are the limits of the media specialist's imagination. Once free from the imposed constraints set by the producer, budgets can be stretched and materials used more effectively.

Media specialists need to be aware of the impact of the concept of mainstreaming upon media programs. Handicapped children, either physically or mentally handicapped, are being placed in the regular classroom setting as much as is possible in accordance with federal mandates. In the past, the handicapped were placed in segregated classrooms or even separate schools and could be effectively ignored by the rest of the school population.

Mainstreaming has changed the total process of educating the handicapped, and teachers and media specialists must adjust their techniques and their ideas of service. Betty Fast recognized and approved of this change. In her *Wilson Library Bulletin* column, she described her experiences in working with classes of retarded students. She said, "Although I didn't know much about them, I thought, well, they're children. And that, it turned out, was the most important thing of all."[6] She used sound filmstrips, storytelling, and improvisational drama, to which students responded very well. She stated also that resources are needed that allow handicapped children to produce their own materials and declared that "production *has* to be one of the strong arms of our media programs with such children."[7]

Handicapped children will need special help in production but will realize the same benefits from working with materials that the nonhandicapped child does. They learn to think critically, listen intently, verbalize better and become more responsive to media. The media specialist has a responsibility to these children and to their teachers and should play a leadership role in mainstreaming.

Money will become available to aid in accomplishing the goals of mainstreaming, and the media specialist should spend that money wisely, remembering to purchase supplies and equipment for student production. Within the limits of their handicaps, these students can make audiotapes, videotapes, do simple photography, and make transparencies. Since handicapped children frequently have difficulty learning to read, it becomes extremely important that they become visually literate. Working with pictures, organizing, dry-mounting, and laminating will help them to read pictorially and to appreciate the importance of pictures and the information they can obtain from them.

Children in the regular classroom frequently have reading difficulties, many times because they are simply "turned off" on reading. James Thomas reports that he used media production techniques to "turn on" his classes. His fourth grade class produced a filmstrip to be shown at the Parent Teacher Organization meeting. In the course of preparing the filmstrip, the students researched their subject in books, encyclopedias, and magazines. The success of their product reinforced the satisfaction the students gained from their research and helped turn the students to reading materials.[8]

Students can begin producing and working with media in the primary grades and continue through high school. The well-equipped media center will make adequate provision for these activities. The media specialist and the classroom teacher will supervise these experiences so that the productions will be curriculum-oriented and competency-based.

The skills acquired will follow on into adulthood and sharpen student response to media.

Children may begin production of simple puppets and other manipulative materials. They can move on to do simple hand lettering or use mechanical lettering equipment. Filmstrips can be made using write-on film, and slides can also be made with write-on techniques. Color lifts can be done to make either slides or transparencies.

Transparencies can be hand-made using felt-tip pens or thermal copiers. Students learn important communication techniques and lay-out skills in the performance of these tasks. More advanced students may use still cameras and copy stands to make slides or prints. Schools with darkroom facilities permit students to learn to develop their own slides and prints. Flat pictures and posters can be dry-mounted and laminated for more permanent use. Students can then arrange pictures to tell a story, evoke feelings and emotions, or motivate discussions.

Cassette or open-reel tape recording has many educational uses and is a rewarding medium for student production. Students may prepare scripts to go with filmstrips, slides, or 8mm films. Tapes may be used for verbal drill and practice, for reviewing material, or for evaluation. Tapes may be exchanged with students in other parts of the world to promote multicultural understanding. Creative students will find many ways to use the tape format.

Motion picture production requires more sophisticated equipment and techniques, but is a highly motivating medium for students. Students can learn film animation techniques or use motion pictures to show social problems in the community. Again, the list of activities is long and constrained only by the limits of the camera and the creativity of the photographer. Many school districts have well-equipped television studios where both elementary and secondary students can learn the basics of television production. They learn to run cameras, operate the videotape recorder, the switcher, and the film chain. In the process, they also learn to write scripts, to critically evaluate performances, and to understand the limitations of the medium.

Computers are an important part of everyday life for most Americans. While computers are not housed in the media center, a terminal may very well be located there and students may wish to use it during their study time. Computer-assisted instruction may be a part of the school district curriculum and the media center may house the terminal and the display system.

In our age of technology, we are doing students a great disservice if we fail to provide them with many ways to experience media. The media specialist, as part of the teaching team, must constantly strive to provide each student with opportunities to produce media or respond to it. If we are to maximize the creative energies of our students, we must take the advice of Betty Fast when she said that "excellence can only result when human beings who care work to help other human beings achieve their true potential."[9]

REFERENCES

1. American Library Association, *School Library Manpower Project, Phase I—Final Report*. Robert N. Case, Director (Chicago: ALA, 1970).

2. American Association of School Librarians and Association for Educational Communications and Technology, *Media Programs: District and School* (Chicago: ALA; Washington, D.C.: Association for Educational Communications and Technology, 1975).

3. Elizabeth T. Fast, "Standards of Excellence in Hard Times," *School Media Quarterly* 4 (Winter 1976): 123.

4. *Media Programs: District and School*, p. 47.

5. Betty Fast, "Mediacentric," *Wilson Library Bulletin* 50 (April 1976): 635.

6. Betty Fast, "Mediacentric," *Wilson Library Bulletin* 52 (October 1977): 133.

7. Ibid., p. 134.

8. James L. Thomas, "Turning Kids On to Print," *Audiovisual Instruction* 22 (September 1977): 34.

9. "Standards of Excellence in Hard Times," p. 125.

THE SCHOOL MEDIA CENTER

From
Wilson Library Bulletin

by BETTY FAST

LOOKING AT THE
"BALANCED" COLLECTION

In the land of the balanced ticket, the balanced diet, and the balanced
T formation, it is probably un-American to suggest that the pursuit of the
"balanced" collection may be retarding program development in school
media centers. After all, our schools profess to offer a balanced curriculum to produce well-rounded students, and the media program has
tried to meet the school's philosophical aims. Library school courses and
textbooks on selection preach the sanctity of the balanced collection as
one of the great truths of librarianship. Since "unbalanced" by definition
means "unstable," how can any sane person challenge the concept of the
balanced collection?

Why not put the eggs in one basket?

It seems to this writer that balance may have led us to a kind of inertia
that is now hurting us, as administrators search for ways to cut expenditures to match low appropriations. Consider one alternative course of
action: spending the entire media budget to develop in-depth collections

Wilson Library Bulletin 50, 5 (January 1976): 370-71.

in specialized areas, so that each class in the school could study one topic the first year with resources sufficient to meet the learning needs of each student.

Imagine the effect of doing even one unit in which each pupil has print materials geared to his or her reading level, enough audiovisual materials to use tapes and filmstrips for homework assignments, and media covering all aspects of the topic under consideration. With this wealth of materials, teachers would have the incentive to plan their unit carefully, to individualize instruction, to help youngsters locate the media best suited to their learning styles. Students would have the opportunity to "employ . . . a variety of media to find, evaluate, use, and generate information," which the new national standards, *Media Programs: District and School,* stress as one program objective.

Allotting budget money in this narrow way would mean that only a few units could be covered each year and that the media collection would have little or nothing for outside interests. It seems, however, that the goal of media saturation would be better than our long-winded explanations of the value of a well-balanced media collection. Teachers, school administrators, parents, and pupils would start to ask uncomfortable questions about why there isn't enough media budget to cover all areas of the school curriculum in the same manner as the one multimedia study. The simple answer would be to point out the need for a vastly larger budget to provide the same scope for every unit of study.

Beginning at the other end with the balanced collection concept, it takes years before we can demonstrate the use of media in anything but a superficial supplementary role. Schools strive to purchase some media for every topic studied in the year, and as inflation and budget-cutting work in a giant pincers movement, there is less and less money available, spread ever more thinly across the entire collection. At this rate the media center will never be able to muster the media for a full-scale study of any topic.

Science fiction, Winslow Homer

Choosing the unit for each teacher requires close cooperative planning since you want to be certain that the teacher will use the media once it arrives. The wise media specialist will spread the units for the various teachers throughout the school year, so there will be more time for the follow-through conferences, which become critical when media is used as a major part of the curriculum. Some teachers may not feel ready to participate the first year; while no one should be coerced into the program, it is best to save some funds for those who may want to join the parade at mid-term when its success has been proved.

For Teacher A's science unit on ocean life, you can provide geological, biological, and science fiction materials. You can even purchase media on oceanography careers, a recording of sea sounds, poetry of the sea, and Winslow Homer art prints.

The reading program could be beefed up by a sizable expenditure of books on sports with enough audiovisual media to answer questions requiring still or motion picture treatment and to motivate student use of the books. In addition to media to expand the breadth of each unit, there would be a myriad of tapes, books, filmstrips, and realia to motivate each student. In other words, everything we always thought should be in the media center but didn't have the funds to get.

Further insanity

Another unbalanced idea to consider is building a media collection by concentrating on a limited number of different media formats rather than trying to buy a smaller number of every new machine and its accompanying software. Money can be saved by limiting the media formats while a collection is in the developing stages, as long as there is at least one format for each learning mode and a variety of types to accomplish the diversified learning objectives.

It's a question of putting all the eggs in a small basket, and it might move us off the dead-center sense of equilibrium in which the media specialist seems to be the only person in the school who is concerned about the media collection. If school boards can cut library book and audiovisual budgets to zero funding because it appears that the media center has a large stock of materials already, we haven't proved much about media use through our purchasing policies.

Our balanced collections will become older collections, increasingly unbalanced as thefts and worn-out materials reduce the number of items. If progress rather than stability is our goal, it might be sensible to scrap the idea of the balanced collection and develop a purchasing plan that encourages post-holing study of a small number of carefully chosen topics. The goal of a larger balanced collection might thus be reached more rapidly.

POLISH UP
YOUR BACKHAND

Some of the recent publications on school media programs emphasize the idea of concentrating on teachers who in turn can influence their students to use media resources. The media specialist, however, must also recognize the importance of reaching the *teacher* through the *students*. This is where the practice of what I call "backhanding" comes in.

In spite of the fact that media centers and their programs are not new, there are still some educators who make little use of AV materials in class activities or assignments. Wedded to the textbook, the workbook, the chalkboard, and the ditto sheet, these people do not even use the books in the media center.

Why do these teachers shun media? Perhaps they do not realize that use of the media can help their students master the skills they are trying to convey. Some instructors are afraid of machines. Others hesitate to make the preparations necessary to include media in their already established plans. Administrative fears that "media use means goof-off time" may be a contributing factor. Developing an understanding that media is an integral part of learning, and not a frill, may come to these teachers most readily through student involvement.

If the media specialist has rapport with the kids, it is not difficult to discover what topics are being covered in the classroom, even though there has been no request to the media center for materials. One technique that usually works is to mention to teachers the excellent materials available on the topic and to suggest that they send someone to the media center to collect them. If you can include student-produced media on the subject from other classes, you can drop a hint to the student helpers that they could develop similar items as part of their work. Few teachers can resist eager kids who keep asking when they can make slides or a tape of the topics they are studying.

A cleverly designed flier on student production as an alternative to the written report should inspire teachers to take the plunge. It is good to remember that the media specialist may need to put aside other tasks to give extra attention to students the first time a teacher makes this kind of assignment, to assure an encore. The second or third project is the time to introduce the idea that the teacher has a role to play in media production. At this point he or she may be receptive to a team-teaching venture, in which the media specialist delineates various ways to use media and explains the necessary techniques, while the teacher checks for content accuracy. As the media specialist works with the class on the best format for presenting the message, the instructor will gain new insight into the value of such materials. It may also help to develop a guide spelling out the responsibility of the media specialist and the teacher in student media production, especially in situations where media facilities and staff time are limited. The best of the student productions can be used by the teacher the next time the topic is covered.

Although we keep hoping that every teacher will become proficient in the operation of equipment, the "backhand" method here is to train kids from each class. Even young children can learn to run machines. One first-grade teacher, who had returned the filmstrip viewer to the media center because she didn't see how it could be used in her classroom, was willing to take it back after each of her students had been taught to operate it in the media center. There will be less wear and tear on 16mm films if projectors are run by pupils who have demonstrated their competence to the media specialist and have been identified as proficient by a license or a formal list. By showing students how to use overhead and opaque projectors to enlarge pictures and maps for classroom displays, some media specialists have demonstrated another use of media to reluctant teachers.

Media specialists can awaken an interest in the use of media in traditional situations by putting together learning packages, learning centers, or clusters of media for use in the media center or for export to the classroom. If the school still operates with scheduled class time in the media center, some of the periods could be devoted to individual and small-group use of media on the topics being covered in the classroom. (Some cooperative planning is recommended for this approach, although the media specialist may have to do most of the work the first time.)

As media programs evolve, frequently the primary responsibility for teaching reference and AV skills reverts to the teacher. Ideally the specialist has procured and developed media for this instruction that can be used in class groups, small groups, and individualized situations. If these lessons are well designed, the teacher who uses them will look for similar materials in other fields. Time spent in making media instruction a how-to-do-it model should pay dividends as teachers observe its value in learning.

With a little help

Instructors who are willing to use the media center for independent study may need assistance to make this a meaningful learning experience. In addition to helping them and their students pinpoint specific objectives for independent study time, media specialists can urge teachers to permit the use of a wide range of materials in independent study and in reports to the class on the activity. Bibliographies and pathfinders produced by the students or the media center staff or adapted from commercially available sheets should also be aimed at a multimedia approach to learning. Although these guides are valuable in helping instructors individualize assignments, they should be made available directly to students as well.

Reaching teachers through kids presupposes that students feel welcome in the media center and come in on their own. The backhand approach only works if the media specialist and the students are already playing ball. In these days when media specialists are an endangered species, it is necessary to convince all the instructors in the school that AV materials are essential to their teaching. Our best teammates can be the students who are already involved and enthusiastic.

PUBLISHERS' CATALOGS: PUFFERY OR RESOURCE?

Each fall the harvest of publishers' and producers' catalogs leaves the media specialist with the choice of carving space in the vertical file or going into the paper recycling business. According to several recent studies, catalogs and fliers are frequently used as selection tools in school, public, and academic libraries in spite of the warnings of instructors in materials selection courses. Perhaps it's time for a serious examination of this whole area.

In his book *Selecting Materials for Libraries,* Robert Broadus states that "the large and colorful catalogs issued by the producers and distributors of nonprint materials often are useful in selection and ordering (more so than are publishers' catalogs for books), hence should be filed for reference."* Although the comparison between catalogs for print and nonprint media may have been true in 1973 when the book was written, the growth of nonprint reviewing sources and improvements in book publishers' catalogs make the difference less pronounced today. Some catalogs of art books offer as much as filmstrip catalogs; on the other hand the cost of color printing has forced some producers to eliminate many of the illustrations that were useful in selection.

Publishers' promotional materials vary greatly in their value to the media specialist. Some have easy-to-use author, title, and subject indexes, while others appear to be intended for browsing, as they lack any index at all. Catalogs of nonprint materials often index their materials by series only, omitting the individual titles that the user may be seeking. Frequently neglected is the information that parts of an expensive set can be purchased separately, which can be important in these days of limited budgets, highly priced prepackaged media, and individualized instruction programs.

An increasing number of both print and nonprint catalogs list favorable reviews (although rarely is the issue of the reviewing periodical cited). One wonders, however, if all the reviews were completely favorable, but the time required to learn the complete story is prohibitive. Lists of award-winning titles are a plus in some catalogs. Suggested grade level, publication date, cataloging information, and LC card number are strengths.

Spotting the genuine thing

Some companies are guilty of deceptive advertising and misleading or erroneous statements in their catalogs and fliers. For example, one company quoted the laudatory review of a picture book in its flier for a filmstrip made from the book, without indicating that the favorable comments were not intended for the new format. In the blurb for a paperback book, a publisher mentioned that another title by the same author had won the Newbery Medal, when in fact the book had been a Newbery Honor Book. One company that produces nonprint materials had a misleading statement at the beginning of its catalog stating that its materials

---

*Robert N. Broadus, *Selecting Materials for Libraries* (New York: H. W. Wilson Co., 1973), p.143.

had been recommended for purchase in *The Booklist* and *Previews,* when this was true of only a small number of the items. More than one promotional piece has claimed recommendations by the American Library Association, when what they actually received was a favorable review in *The Booklist.* Even though such inaccuracies are rare, they do point up the difference between catalogs and standard selection aids.

What information would we like to find in a catalog? Complete bibliographic data (including the author, title, edition, series, pagination, place, and date of publication for books; producer, title, series, release date, details about format, and length for nonprint media) should be standard. Unfortunately, we can't take this for granted now. Publishers and producers do better with such ordering information as the publisher's address and price of the item, although I have seen fliers that lacked one or the other. The LC card number is usually given for books, but should be included in AV catalogs as well. (The value of the ISBN is still being debated for the library without computerized ordering.) Now that Cataloging In Publication is more widespread. Dewey Decimal number and/or LC classification and subject headings could be given along with the information that a title has CIP. Availability of catalog cards from the publisher or producer should be indicated.

Is it too much to ask that each item be accurately and fully described without excessive praise? Jobbers' catalogs should identify the original publisher or producer to aid in searching for a more complete description of the items listed. Although newer titles need a longer description, annotations of the backlist are also useful. In fact, thoughtful descriptions of books and other media are one of the major services performed by catalogs. Comments about AV materials should include all necessary details about the format and should tell whether the visuals are photographs or artwork, animated or live action, and give other pertinent information. Illustrations are helpful as examples of the artwork used in filmstrips, transparencies, and slides; if media have been produced to meet specific teaching objectives, these should be listed.

A complete author-title index is an absolute must, and subject access to items in the catalog is highly desirable. Curriculum-related subject guides enhance the value of the catalog for schools. If abbreviations, color-coding, or pictorial symbols are used, a key should be easy to locate and clearly explained.

Citation of reviews and awards make catalogs worthy of consideration as selection tools. Even though we can never expect producers and publishers to list unfavorable reviews, full information about the ones they do mention would enable the user to locate the complete review more readily. Naturally reviews of new materials cannot be given, so here catalogs simply call our attention to them.

Valuable but limited

What conclusions can we draw from our reappraisal of publishers' and producers' publications as selection tools? While it is difficult to generalize because of the vast differences in catalogs, these items, along with fliers, remain most valuable to alert us to new or overlooked materials and to give acquisitions information. If the catalog provides accurate visual information about such items as transparencies, slides, or art prints, it may serve as the sole selection tool for someone who can judge the quality based on the reproduction. Catalogs can be invaluable as a source of items to preview or examine for possible purchase; and they are important for items that are not reviewed. Their major limitation as selection tools is their built-in lack of scope. Although promotional materials can serve some purposes in the selection/acquisitions process, they cannot replace standard selection and reviewing sources.

THE CASE FOR
MULTIPURPOSE MEDIA

The behavioral objectives bandwagon and the quest for learner verification have encouraged the production of media with narrow, specified purposes. This movement had its roots in programmed instruction, so it is not really new. While instructional development that is aimed at helping an individual or group master precise cognitive objectives has a valid place in the educational program, a real case for multipurpose media can also be made, especially when budgets are tight and are not likely to become looser for a good long while.

Although the cataloging background of the media specialist gives strong impetus to the idea of placing an item in one or another category for shelving purposes, the art of being a good media specialist lies in making multiple connections for media. A fresh look at the collection should reveal a variety of new uses for items purchased in previous years. Novels and poetry are not the only media that can be appreciated on more than one level of understanding.

The connection within the collection

In the elementary school media center Robert McCloskey's *Time of Wonder*—available as an award-winning book, a sound filmstrip, and a film—is classified under MAINE. After watching the sound filmstrip, some Groton (Conn.) sixth-graders identified more than ten places where this story would fit into the curriculum. Among other things, they saw it as a work of art, a graphic and accurate description of a hurricane, and a warm family story.

As media specialists we need to open our minds to the wide range of possible uses for a well-made media item. Some connections seem obvious, such as the suggestion to an intermediate grade teacher whose class is studying ancient times that *The Egypt Game* might be read aloud to the class. Although the book will not teach many facts about Egypt, it may motivate a keen interest in learning more about bygone civilizations at the same time that it develops positive values.

Other connections necessitate a much greater knowledge about the collection than the title and call number. The media specialist who is a walking analyst of his/her collection can call the attention of a social studies teacher to a section on how people live at high altitudes in the *Life* science volume on mountains (*The Mountains*) or suggest that a portion of a filmstrip on housing in the series *Man: A Cross Cultural Approach* will answer a reference question on the design of a pygmy hut in the Ituri Forest.

Traditionally school district, regional, and university rental collections of 16mm films have concentrated on the "educational" film, which explained to the viewers the things they would see, proceeded to show these, and gave a follow-up review of the concepts that had been developed. In recent years teachers and media specialists have discovered the greater impact of more open-ended films. Films such as *A Place in the Sun* and *Boomsville* are not limited in use to a particular grade level or curriculum area; nor do they evoke the critical comment, "We've seen this before; do we *have* to watch it again?" Two ways to acquire this type of film for school use are to change the philosophy of purchase for school district collections and to borrow films from public libraries. With networking, cooperative agreements, and rulings that LSCA-purchased films cannot be barred from school use, more public libraries have accepted the notion that schools are part of their public.

Needed: flexibility and ingenuity

Most of the career education materials that hit the market as special funds for their purchase became available are narrow in scope, simplistic in treatment, and outdated almost before they are used. Media specialists can recommend that career education money be spent to purchase materials that genuinely motivate people toward careers, even though the creators did not produce them for this purpose. *Frank Film,* a top award winner which tells how one boy became a filmmaker using innovative filming techniques, can spark livelier discussions of career choice than any of the many films on how to choose a career. An inspirational film like *Helen Keller* will give a clearer picture of the intrinsic rewards of teaching than media designed to show career clusters in the field of education. When not employed for career education, these fine films will have multiple uses in the school program.

Another way to extend the use of media is to produce new taped soundtracks for filmstrips or films that have scripts which limit their use to a small number of grades and visuals that offer greater utilization possibilities. Even so-called single-purpose 8mm film loops have great versatility, since students of varying ages gain different insights; these loops, too, can be increased in usefulness by separately taped commentaries or question cards geared to various grade levels.

Our ideas about equipment can become stereotyped. For example, we tend to regard the overhead projector as an instrument for large-group lecture presentations. Looking at the overhead in a new light, we notice that it is a marvelous device for small-group manipulative exercises. Students can move letters and numbers around on the stage to make words or solve equations. A series of individual sentences can be placed in proper sequence without scratching holes in the workbook through repeated erasures. Some of our other equipment is more versatile than our present limited use of it indicates.

The key to multipurpose media is the creative imagination of the media specialist who envisions a myriad of uses for a particular item. If school budgets must be reduced, it is better to cut materials than personnel, for it is only through the talents of the professional staff that we will succeed in getting full mileage from our media collections.

MEDIA MENTIONED IN THIS ARTICLE

Boomsville. National Film Board of Canada, 1970. (16mm film)
Frank Film. Pyramid Films, 1973. (16mm film)
Helen Keller. McGraw-Hill, 1969. (16mm film)
McCloskey, Robert. *Time of Wonder.* Viking, 1957. (Book)
McCloskey, Robert. *Time of Wonder.* Weston Woods, 1960. (Sound filmstrip)
McCloskey, Robert. *Time of Wonder.* Weston Woods, 1965. (16mm film)
Man: A Cross Cultural Approach. Educational Resources, 1970. (Sound filmstrip set)
Milne, Lorus J. *The Mountains.* Silver Burdett, 1970. (Book)
A Place in the Sun. Pyramid Films, 1965. (16mm film)
Snyder, Zilpha K. *The Egypt Game.* Atheneum, 1967. (Book)

MEASURING MEDIA SERVICES—
A GUIDE TO BETTER
PROGRAM DEVELOPMENT

by BLANCHE WOOLLS

Planning media services is ultimately the responsibility of the school library media specialist. Many persons have definite ideas and widely varying conceptions of just what these services should include. The collective wisdom of members of several task forces is reflected in current American Association of School Librarians standards, which state that the media program should

> support and further the purposes formulated by the school or district of which it is an integral part, and its quality is judged by its effectiveness in achieving program purposes. A media program represents a combination of resources that includes people, materials, machines, facilities, and environments, as well as purposes and processes. The combination of these program components and the emphasis given to each of them derive from the needs of the specific educational program.

The more purposeful and effective the mix, the more sensitively it responds to the curriculum and the learning environment, the better the media program.[1]

For too long school library media specialists have planned programs using the blueprints they were given by (1) observing librarians when they, as students, went through school; (2) their teacher/librarian training programs and the texts and articles they were assigned to read during this period; (3) their student teaching practicum experience, and (4) colibrary media specialists presently employed who, observed on-the-job today, become role models. While some of these have provided satisfactory patterns of service, many have not.

School media specialists, like their programs, vary in quality. Until reaching high school, many school library media specialists may have attended schools with no libraries. The librarian at the high school may have been functioning in an inadequate facility with limited time and budget, collection and equipment. The university training program may have espoused a blueprint for a mythical school, its teachers, students, and administrators, but adaption in the real world might be difficult, if not impossible.

Obviously, working with real children and adults in real situations poses problems that cannot be anticipated through case studies, role playing, or games and simulations. It is apparent that programs visualized through these techniques must be modified when the library media specialist is at work. One of the first opportunities for the media specialist to put theory into practice is in the student teaching or practicum experience. In spite of care taken when choosing practicum locations, student teachers in media services are sometimes assigned to schools whose library media programs are traditional book distribution centers or are otherwise uninspiring. In fact, some school library media specialists today are inadequate role models.

Media programs today must be tailored to meet the needs of each group of teachers, students, and administrators. These needs change as students, teachers, and administrators change. Because needs vary, constant appraisal is essential if the library media center is to function to meet today's needs rather than yesterday's or the hypothetical needs that were discussed in library training programs. Careful assessment will help media specialists plan for the future. Measurement of individual facets of the school media program will provide the evidence necessary for decision making and program planning. This measurement starts with what is there and moves to what should be, with recommendations as to how to get there. Before this measurement is begun, however, one must look at the environment of the school library media center.

Individual parts of the school program should not be measured alone, for individual programs cannot exist in isolation from other programs. The library media program is an integral part of the total school setting and one cannot disregard this environment.

What is there?—The school setting

The school library media specialist is the most isolated of all other types of librarians except, perhaps, the special librarian. Few public or academic librarians are a staff of one. Most school libraries are staffed by one professional (and this may be on a rotating basis, as one person manages more than one school) with minimal clerical support. The program that they design must, therefore, operate with little additional professional librarian input, unless the school system has a coordinator or supervisor of the school media program. One of the most difficult tasks confronting the school library media specialist is that of educating the students, teachers, and administrators of what to expect from the media program.

The most important person in the support of a strong media program is the chief school administrator. The school superintendent must be proud of the district media program. It must be a priority item. This program must also be deemed important by other members of the central office staff.

Another important administrator is the school principal. A principal who is an advocate of a strong media program is a joy to know. One with less enthusiasm may be a joy to educate. An administrator with negative feelings toward media programs, for whatever reason (and it might be wise to discover the reason), is a challenge one must accept.

It will be helpful to the school library media specialist to discover the educational and professional backgrounds of the administrators, staff, and teachers. If these persons have attended or observed schools with poor media programs and have taught in schools with traditional media programs, a great deal of in-service training, both formal and informal, will be necessary to change their perception of the media program. Informal in-service is not difficult to carry out; more formal in-service programs might be considered unnecessary by many teachers or administrators. The media specialist must test the climate for provision of in-service and plan carefully the methods of presenting this training, so that the information will be accepted by the audience.

The teaching competencies of the faculty must be known. Many teachers may be teaching in a second or minor area, rather than their first choice. Reassignment of teachers to secondary areas will continue as staffs are cut back because of reduced enrollments. These teachers will be in more critical need of the support services of the school library media specialist. The media specialist must also be aware of the teaching styles of the faculty. If all of the faculty have adopted the lecture-text, options to this method must be presented and accepted before students will be encouraged to make much use of the media center.

The program planner must also be aware of the composition of the student body. If students are living in a neighborhood with a great many cultural opportunities, with an overload of out-of-school activities such as Girl Scouts, Boys' Club, bowling, dancing lessons, piano recitals, church activities, and Little League, the climate of the school will be different from the child who lives in a crowded home with no place to study or with no one home when the child returns from school. Furthermore, the school media specialist should know the achievement level and the intelligence quotient range of the students attending the school. Abilities of students must be taken into consideration when choosing materials. In the high school, if most of the students are in a vocational track rather than the academic track, a different media collection may be needed than for a school where all students are planning for further education immediately after graduation.

Students who come from homes where parents have little education create possibilities of sharing resources from the media center to encourage the transfer of learning. Providing materials to take home is even more critical for these students than for those who come from homes where family members have been or are attending college.

In addition to the human factors, some other information is necessary. Certainly the media specialist should be aware of the information agencies in the school's vicinity. Students may use the public library collection or the local community college or university library. Even the schedule of the school is a factor. If students have a schedule that does not permit "free" time for research, or who must leave the school at a given time (perhaps to meet a bus or work schedule), a different program must be planned. If the media center is scheduled to meet an arbitrary assignment of students to the center, little flexibility in program planning exists.

The curriculum of the school also impinges upon the media program. If the semester is made up of long units that are repeated each semester or once each year, one kind of planning can be done. If students are taught through mini-units or other forms of short curriculum periods, another plan is required. Topics that are taught only occasionally may be covered with a minimal number of materials, while expanded interest may cause the media specialist to search outside the school for resources. Few of the above factors are within the control of the school library media specialist, but once the school setting is identified, measurement of the media center program can begin.

What is there?—The school library media program

The process of assessment of program has been termed "measurement" by the author because it seems less threatening than the term "evaluation." Evaluation has been interpreted as the assigning of a rank order on a scale from good = A, to bad = D or F. Often this becomes a comparison with another like object, as, in the case of students, one student who is judged better than another is thus given an A, the other assigned B. The choice of scale—points, percentages, letters—and the choice of cut-off level on the scale determine scores. Assigning a rank order for school media program components is not so easy, since rank order program scores have not been designed, and it is even more difficult to compare performance to like objects.

Since school library media programs cannot be analyzed by comparison to a like object, an arbitrary goal may be set. With students, this goal may be described by giving everyone who scores at least nine points an A or assigning those who have 130 points on a particular intelligence test the rank of "genius." With the school library media program, the AASL (American Association of School Librarians) standards set 40 items per student as such a goal. One flaw to this form of measurement is that measuring is treated as a quantity count—tabulation of how many of specified objects exist: books, filmstrips, tables and chairs, 16mm projectors, or staff members. The first step in this type of analysis is to find out what is available. A variety of evaluation models exist to measure existing resources by this numerical count.

The second step is a prediction of what should be available, again using several methods to determine what should exist in the media program. If one is using AASL standards to measure, one can only assume that the standards describe the adequate, if not the ideal. Since most standards are developed for a wide geographic area, such as state or nation, it may be that each school district will wish to adapt such standards for the local school. A locally developed needs-assessment instrument may generate the quantities needed for a quality program.

The third step in this measurement process is the determination of what is needed. This is a simple arithmetic calculation that occurs when the total number of items available is subtracted from what should be available. This number of "missing" items can then be multiplied by the cost of a single item and a cost analysis has been completed.

Quantitative assessment is relatively easy; few persons attempt the more difficult test—a measure of the quality of the books, filmstrips, tables and chairs, 16mm projectors, staff, facilities, or collection.

In his landmark publication, Lancaster divides library services into catalog use, reference service, literature searching and information retrieval, collection, document delivery capabilities, technical services, and automated systems.[2] He also discusses the relevance of standards, effect of physical accessibility and ease of use, and cost-performance-benefits considerations. While school library media specialists may be interested in automated systems, few school media centers have automated program elements. Catalog use and technical services may not receive as high a priority ranking for evaluation in these centers as the need to evaluate reference service, literature search, document delivery capabilities, ease of use, and cost-performance benefits. These elements in turn must be considered in relation to those that are essential to programming: collection content and size, available facilities and equipment, and the number, composition, and training of staff.

Measurement of collections

The measurement of the collection has been most often done by counting the numbers of books, filmstrips, reference books, vertical file drawers, globes, slides, and other items available for use by the school population. This statistic is the one most often required by state departments of public instruction and other accrediting agencies that set an arbitrary number that a school must own to be accredited. Often this number is tied to the number of students, the average daily membership. Therefore a school library media center must have 10 books per student or 6,000, whichever is smaller, or 20 books per student and 6,000 minimum, or some other combination of numbers. Administrators then work to attain that number of volumes for the shelves in the media center with little concern for the value or relevance of the contents of the volumes in relation to the school's curriculum. Having 60 file drawers of outdated, unused pamphlets, clippings, or pictures is of little use to anyone except the principal, who must have 60 file drawers to be accredited.

It is not the purpose of this article to discuss how, why, or even if such an arbitrary quantity count of any item will determine the effectiveness of a collection. Certainly it would be difficult to provide an information program with only 50 volumes, but no research has been done to show statistically how many volumes are necessary to provide "adequate" information. With the national emphasis on providing information for all through shared resources and networks, information might be available and accessible from library collections other than building holdings or even the district or city library collection. This will be of great assistance to students who may be able to wait for information from other sources; but some analysis must also be made of the immediate usefulness of a building's collection to the users.

The school library media specialist should analyze at least part of the collection each year, with each item in the total collection reviewed at least once every five years. Materials that are worn out, outdated, or, perhaps because of curricular changes, have not been used in the past three years should be removed from the shelves. If these materials have any potential for the future, they could be stored until the curricular area or interest is restored. In many instances, newer materials will be produced that may replace unused materials and save the cost of storage. Therefore, the age of the material is one factor to be analyzed.

Certainly one does not automatically discard a volume or a filmstrip because the library has owned it for five years or the copyright date shows that the material was published five years before (which means that it was written or photographed or taped *more* than five years before). Yet the date of the information is important.

Different subjects have different age requirements. Almanacs become outdated annually. Information on geographical areas of the world become obsolete quickly. The nations of Africa and South America are undergoing constant change in governments, boundaries, and names. Science materials also become dated quickly. On the other hand, a history of the Civil War, if accurate and well written, if the topic remains part of the curriculum and the material suitable to the reading ability of the students, might be of use indefinitely.

Another factor in the analysis of the collection might be in terms of usage. If materials are not being circulated or have not been circulated for three years, a determination of their value should be made. Perhaps the materials were used in the media center rather than taken for out-of-center use. Checking the circulation card, date due slip, or automated circulation system records will indicate if the material has been circulated, even though it will not assess the use of the material after it was taken from the center. Any records to determine quality of materials and appropriateness of material to the user will require information that is much more difficult to obtain. One method is to interview faculty and students concerning their assessment of materials as they return them to the media center. Another method is to get students and teachers to rate the materials they selected on a checklist, indicating their analysis of the relevance and usefulness of the items used to their topic. This analysis might question whether they made use of all of a book or filmstrip or only specific parts, and why or why not items were useful.

The citation count, a favorite method utilized in academic research, could be used to analyze the references cited in student papers. Teachers should be willing to comment, at least verbally, on the quality of materials that they use in presentation of units or in the classroom collection. Teachers and students could comment upon those items listed on a bibliography that was developed and utilized with a curriculum unit.

Just as actual usage must be measured, the inability of the media center collection to meet teacher and student needs should be recorded. While document delivery is important and clientele are sensitive to materials that are missing from the shelf, an accurate record must be kept of any subjects or topics that cannot be found in the media center and the appropriateness of such material. In the analysis of those topics, for which little or no relevant information was available, a search must be made to discover the extent of need for information on the topic, the materials that are available for purchase or that should be produced, and what information could be secured elsewhere.

Facility evaluation

Facility evaluation should cover three elements of the room(s): ambience or atmosphere, room arrangement, and size. Obviously if a room is unattractive, crowded, and dull, it will be less enticing than one that is inviting and attracts and welcomes the user. The room should be well marked with directional signs so that users can easily locate materials, equipment, and staff.

Room arrangement includes the location of furniture, shelves, charging desk, card catalog, listening and viewing areas, production room, and others. These various components of the facility have a logical traffic pattern. The patterns will vary from facility to facility, since media centers were not built from a single plan and change not only in size but in configuration. It is important to any facility that the most practical traffic pattern be designed and utilized. An analysis of ease of use of materials will be related to this traffic pattern. The arrangement of the room—for example, placing equipment near electrical outlets—will facilitate use.

Adequacy of size means that the media center is large enough to accommodate an appropriate number of students who will be in the room at any given time. These students should be able to move about the room easily with sufficient space between shelves and tables. If some students wish to view a film, that section of the media center should be able to be darkened without turning off all the lights in the room. A final check of room size is an analysis of the size of the furniture. Does it fit the intended user, or has hand-me-down furniture been used and is it too large or too small for most users?

Measurement of staff (performance appraisal)

Football players are measured by easily determined facts—height, weight, age. Their "success" can be calculated by yards gained, passes completed, or number of tackles. The ultimate test for the team (but not necessarily for the success of an individual player) is the win/loss column.

Such vital statistics for the school library media specialist and other media center staff are not as easily determined, and the win/loss column is even more obscure. It would be impossible for any human to adjust to the variant requests from an everchanging student body. Students and faculty are human, and qualities that appeal to one student or teacher may not to another. However, the basic rule for any staff member involved in the program was stated by Frances Henne:

> For some students, and in certain schools this may be many students, the only library skill that they should have to acquire is an awareness, imprinted indelibly and happily upon them, that the library is a friendly place where the librarians are eager to help.[3]

The test of this measure may be the numbers of students who do seek the advice and counsel of the school library media specialist not only on curriculum topics and reading guidance, but on matters that go beyond the scope of the classroom.

Elizabeth Fast has suggested that performance appraisal or evaluation must have self-evaluation as an important part of the process. She lists the basic components of performance evaluation, as developed by George B. Redfern:

1. Clarification of performance criteria or definition of the scope of the job;
2. Establishment of performance objectives or job targets;
3. Formulation of performance activities or a plan of action for implementing the objectives;
4. Agreement on monitoring techniques for measuring the effectiveness of the activities;
5. Development of a means for assessing the monitored data; and
6. Arrangement for one or more conferences with follow-up to utilize the feedback gained from the process.[4]

These statements could be interpreted to mean that the media manager should analyze the job and then choose the management style that is comfortable and yet would accomplish the task. Choosing a style is difficult, since many persons have personality traits that may not permit one style. For example, an individual who is only comfortable as a dictator will be less likely to permit democratic decision making for media center activities.

While human beings react at different times to different leadership styles, choosing a management style and attempting to adhere to it is as important to the media manager as it is to the manager of a commercial enterprise. The dictator may set rules that seem arbitrary to the students or teachers and the reaction may be avoidance of the media center or attempts to circumvent or overturn the rules. On the other hand, a laissez-faire manager may permit the media center to become so chaotic that, while students and teachers enjoy coming to the center, they may be unable to sort through the confusion to locate the materials needed. Certainly the managerial style is one that must be evaluated in assessing staff performance, since the style may predict the success or failure of communication with the school.

Another measure of staff performance is the capability of the center to provide resources. Since school library media centers exist to provide information, one would assume that the staff should provide organized, efficient, and ready access to the information collection. One measure might be the success of the clientele to get correct and pertinent information in an efficient manner and with a minimum of difficulty. Another method for measuring user satisfaction with reference retrieval is the analysis of the willingness of students and teachers to ask for help. If they are reluctant to "bother" the school library media center staff, performance of the staff is below necessary achievement.

There are occasions or circumstances in which information may not be available in the existing collection. At this point it is the responsibility of the media center staff to help locate information elsewhere. With a national emphasis on networking and resource sharing, students and teachers should be directed to or assisted in securing materials from sources of information other than the school library media center. To do this efficiently, the numbers of staff in the media center should be large enough to carry out this service. Size of staff can affect the number of services and the quality of services offered. Mary Virginia Gayer verified this assumption—that larger staffs offer more services than smaller staffs.[5]

Another assessment of staff may be an evaluation of the education of the staff. If a particular state requires a master's degree for permanent certification, tenure, or the life license, the school library media specialist will have completed advanced training. In other states such certification may be granted to persons holding the A.B. or B.S. degree. Lucille Wert's study confirmed the fact that librarians with more library education attracted more teachers and students to the library, perhaps because these librarians developed more extensive programs.[6] Where the librarian had completed the master's degree in library science, students used the library and its collection more frequently to complete class assignments.

The setting for the school library media center has been described in terms of the environment of the school or parent institution itself and in terms of the ingredients: collection, facility, and staff. These are all required if the school library media center is to have any educational program beyond that of a repository of materials in a building.

Measurement of services

Many school library media specialists have never systematically listed the services they are offering. They are certain that they provide new materials because they prepare orders and see that the items are received, processed, and placed on shelves for users. They also realize that library media skills are taught, that reading guidance is given through story hours or book talks (even to individual students), and that reference inquiries are answered. (Since most school library media specialists are tired at the end of the day, *some* services must be given.) However, in many instances these services are offered with little regard as to the relevance or the need for the service.

Several researchers have attempted to measure services.[7] Their lists of services offered and their methods of analyzing the data are invaluable to the school library media specialist as a method to pursue and as data to compare to the results. Whatever method or checklist is used, however, there are some common elements to consider.

When the school library media specialist analyzes services offered, some indication should be made of the priority given to the service, e.g., whether the media staff works with teacher/counselors to help improve student progress in learning. If the service is not provided, teachers should be given an option to rank this service as a high priority to be implemented immediately, priority to be implemented as soon as possible, or low priority. It may be that the media specialist will find that the *only* service desired by faculty is "maintenance of students from study hall" or "baby-sitting" while the teacher takes the contract-entitled break. While this finding would be discouraging, it would indicate that a full-scale awareness and public relations campaign should be planned and implemented immediately. No longer will the media specialist be expending energy upon services that are not seen as essential by students or teachers; instead, services can be offered that are requested by media center users.

Two services always offered by the school library media specialist that need much reassessment are "inventory" and "cataloging." Teachers and students do not welcome the early closing of the media center to provide the media specialist the luxury of taking inventory, and few understand the time constraints of cataloging and processing materials. To find the media specialist secluded in a quiet corner attempting to process materials is not viewed by most individuals as important as helping in the congested reading room.

The measurement of services in the media center is a very necessary exercise for the media specialist in the present climate that stresses accountability. Yet this will be a very frustrating experience if it is only an exercise and nothing is done with the results beyond analyzing them in terms of "where we are." The next step is to determine where the program ought to be and to set a time frame and a methodology for getting there as quickly and economically as possible.

What should be?

As stated earlier, most often program elements are measured against standards—local, state, or national. Since these standards are usually quantitative, the only guidance provided is for the addition of things. While these standards may provide a temporary document for assessment when no other means is available, a self-study should be designed by the media center staff with input from the school community. All facets of the program can be viewed in relation to the services offered, and it is this element of the program that should be tested in order to determine what is missing.

If an analysis of services is provided and services desired can provide some indication of what is needed, the results of the study must be more than a comparison of numbers of items available or the number of staff working in the center. If the teaching staff and students give high priority to such service as help from the media staff for locally produced AV materials, a facility must be provided for production. This may necessitate addition or reallocation of full or part-time staff, increase or reallocation of space, and purchase of necessary equipment and supplies. If the use of the media center by small groups upon teacher request is a high priority, it may be that classes that have been regularly scheduled in the small media center to relieve the teacher for a 30-minute break may need reassigning to another area of the school to be overseen by paraprofessional or other staff.

The final analysis of "what should be" must be the consensus of faculty, students, and administration. All three groups must have input into the planning of "what should be" or it will be the media specialist's "impossible dream." If the entire faculty, student body, and administration cannot participate in this planning (and if the school is very large this might be impossible), it is the responsibility of the media specialist to choose a committee that is truly representative of the school and one with membership in the strongest political arenas so that the planned program can be sold to the constituents. Certainly the implication of "what should be" measurement can be pointed out.

How to get there?

Subtracting what is there from what should be there can indicate how much quantity is needed. If a dollar amount can be placed on each missing item, simple multiplication can determine how much it will cost. In most instances it will be impossible to get everything in one year. The attainment of missing items can be built into a three-, five-, or ten-year plan with rationale for each step of the process built into each year.

Again, the development of such a document should not be done by the media specialist alone. It must be based on a careful analysis of what is available. This may be the responsibility of the media specialist, who will decide how to go about this beginning measurement. Then, with the planning committee, the goals and objectives should be set.

Finally, plans must be made, with costs and a lucid rationale for each step attached, to show why and how much it will cost for the objectives to be met. The necessary time frame should also be stated. This document can help evaluate progress through the year. At specified points in time the plan must be reviewed to determine progress and to reassess the needs, goals, and objectives. It well may be that some services, after implementation or after reassessment, were not as effective as predicted or desired. These should be given a lower priority and another service increased or begun. A service that is offered should be assessed for the quality, and if the service isn't effective but still needed, it should be analyzed for a more efficient and effective method for offering.

To some, this process may seem to be very time consuming and impractical. After all, school libraries have been in existence for some years now; they are required for high schools in most states. Others feel that it doesn't really matter much what is or isn't done, because the school library media specialist is tenured with longevity over most other school personnel.

While the above may be true in some cases, for many others the positions, the facility, and the services are in jeopardy. In many areas the elementary school library media specialist is an endangered species, being reassigned to the classroom or furloughed as the reductions in student population reduce revenues for school districts. Such conditions demand a careful analysis of what is currently available compared to what school personnel desire. The resulting data can be built into a logical plan for implementation for continuing services, revising services, or discontinuing services not only to preserve the school library media program, but also to increase its effectiveness.

REFERENCES

1. American Association of School Librarians and Association for Educational Communications and Technology, *Media Programs: District and School* (Chicago: ALA, 1975), p. 4.

2. F. W. Lancaster, *The Measurement and Evaluation of Library Services* (Washington, D.C.: Information Resources Press, 1977).

3. Frances Henne, "Learning to Learn in School Libraries," *School Libraries* 15 (May 1966): 17.

4. Elizabeth T. Fast, "In-Service Staff Development as a Logical Part of Performance Evaluation," *School Media Quarterly* 3 (Fall, 1974): 35.

5. Mary Virginia Gaver, *Services of Secondary School Media Centers* (Chicago: ALA, 1971), p. 39.

6. Lucille Mathena Wert, *Library Education and High School Library Services* (Ph.D. diss., University of Illinois, 1970).

7. Gaver; James W. Liesener, *A Systematic Process for Planning Media Programs* (Chicago: ALA, 1976); David V. Loertscher, *Media Services to Teachers in Indiana Senior High Schools 1972–73* (Ph.D. diss., Indiana University, 1973); David V. Loertscher and Phyllis Land, "An Empirical Study of Media Services in Indiana Elementary Schools," *School Media Quarterly* 4 (Winter 1975): 8–18; and Janet Gossard Stroud, *Evaluation of Media Center Services by Media Staff, Teachers, and Students in Indiana Middle and Junior High Schools* (Ph.D. diss., Purdue University, 1976).

THE ESSENTIAL ELEMENTARY SCHOOL LIBRARY MEDIA CENTER

by ALICE E. FITE

The annals of public education in the United States record the principles of educational thought for each generation of American educators. Each ethos providing for quality education through instructional attainment was based upon that generation's acceptance of how learning took place and its appreciation for the nature and extent of knowledge. Although there exists an evolution in the methods and teaching strategies applied to the continuous process of learning in American education, a definite trend appears in the singular definition of an educated person. Basic to an understanding of the goals of education is the underlying American ideal for equality and the right of every student to achieve the best that is possible.

It is through this response to a critical need for the improvement of the human race that education has looked for new ways to maximize the individual competencies of teachers and provide better instruction for students. Mid-twentieth century educators had to react to the critics who firmly believed that only a massive upgrading of scholastic standards would guarantee future prosperity. The launching of Sputnik by the Russians thrust American education into a turbulence of reactions in the late 1950s and 60s as realization came that we were behind in the space race. The critics reacted by addressing the need for standards of excellence. Those scholars who spoke were representative of three centuries of educational thought with some placing more emphasis upon the social and emotional development of students, while others were demanding a greater degree of academic rigor within the curriculum.

Admiral Rickover, an adherent of the liberal arts curriculum dedicated to the training of the intellect, asked educators to focus their attention upon gifted and talented youth by educating superior minds in fields of special competencies. Although he advocated advanced technical and scientific training for the nation's youth, he supported a broad terminal education for the average and below-average student. He asked for a central authority to set uniform standards for curriculum development and teacher qualifications.

Not every critic agreed with Rickover's philosophy for excellence. John Gardner accepted a less rigid approach. He believed that American democracy was nurtured upon a diet of innovation and individualism coupled with internal motivation. It was because of this philosophy that he asked educators to encourage self-development through a continuous process of individual evaluation. In his mind, rigidity brought decay. His idea of curriculum revision was built upon his philosophy of the self-renewing person. The design of such a curriculum would be based upon the process of self-discovery, with students being asked to "know themselves." Standards of excellence were essential when it was possible to translate them into maximum development of each student at an appropriate level of ability.

This concept of Gardner's, that asked for the full development of each child through enabling every person to achieve to the greatest extent possible, became the central focus of thought for elementary educators during the 1950s and 1960s. The leadership in elementary education turned to the individualization of educational programs. Research implied that learning differences among children of the same age were greater than educators had believed a generation earlier. There developed from this an intrinsic concern for coping with individual differences. New methods of instruction placed added responsibility upon the learner.

Teachers accepted the proposition that no single approach or method brought the same results for each student. Standards and guidelines for excellence in education were written to advance patterns of individual and institutional diversity.

It was within this element of major review in educational pedagogy that the elementary library media center received a new significance and an increased level of concern among American educators. Elementary library media centers were not characterized as essential in American education until the emphasis in educational thought fell upon the learner rather than the tasks to be learned. When the primary objectives for educating the elementary school student were nurtured in a demand for maximum development of individual potential at all levels of ability, the learning experiences inherent in the media program of an elementary library media center became essential and were in concert with that primary objective.

First comprehensive school standards

The leadership in the field of school librarianship answered the challenges of the critics by establishing criteria for quality library programs that were to shape the thinking of elementary educators for the next two decades. At the 1953 Midwinter Meeting of the American Library Association (ALA), a committee co-chaired by Frances Henne and Ruth Ersted was appointed by the American Association of School Librarians (AASL) to revise the 1945 school library standards, *School Libraries for Today and Tomorrow*. The result of this committee's work was a mandate for excellence, *Standards for School Library Programs* (ALA, 1960). This publication provided the impetus for the rapid growth of school libraries since 1960. This rapid growth was especially true of libraries in the elementary school.

Prior to this date, elementary school libraries were few in number and existed as an area supplemental to the school, rather than an integral part of the instructional program. In most instances where such facilities existed, the room and the collections were small and consisted solely of books. For the year 1953–54, the United States Office of Education indicated that only 28.89 percent of the elementary schools were served by librarians. The figure of 34.1 percent of the elementary schools having centralized libraries was reported for the 1958–59 school year. Within fifteen years, it was possible to report from statistics obtained from the National Center for Education Statistics, *Statistics of Public School Libraries Media Centers, Fall, 1974,* that 81.1 percent of all elementary schools had centralized library media centers. Some authorities believe that a large number of the 12,000 elementary schools remaining without library media centers are small schools with possibly fewer than 75 children per school and exist as special purpose schools with a policy of providing classroom-level collections of specialized materials.

Statistics document the extent of growth of libraries and library programs in elementary schools. They may even attempt to explain and clarify the degree to which library media centers are an integral part of the school's educational program. What they cannot do is justify or give credence to the premise that the library media center is basic to a sound instructional program. A rationale for this essential contribution of the media program to elementary education became possible when standards were translated into evaluative principles that served as determinants of quality media programs.

The principles described in the 1960 standards for library programs concentrated on the directions necessary for reaching desired change. Ten years later, Alvin Toffler in *Future Shock* asked educators to shift into the future tense. He was asking that the schools teach not only data but ways to manipulate it, that students learn how to throw out old ideas and when to replace them with the new, and, in essence, he was asking teachers to guide students in learning "how to learn." To a certain extent, the 1960 standards for school libraries are analogous to Toffler's message. They were futuristic in that they tested the ability of the institution known as the school to adapt and cope with change. The manner in which the field of school librarianship responded required many educators to develop a new stance toward the future of library programs. This attitude provided the stimulus for rapid change.

National studies create awareness for future development

The new guidelines of excellence for library programs anticipated that soul-searching regarding the education of youth would eventually lead to the investigation of the adequacy of library materials in the schools. The writers believed that in the education of all youth, an abundance of printed and audiovisual materials was essential. The ideas expressed were based upon the historical concept of common skills (coupled with the accepted objectives required for human communications and social integration). The message was that schools without libraries and professional librarians were schools without the basic instructional resources required for quality education. The school library became fundamental in the organizational pattern of the elementary school and its program of services, because the substance of elementary education was found in the goal of developing a desire to learn within the individual.

Future projects and educational studies demonstrated that schools without libraries and professional librarians were schools unequipped to meet the educational objectives of the last two to three decades of the twentieth century. The 1960 standards provided the conceptual foundation for school library programs and paved the way to a series of events that were to define the essential role of the new elementary library media center. National projects, philanthropic grants, and new federal legislation directed to improve school librarianship on the elementary level enacted subsequent to these standards became tangible evidence of the unique contribution of media in the instructional process.

It has been said that change is the process by which the future invades our lives. Change in school librarianship took its direction from the implementation of the 1960 standards. School library improvement was initiated through the School Library Development Project, a project supported by the Council on Library Resources. Under the direction of the American Association of School Librarians, this national endeavor brought a total program of public awareness to the changes recommended for school libraries through a massive campaign of written publications and speeches before educational associations, citizens groups, and other interested organizations. The nation was tuned in to the need for school library development.

Knapp School Libraries Project

Telling the library story was important; however, it was not sufficient in and of itself in preparing people for ways to adapt to the future. Educating for change required demonstration and research into the effects the new philosophy would have upon the schools and the learners in them. In 1962 the Knapp Foundations, Inc., awarded the American Library Association a $1,130,000 grant for a five-year project to demonstrate the effect of the attainment of standards as stated in *Standards for School Library Programs* in a total of eight demonstration schools. Five of these schools were on the elementary level.

In these Knapp schools, the standards were transformed into principles of learning that became the determinants of a successful library program. The results of this national project, also administered by the American Association of School Librarians, demonstrated that schools could give better instruction, maximize the competencies of teachers, and increase the avenues of individualized instruction through the implementation of the new national guidelines for library programs. The attainment of these guidelines demonstrated through an operational manifestation that students learn from various sources and not from a single text of information, even when enhanced by an explanation from the teacher. A stronger commitment to a multimedia, multisensory approach to learning developed. More attention was given to all of the communications skills. The library became a place for learning, a place in which teachers and students became partners in the design and development of learning experiences.

The attainment of these guidelines further demonstrated that a systematic organization of a wide range of instructional materials provided the resources for prescribing individualized learning activities. Teachers assumed greater responsibility in the preparation of instructional programs when they were involved in developing the philosophy of the library program as it was organized. This included the reasons why the library was to be established, how it was to be used, and when it was to be used.

The further attainment of these guidelines through the establishment of a quality library program brought credence to the belief that students learn as a result of their own activities. The library became a place for them to learn on their own and to reuse the concepts presented in a formal classroom situation. The goal—to impart a desire to learn in every student—was made possible through avenues of independent study in the library where instructional resources were readily accessible and where students were able to satisfy their need to know.

A large percentage of learning is acquired as an outgrowth of classroom activity. As elementary school libraries continued to demonstrate their usefulness to the learning process, educators of all types became convinced that the principles introduced in the standards uniting teaching and learning with the support base of a media program were far better than what had previously been accepted as normal practice. School library programs became essential because they provided a better means of developing and instituting a wide range of teaching and learning strategies for many philosophical and educational sets. It was clearly demonstrated that a well-designed program in elementary school libraries taught children how to think. Programs were planned where students received instruction in how to organize their thoughts, analyze problems, and seek solutions. Students experienced self-fulfillment, as a meaningful understanding of an educational concept was attained through the instructional support base known as a library program.

Federal legislation supports elementary libraries

Peggy Sullivan, director of the Knapp School Libraries Project, focused national attention upon the educational importance of these library standards through many articles and addresses at state and national meetings. Prior to the completion of this project, federal legislation supporting school libraries in the form of funding was made possible through the Elementary and Secondary Education Act of 1965, which authorized the purchase of school library resources, textbooks, and instructional materials. While it is not possible to state that this funding came solely as a direct result of the Knapp Project, it is more than likely that the experiences acquired through the planning and evaluating of effective library programs in the demonstration schools identified the learning capabilities made possible when such programs are adequately funded and maintained. It is safe to say that the 1960 standards and the research obtained from the Knapp Project supplied the major influence for the extensive support for school libraries by the federal government.

Expanded guidelines for media programs

The increase of federal funds resulted in both an increase of facilities and the level of adequacy within the library media centers. This pattern of physical and fiscal growth, coupled with the natural enthusiasm engendered by the demonstration centers, created the need for an expanded set of evaluative principles and standards. Although the basic philosophy expressed in the 1960 standards remained somewhat constant, *Standards for School Media Programs* (1969), prepared jointly by the American Association of School Librarians and NEA's Department of Audiovisual Instruction (now known as the Association for Educational Communications and Technology), placed a greater emphasis upon the definition of the unified media concept. The justification and the logistics of print and nonprint materials in a systematic instructional pattern of development, organized under a central administration, were described within the framework of instructional patterns, resources, facilities, and staff.

The expansion made possible by the 1969 standards was further enhanced with the publication of the latest and most current guidelines, *Media Programs: District and School* (1975). These new guidelines appeared a little more than twenty years after the major revision of educational thought in elementary education, and their impact was questioned by critics within and without the field of school librarianship. The need for maintenance of personnel and unusual budget constraints were beginning to appear in all areas of school media programs; however, the reason for the existence of these guidelines was based upon the premise that education in all its aspects was a continuous process and that the striving for excellence was possible within a framework of diversity for each institution representing a school program.

Current constraints

The media professional at the end of the 1970s is being asked to respond to a different set of values and to a restless public. The public objects to increased taxes and is concerned with the quality of services purchased and delivered by local school communities. Educators are entering a decade in which they are going to be asked to do more with less in public education. Segments of the public have turned cynical, and a large portion of the populace seems willing to believe that educators have received more than enough money to achieve quality education.

The temptation to regress from the goals once established for elementary media programs is prevalent. An attitude of pessimism upon the part of library media specialists will become pedestrian if the response to budgetary constraints becomes defensive and apologetic. The elementary library media specialist must continue to believe that media professionals are resource people with the capability of providing some of the answers to the problems of reading achievement, literacy, and the attainment of the identifiable basic skills.

Elizabeth Fast developed a rational defense in response to the expanded programs described in *Media Programs: District and School* at a time when budgets were beginning to be questioned by local taxpayers and holding the line for the maintenance of personnel and materials was a difficult task. In *School Media Quarterly* (Winter, 1976), Betty Fast answers the critics by comparing standards of excellence to program goals and priorities. She states:

> Although some people dismiss the concept of standards of excellence as unrealistic in the actual world, there is a need for a vision of the educational program as it should be, even though its achievement may seem impossible. . . . We need standards to help us determine if our present course is a wise one; program goals provide a sense of direction even though we may be able to move only a short distance.

Ernest L. Boyer, U.S. Commissioner of Education, views the library as essential to the advancement of education. Although he states that 85 percent of the nation's schools have libraries today, he does not dismiss the need for continued growth. Asked to respond to issues facing school library media centers today, he wrote for *American Libraries* (November, 1978, p. 585):

> Good books must be available to all children. Librarians must be supported in their role as teacher, and the relationship between the library and the classroom must be strengthened.

It is at this point that the essential quality of media programs becomes crucial. The link between media programs and the classroom is found in program goals that are learner-oriented or learner-centered. Media programs that are learner-oriented and complete with learning alternatives and options are only possible when there is a fusion of media services within the instructional program. When the library media specialist can develop a media program directly related to the learner's objectives, it may also be possible to prove that reduction in that media budget will lead to a reduction in the level and quality of learning within the school environment.

The American Association of School Librarians has long been a proponent of accountability and competency-based instructional programs, accepting as the essential criterion of the media program that program's role within the instructional program. The association has supported the concept that every student has the right not only to abundant, high-quality instructional resources, but also to a professional library media staff sufficient in number and diversity of competencies to administer a wide range of media services and a well-planned program of developmental library media skills instruction. A commitment to this philosophy will enable the media professional to move more easily into the decade of the 80s, when declining enrollments, budget crises, and the goals of a job-oriented society will influence the decisions of educators and those responsible for providing the necessary resources to match those decisions.

Library media specialists must be willing to submit their philosophy for quality library media programs to the scrutiny of those who ask for continuous improvement in the educational system. It is still necessary to apply the criteria of excellence to school library media programs. If it were possible to meet the minimum standards of the American Association of School Librarians at this time, 100,000 qualified library media specialists would have to be employed by public local education agencies. A level of mediocrity will exist among elementary media programs if we lack vision for continued growth. Library media specialists must place their emphasis upon the direction of change rather than the rate of change. A striving for standards of excellence must pervade every facet of media program development in schools if we are to influence the behavior of the members of the profession.

BIBLIOGRAPHY

American Association of School Librarians. *Position Statement on Need for Maintenance of Professional Media Staff at Elementary, Secondary and District Levels.* Chicago: American Association of School Librarians, 1976.

American Association of School Librarians. *Standards for School Library Programs.* Chicago: ALA, 1960.

American Association of School Librarians, American Library Association, and Association for Educational Communications and Technology. *Media Programs: District and School.* Chicago: ALA; Washington, D.C.: Association for Educational Communications and Technology, 1975.

American Library Association, Committee on Postwar Planning. *School Libraries for Today and Tomorrow; Functions and Standards.* Chicago: ALA, 1945.

Darling, Richard L. *Public School Library Statistics, 1962–63.* Washington, D.C.: U.S. Department of Health, Education and Welfare, Office of Education, 1964.

Davis, Harold S., ed., *Instructional Media Center: Bold New Venture.* Bloomington: Indiana University Press, 1971.

Fast, Elizabeth T. "Standards of Excellence in Hard Times." *School Media Quarterly* 4 (Winter 1976) : 121–25.

Fite, Alice E. "A Statement in Honor of the Twenty-fifth Anniversary of AASL as a Professional Organization." *School Media Quarterly* 4 (Summer 1976): 293–95.

Gardner, John W. *Excellence: Can We Be Equal and Excellent Too?* New York: Harper, 1961.

Gaver, Mary Virginia, *Effectiveness of Centralized Library Service in Elementary Schools.* New Brunswick, New Jersey: Rutgers University Press, 1963.

Hannigan, Jane A. "The Promise of Media Programs: District and School." *School Media Quarterly* 2 (Fall 1973): 9–14.

Joint Committee of the American Association of School Librarians and of the Department of Audiovisual Instruction of the National Education Association. *Standards for School Media Programs.* Chicago: ALA, 1969.

Kennon, Mary Frances, and Doyle, Leila Ann. *Planning School Library Development; A Report of the School Library Development Project, American Association of School Librarians,* February 1, 1961–July 31, 1962. Chicago: ALA, 1962.

Liesener, James W. *A Systematic Process for Planning Media Programs.* Chicago: ALA, 1976.

National Center for Education Statistics. *Statistics of Public School Media Centers, Fall 1974.* Washington, D.C.: U.S. Department of Health, Education and Welfare, 1977.

Sullivan, Peggy, ed., *Realization: The Final Report of the Knapp School Libraries Project.* Chicago: ALA, 1968.

DISTRICT LEVEL SUPPORT
OF SCHOOL MEDIA
CENTER PROGRAMS

by RICHARD L. DARLING

Support from the district level for school media service, a type of service to which Betty Fast devoted much of her professional career, has been a major force in achieving excellence in school media programs. Although there has been no systematic research to verify the extent to which central supervisory and support services for school media programs enhance their quality, a considerable amount of observation and testimony provide evidence that such is the case. While there are many superior individual school media programs where there is no district level media staff, a list of local school systems with a reputation for excellent media programs district wide is a list of systems with effective centralized services to support the building level media program.

No history of school district media center supervision has been attempted and, indeed, the literature of school media service supervision is inadequate. In 1964 the U.S. Office of Education reported that in the 1960–61 school year there were 2,591 positions—1,100 professional and 1,491 clerical—in a variety of school system-level support services for media programs, including supervisors, librarians administering centralized processing, librarians of professional libraries, and clerks serving each category.[1] No subsequent official national estimate has been gathered, but throughout the 1960s it is probable that the number of positions increased rapidly as unprecedented sums of money, much of it from the federal government, poured into school media center development. Much of the increase in supervisory level positions after the passage of the Elementary and Secondary Education Act of 1965 can be attributed to the need to cope with the avalanche of materials purchased with ESEA funds, rather than to achieve excellence in school media programs, but the effect of creating district level services was to increase the number of good programs.

Although there have been no systematic studies of centralized school system services to support building level media centers, several articles have appeared that describe the programs in particular districts. The April, 1968, issue of *Library Trends,* edited by Sara Krentzman Srygley, was entitled *School Library Services and Administration at the School*

District Level.[2] In addition to several studies of particular aspects of school system-level media services, the volume includes descriptions of the programs in Webster Parish, Louisiana; Shaker Heights, Ohio; Fulton County, Georgia; and Lansing, Michigan. These articles, each written by the long-time supervisor of the program, provide insight into ways that system supervision can promote excellence in school media service.

The most extensive study of a school system media program is John T. Gillespie's *A Model School District Media Program.*[3] In his detailed analysis of the centralized media department of the Montgomery County Public Schools in Rockville, Maryland, Gillespie explores the evolution of the county's school media program, its services, staff, and other resources, its problems, its successes and failures. If read in conjunction with Gillespie's earlier unpublished New York University Ph.D. dissertation,[4] this study gives the most extensive picture we have of the impact of a good central program in achieving excellence in individual school media programs. Still more information on the Montgomery County program can be found in articles by James W. Jacobs and by the present author.[5]

These case studies provide an account of program developments in individualized systems, to be sure, but they also provide a basis for a generalized statement of the ways in which school district media services can contribute to excellence, as well as goals for those programs to establish in serving school media centers.

The school system media program functions at two levels to promote excellence in the individual school media center. At the system level, itself, the district media office works in many indirect ways that affect the building center as well as directly in service to the school. Both are significant in improving the quality of the program.

Indirect services

The indirect services for the school media programs relate to the leadership function of the district media office. The staff of the office interpret the media program and its importance in a variety of ways. As a member of the staff of the district superintendent, the media director has access to policy making at the district level and, through the superintendent, has a direct line to the board of education.

The effective director uses every opportunity to exploit this access to increase the visibility of the media program. One opportunity lies in the preparation of the annual budget and its presentation to the superintendent and the board of education. By presenting the budget directly to the superintendent, the media director can win the superintendent's support for needed expenditures for the program, and provide more cogent arguments to support them.

The budget can also be a valuable vehicle for educating the board and, through it, the public. The media director should seek the right to present the media sections of the budget to the board. Assisted by appropriate members of the media department staff and representatives of the building library media specialists, and armed with up-to-date factual data, the media director can answer board members' questions, assisting the superintendent in supplying necessary information and justifying requests for funds for materials, equipment, and staff.

At budget hearings the board of education is under particularly great pressure, with the necessity to develop an expenditure budget in balance with its estimated revenue, and may be less responsive than at times when the budget is not under consideration.

The annual report of the media department should be presented at a time when there is no budget pressure. Such a report should inform the board and superintendent not only of the accomplishments and problems of the district media department but also, and especially, of the current status of staff, collections, and services of the media centers in the individual schools, and of their needs, in order to make the most significant contribution to the education of the boys and girls of the community. When the director and other members of the media department staff can present this report in person, they gain additional opportunities to interpret the media program.

Still another device used successfully in at least one school system is the presentation of media standards for board of education adoption. In Montgomery County, Maryland, Public Schools, the media staff has prepared standards for staffing, for collection size, for annual expenditures per student, and for media center facilities. They have always presented their standards and periodic revisions at times as far removed as possible from budget considerations so that the board would consider them on their own merits and not in terms of fiscal exigency. These presentations have been the occasion for fruitful discussions of educational needs and system policies. Even when the board of education reduced the standard to a level below professional recommendation, it was with a conscious commitment to seek funding that would move the system toward its adopted goals. Though the board was unlikely to immediately adopt a budget that would achieve a newly adopted standard, the media staff had succeeded in securing general agreement on goals that made planning for excellence possible.

The media department can also help educate the general public through a public relations program that can systematically keep the media program before the public eye. Through news releases, personal contacts with the news media, speeches before parent associations and other groups, and exhibits, the public can be informed of interesting developments and special programs in both the school media centers and the district department.

Direct services

The direct services of the district media department, while no more important than the indirect ones, are more immediately visible. They differ in different districts, but may include a wide variety of functions that can be performed more efficiently or more economically at the district level, or which cannot be done at all in each school.

A common and valued service is centralized purchasing, cataloging, and processing. These functions can be performed by each school, but when the district does them they can be done more professionally by an expert staff that specializes in technical services. As a result, the students and teachers can work with a better conceived and prepared catalog to the benefit of their learning and teaching. In addition, considerable money is saved. Larger discounts on combined orders extend school materials budgets and permit the purchase of additional materials. Efficient production methods further reduce total school system costs for cataloging materials.

More important, however, is the impact of centralized technical services on the service program of the school media center. Freed from cataloging and classification, and from the mechanical preparation of materials, school media specialists can devote vastly increased time to planning with teachers, to guiding the research, reading, listening, and viewing of students, and to selecting appropriate new materials for purchase. It is in better service to students and teachers that centralized technical services most contribute to excellence.

Another important direct service the media department provides is in-service education. The department can organize and present workshops to teach media specialists about new media and new techniques using the district staff or securing outside experts to do the teaching. Not only can it help media specialists keep abreast of new developments, but also the media department can train library aides and clerks to provide the necessary support for new programs and can give workshops for teachers on the use of new media in the classroom.

The media department can also develop collections of very expensive or infrequently used materials, or materials requiring special care and handling, from which individual schools may borrow. When a school media center secures films, video tapes, professional books and periodicals, large type and braille books from the district central media department, its own service is enlarged and the district service integrated into a single one, to the benefit of users.

Some services are the joint responsibility of the central media department and other school system units. The media director and staff work with a school facilities department to be sure new schools have media centers that promote excellent programs. They work with the purchasing department to make certain that specifications for bids for furniture and equipment will be appropriate for the school's program. They secure the cooperation of subject supervisors, building principals and media specialists, and classroom teachers in selecting collections for new schools, and then use the full resources of the central media department to purchase and prepare collections and have them ready for use on the first day of instruction in the new school.

The central media staff works with the personnel department to recruit effective professional-media specialists and supporting staff, and advises on placement and transfers that will be most appropriate for developing media programs. They also assist the personnel department in writing job descriptions and in developing criteria for evaluating job performance in the media center. They work with curriculum directors and supervisors to be sure that the media program is represented in curriculum development and revision. In nearly every aspect of school system-level administration, the district media department makes sure that decisions that will affect the media program are going to improve it.

Service in the schools

Some of the direct service to the school media centers takes place in the school itself. An important function of the district media staff is to serve as consultants to the media specialists in the schools. Frequently central office staff members assist the building staff in evaluating the ongoing media program and in planning new services or improvements in existing services.

The guidance of the central department is particularly valuable to the new media specialist unfamiliar with policies and procedures of the school district. While much of the information needed by the new media specialists can be presented in an orientation workshop for new staff members at the beginning of the school year, on regular visits to new media specialists the central department staff can answer questions and help new staff members solve problems that the planners of the orientation workshop did not anticipate.

The consultant visit can be equally useful to experienced media specialists. When introducing new services, altering old ones, or when trying to persuade the principal and teachers to use media in new ways, the building media specialist may find that the central office staff can help present the program and influence the needed decisions. That the central office consultant comes from outside the school gives his or her advice the enhancement of seeming more objective. The consultant is able to describe the program in other schools and explain the ways other schools solved any problems that arose.

Sometimes the central office media consultant helps to assure excellence in school media programs by evaluating the existing service and by advising the principal on the shortcomings of the building media center and staff. In extreme cases, such work with a principal could end in the replacement of staff, but more often it would result in joint planning and counseling with the principal, the media specialist, and, sometimes, with teachers, to plan improvement of the program.

There are many elements that contribute to excellence in school media programs. Good staff, good collections, good facilities, adequate funds, and imaginative services are among the important ingredients. There is no magic formula for mixing these ingredients to get the desired outcome. The presence of a good school system-level media service to support the efforts of the individual schools, however, is often the catalyst that changes the available ingredients and infuses them with excellence.

REFERENCES

1. Mary Helen Mahar, and Doris C. Holladay, *Statistics of Public School Libraries 1960–61, Part 1, Basic Tables* (Washington, D.C.: U.S. Department of Health, Education and Welfare, Office of Education, 1964), pp. 72–75.

2. Sara Krentzman Srygley, ed., *School Library Services and Administration at the School District Level. Library Trends* (April 1968).

3. John T. Gillespie, *A Model District Media Program; Montgomery County as a Case Study* (Chicago: American Library Association, 1977).

4. John T. Gillespie, *A History and Descriptive Study of the Media Centers of the Montgomery County Public Schools, Montgomery County, Maryland 1948–1969* (Ph.D. diss., New York University, 1970).

5. James W. Jacobs, "Organizing Instructional Materials Services at the System Level," *ALA Bulletin* (February 1968), pp. 149–52; Richard L. Darling, "Nonprint Media in Montgomery County Public Schools," *Drexel Library Quarterly* (April 1971), pp. 121–28.

PROFESSIONALISM OF
SCHOOL LIBRARIANS AND
MEDIA CENTER MANAGEMENT

by EVELYN H. DANIEL

A few years ago a friend of mine and I were casually watching television. On the screen Evel Knievel was being interviewed sitting astride his motorcycle after just jumping over seven city buses. The interviewer asked, "Why do you endanger your life by jumping over buses?" Knievel replied, "Because I'm a professional and this is my profession!"

Do a professional bus jumper and a professional school library media specialist share a common self-perception? Do they regard their occupations in similar ways? Perhaps they do. By his use of the term "professional," Evel Knievel meant to convey to his audience certain qualities about himself and his attitude to his "profession." In addition, he may also have suggested a few things that were not intended.

For example, a professional is seen by our society as someone who has undergone a long and specialized training before attaining this status. The professional is expected to live by certain standards of behavior and have an internalized code of ethics so that he or she may be trusted by the public to work for the public good rather than for individual self-interest. The professional is expected to exercise autonomy in work definition and in the manner of accomplishing work with very little evaluation and control from lay people. The professional is accorded high status by society because the professional is expected to work with the mind, primarily for rewards that are symbols of work achievement, and thus ends in themselves, and not only for money as a means to some other ends.

Partly because of the high value that society has placed on this term, many individuals and groups apply the label to themselves as a status-seeking ploy. At other times the term is used as an accolade, that is, doing something "in a professional manner," meaning concerned with an efficient and superior performance for its own sake, rather than for external rewards of money or recognition. In the frequent appropriation of the term "professional," Evel Knievel and others doubtless intend to convey a sense of dedication, rigorous prior training, and a concern with achievement at self-set standards often combined with a sort of lofty disregard to the monetary gains involved.

There seem to be some similarities and some differences between the perceptions of the professional school media specialist and those of our exemplar. School media specialists have many of the attributes of the professional, but can the occupation be styled a profession? Perhaps there has been a shift in emphasis, from a concern with the technical aspects of the job to a larger perception of it. As school librarians have donned a new name, becoming media specialists, perhaps they have also donned new professional responsibilities. If the school media specialist is considered to be a practicing professional, what is the profession? Is it librarianship? Or is it teaching?

In an exploration of these questions, this paper first discusses the nature of the professional orientation and its significance for the practicing school media specialist. The second section deals with media center management and the need for a different perspective toward the tasks of running a modern center. The last section returns to the question of professionalism and considers what the profession of the school librarian qua media specialist really is and how to enhance its future development.

Professional orientation of media specialists

We are not at our best perched at the summit; we are
climbers, at our best when the way is steep.

—John W. Gardner

Approaching the job "in a professional manner" for the media specialist is probably both useful and necessary in order to do the job well. Three important attributes of this professional orientation will be discussed here—the belief in growth and progress, the need for autonomy, and the realization of the importance of status.

Gardner's statement reflects a belief, almost a faith, in growth and progress, an unwillingness to accept things as they are, a vision of some "ideal" future. This futuristic outlook is interwoven throughout any professional education. The master's program in librarianship, for example, consists of a number of things—a strong theoretical background, a sense of the past history and traditions of the field, some problem solving on current issues, some skill acquisition, and, mixed with all these, a substantial amount of philosophy toward life and work. This socialization (some would say indoctrination) introduces the element of the "ideal." The present is always seen as unsatisfactory but with patience, work, and vision, there is a strong faith that the future will become more nearly perfect.

This outlook on the present as not quite satisfactory, combined with the sense that one possesses the necessary skills to reshape events to a more acceptable future, is a strong motivator. If one lacks this future orientation, then the *joie* departs, accommodation becomes the order of the day, and the world seems smaller, grayer, older. The job becomes a nine-to-five cage that supports us in our life outside the work sphere. So the professional outlook, with its belief in growth and progress and in the ability of professionals to make positive change, not only produces a more acceptable personal life style but also introduces the altruistic possibility of working for the greater good of other human beings, another powerful motivator.

To support this general philosophy and to help practitioners in the implementation of it, the professional generally is given standards and guidelines that articulate the necessary vision of the future. The professional journals and conferences that we read and attend add to that vision and provide practical methods for achievement. Perhaps most of all, a professional orientation provides us with an inner perception of self that leads us to work toward the achievement of often intangible goals in ways that bring self-satisfaction, whether or not the achievements are acclaimed or even noticed elsewhere.

Philosophy and vision, however necessary, are not sufficient. The professional stance is one that insists on autonomy. In order to effect change in accord with a given direction, it is necessary to have a high degree of control over the job. Within the school, for example, who but the media specialist knows what must be done and in what way in order to develop a media program that helps "learners to grow in their ability to find, generate, evaluate and apply information that helps them function effectively as individuals and to participate fully in society."[1]

Society grants autonomy to the professional. And autonomy provides the necessary freedom to set objectives and to select the best ways to achieve these objectives. Many media specialists who arrive at the beginning of the new school year have handed to them a full schedule of classes with perhaps only one or two "free" periods during the entire week and no opportunity to interact with other teachers. Whether or not scheduled classes are good or bad is not the issue. Rather the point is that it should be the media specialist's professional prerogative to decide whether classes should or should not be scheduled and with what frequency intervals in order to best help students become independent gatherers and users of information.

To grow in competence and to progress in achievement requires a high degree of autonomy in job performance. A professional orientation calmly assumes that autonomy will be granted once credentials are established, authority is demonstrated, and trust is earned. Thus the media specialist may stress the professional aspects of previous education and the professional character of the occupation. This can be done in a variety of ways:

1. Through the dissemination of a detailed plan of action via many communication channels—a written document for principals and teachers, a slide-tape orientation for students and parent groups, periodic progress reports showing accomplishments and deviations from the media specialist's self-set goals, oral presentations in faculty meetings and the like.
2. Through concrete demonstrations of the benefits to be gained by teachers in the performance of their tasks and by students in their increased sophistication in gathering and using information.
3. Through the use of a specialized vocabulary (jargon to the noninitiates but useful discrimination to those within the field) when discussing aspects of the media center with administration and other faculty.
4. Through the willingness to be held accountable for the achievement of self-imposed, published goals.

All these attempts to demonstrate competence and authority also have the effect of building status within the school. To be termed a status-seeker is pejorative, as it connotes a concern with title and perquisites but not substance. Yet the achievement of status is extremely important to the professionally oriented media specialist. Status has a dual meaning. At times it can mean recognition by others of the requirement for a special role or position in the organization; at other times or in subtle connotation, it also means standing or rank in comparison to others within a particular setting. Both meanings are salient for the school media specialist.

Status concerns are also power concerns. Those with a professional orientation recognize the need for some source of power in order to be able to influence events and people in congruent ways. One accepted categorization of the sources of individual power in an organization is that proposed by French and Raven.[2] They discriminate among physical power, resource power, position power, expert power, and personal power. Although there is a great deal of overlap among these, two of these sources of power can be singled out as particularly pertinent when discussing professional status within an organization—position power and expert power.

Position power is legitimate power that comes as a result of a recognized, established role in an organization. The occupancy of that role entitles one to all the rights of that role in the organization. Position power gives the occupant potential control over the flow of information, access to a variety of networks (for example, the curriculum committee for the school media specialist), and the right to organize the way one's work is to be accomplished.

Expert power is the power that is vested in someone because of his or her acknowledged expertise. If a specialist is acknowledged as an expert, the expert's suggestions or instructions will usually be implemented. Only when this expertise is questioned will it be necessary to fall back on other sources of power to implement the wishes of the specialist. Expert power is also comparative—anyone is an expert who knows more than anyone else around and has that claim recognized, explicitly or implicitly.

Status for the school media specialist within a school is achieved when the position of school media specialist is recognized as a necessary and unique role in the organization and when the media specialist is recognized as an expert in certain areas that are essential to the proper functioning of the school. Without this recognition, it is unlikely that the media specialist will be able to progress in achieving the accepted ideals of service.

Thus, the media specialist with a professional orientation holds a fundamental belief in the possibility of positive change through autonomous program planning within an organization that recognizes the rights and responsibilities of the media specialist to provide leadership and guidance in the provision of media services to all who work in the school. Believing in progress, striving for autonomy, recognizing the need for status, those with this professional orientation possess the enabling attitude that serves to create a positive climate for work achievement.

A perspective on media center management

One of the most frustrating and discouraging things in this life is to do good work and have it fail for reasons which have nothing to do with the quality of effort.

—*Bits and Pieces* (Jan. 1978, p. 8)

This quotation carries an important message. Often we define our jobs narrowly, focusing so completely on the technical performance of our tasks that we neglect the necessary facilitating aspects of the job. Within the service sphere, once a certain level of autonomy is reached over the ways in which a task is to be accomplished, it becomes essential to spend nearly as much time educating and interacting with others as on the accomplishment of the task. Time invested in this facilitating function is important in order to make sure that the ends to be achieved are appreciated and expected by the significant others in the organization and that the ways of accomplishing the tasks mesh with other activities to become an integral part of the organization. The school media specialist will find it helpful to look holistically at the school using a systems approach to plan and accomplish work goals.

In the *Last Whole Earth Catalog,* there are three "Laws of Life" that are supposed to embody TRUTH:

> Everything is connected to everything!
> Everything has to go somewhere!
> There's no such thing as a free lunch!

These three maxims stress the interrelationships of things, the need for organization, and the importance of examining work with a cost-benefit ratio in mind. The school library media center does not exist in isolation. It has a place within the total school environment. The way it functions affects, and is affected by, the other elements of the school. Together, all the elements affect the nature of the whole. It is easy to get so wrapped up in our own immediate problems that we see other parts of the organization only as they relate to us. Remember Pogo's classic phrase, "We have met the enemy and he is us!" One way to avoid that dilemma is to move outside our small world and try to see the entire system.

Talcott Parsons, the sociologist, suggests that there are three levels of management—the technical level, the developmental level, and the institutional level—each of which has a different perspective, a different view of time, and a different approach to problem solving.[3] The technical level of management has a somewhat narrow perspective, focuses on the immediate day-to-day problems, and is concerned with the nuts and bolts of the operation, the application of resources of time and materials in very concrete and specific ways. Many school media specialists are technical managers and may, as a consequence, be adversely affected in ways suggested by the quotation that introduced this section.

The developmental level manager, or the "middle manager," usually stands in the middle of a hierarchy with subordinates and superiors and relatively few peers. The developmental manager has a longer time frame, perhaps year-to-year rather than day-to-day, and he or she has a concern with taking broad policies articulated at a higher level and translating them into operational guidelines. The principal of a school frequently has this perspective.

School media specialists rarely view themselves as developmental managers. One research study conducted by the author on the communication patterns of media specialists involved asking several media specialists to complete a questionnaire in which they specified five people above them in the school hierarchy, five peers, and five subordinates or people below them in the school hierarchy. One plaintive reply to the last query made a significant impression. This school media specialist wrote across the form, "There is no one below me in this school!"

At the third level of management, the institutional level manager has a systems perspective and a sense of mission. He or she looks to the future—five or ten years, a generation, a lifetime—and formulates the broad policies and goals for the organization. The institutional level manager takes a long view and a wide view, considering the impact of the organization on the environment, and vice versa. If one wanted to sketch these various perspectives in a few words, risking some oversimplification, the technical manager looks within and down; the developmental level manager looks both up and down but still within; the institutional level manager looks around the organization and beyond. Parsons says we can allow our positions within organizational space to restrict our viewpoint, or conversely we can consciously assume the perspective of the institutional manager and take a systems view of the total organization.

It is important to adopt a systems approach and a managerial perspective to the work of the media specialist. When school librarians became media specialists, they also became media managers. As the duties, the collections, the facilities, the staff, and the responsibilities have become greater (and they have been consistently increasing in all areas over the past decade), then it has become the media specialist's responsibility to coordinate all these diverse elements and to create a smoothly running program with carefully articulated goals and objectives and a plan for achieving them. This coordinating-planning-managing role requires a managerial perspective in much the same way that the media specialist requires a professional orientation.

The profession of the media specialist

The school media specialist's services to the school community may be divided into several broad areas of responsibility. These responsibilities will, at various times, cast him/her in the role of teacher, consultant, librarian, organizer, leader, designer, or administrator.

—*Conceptualization of the Media Professional* (Syracuse University Press, 1977)

Butcher? Baker? Candlestick maker? What is our profession? What basic principles and values do we profess? Some would say that we are teachers; I will argue that our true profession is librarianship.

The work of the school media specialist has changed signficantly over the past several years, increasing in scope, complexity, and responsibility. As is often the case in periods of great change, other people's views of the school media specialist's position have not kept pace with these changes. Those with whom the media specialist interacts—teachers, principal, parents, even children—hold a very limited and one-dimensional conception of the media specialist's role, seeing it predominantly as materials provider. A natural step to take in trying to remedy this misperception is to identify with the dominant role within the school—that of the teacher. This may have the effect of reducing some of the isolation and also may seem to give status in the sense of providing a recognized position within the school organization. However, it does not alleviate the misperception and may perhaps contribute to a greater one.

Teaching is only one dimension of the librarian's role. To call oneself a teacher and to have others perceive us as teachers does violence to the many other dimensions of the role of school media specialist. The media specialist has no real discipline to teach. Information gathering and using skills do not seem to be taught effectively isolated from a subject context. Yet, how to find and use information is probably the most important skill that children should acquire before leaving school. Because of its central importance, it is a skill that must pervade the curriculum. It must be taught by *all* the teachers and cannot be the unique teaching province of the media specialist. Because the media specialist has greater knowledge of "library" skills, he or she must assume a consulting role with the teachers, advising them and helping them to design instruction around these skills. The media specialist must assume a managerial role in organizing resources and scheduling activities to enhance the probability that the information gathering and using aspect of problem solving is the center of all learning activity.

The primary client of the teacher is the child. The primary expertise of the teacher is subject knowledge. The primary responsibility of the teacher is to organize that knowledge in a coherent way and to lead the children systematically at ever deepening levels into that subject knowledge. Conversely, the primary client of the media specialist is the teacher. The primary expertise of the school media specialist is metaknowledge—knowledge about knowledge. The primary responsibility of the media specialist is to diagnose teaching/learning problems, to prescribe ways that information can help solve these problems, and to organize the knowledge about knowledge in such a way that teachers and students can acquire it, evaluate it, and use it independently.

The closest counterpart to that role is that of the librarian. It is the profession of librarianship that is concerned with knowledge about knowledge and with the central process of diagnosing information needs and guiding users to information that will satisfy those needs. It is this conception of the school library media specialist's profession by those who practice and by those with whom the media specialist interacts that will best reduce the ambiguity and enable the media specialist to realize the powerful contribution that exists in the role's potential form.

Without a sense of professionalism, much will be lost. If one looks to others to define a role or a status, it should be not surprising if that role is reduced to a minimum with very little status attached to it. If the school media specialist looks to the principal and teachers to tell him or her what is wanted, the principal and teachers will often exert pressure to schedule the greatest number of classes in the media center and require the media specialist to handle the greatest number of students, to produce the largest number of mediated materials, or some other arbitrary objective. These objectives seem to others to be instrumental in achieving the end of equipping children to cope with life. But school media specialists who exercise their professional sense realize that the means to this end are more complex, that more is not necessarily better, and that possibly smaller, shorter contacts of a higher order with an intelligent plan underlying the provision of services will be a more effective way of attaining the end goal.

To summarize my point of view on professionalism and the school media specialist, consider the following five points:

1. Nobody knows more about the media center and its potential contribution to the total school program than the school media specialist. One cannot ask others what to do but must assume a leadership role.
2. The responsibility for the successes and failures of the school media program rests with the media specialist. Because the responsibility rests there, one must act with the necessary authority to make sure that there are more successes than failures.
3. There is an ethical code that undergirds the profession of school media specialists. This code presumes that media specialists will provide equal treatment for all, will speak for intellectual freedom, and will work to guarantee each child's right to free access to information. Access is here used in the larger sense of being able to find and use information whenever and wherever it is needed.
4. The work of the media specialist is more than a nine-to-five job. It is a full-time, lifetime occupation. One is a library

media specialist all the time, whether actively practicing or not. It is a true life commitment.

5. The umbrella profession of the school media specialist is that of librarian. The nature of the work with the client is a consultative one rather than a direct teaching one. The stance of the school media specialist is *in* education but not *of* education. There are more similarities between the work of the school media specialist and the public librarian or the academic librarian or the information specialist than there are with teachers where the role is more complementary than analogous.

To see the role of the school media specialist as really professional can be somewhat frightening without the concomitant attitude that professional development means lifelong learning. One never knows enough. Knowledge of the curriculum, of the clientele, of materials, of better methods of organizing and promoting services can never be achieved in full. And there is, of course, the professional challenge and the final reason why it makes an enormous difference to regard oneself as a professional. It is in the growing and learning that life becomes vital and exciting, that one wakes up in the morning eager to rise and face the challenge.

Perhaps in the largest sense, professionalism is caring. Our world needs those who care and who commit themselves to collective goals over individual goals. Gould put this well, when he said:

> I do not believe the greatest threat to our future is from bombs or missiles. I do not think our civilization will die that way. I think it will die when we no longer care, when the spiritual forces that make us wish to be right and noble die in the hearts of men.[4]

REFERENCES

1. *Media Programs: District and School* (Chicago: ALA; Washington, D.C.: Association for Educational Communications and Technology, 1975), p. 4.

2. J. R. P. French, Jr., and B. H. Raven, "The Bases of Social Power." *Group Dynamics: Research and Theory.* 2nd ed. D. Cartwright and Z. A. Zander, eds. (Evanston, Ill.: Row, Peterson, 1960), pp. 607–623.

3. Talcott Parsons, *The Social System* (New York: Free Press, 1951).

4. Lawrence M. Gould, as quoted on pp. 14–15 of Ruth Ann Davies, *The School Library Media Center; A Force for Educational Excellence.* 2nd ed. (New York: Bowker, 1974).

THE INSIDE STORY:
SCHOOL MEDIA SPECIALISTS
AND THEIR PUBLIC RELATIONS
EFFECTIVENESS

by COSETTE N. KIES

The degree of success of school media centers within various school settings has always depended, in large part, upon the level of understanding of the potential patrons regarding the materials and services available. From the early days of the implementation of the school media center concept, theorists and practitioners in the field have been concerned with the effectiveness of the information being disseminated about school media center services and materials. This area of communication, or internal public relations, with the users and potential users of media centers has long been recognized as an appropriate field for examination, but only recently have standardized methods been developed that can be used by media specialists for accurately determining the effectiveness of their internal public relations.

The close interrelationship of public relations with the entire communication process is cited frequently in definitions of public relations. "Public relations is the planned effort to influence opinion through socially responsible performance based on mutually satisfactory two-way communication."[1] The authors of this definition, Cutliff and Center, also point out further considerations of communication by suggesting the seven "C's" of communication:

1. Credibility	5. Continuity and Consistency
2. Context	6. Channels, and
3. Content	7. Capability of Audience.[2]
4. Clarity	

Applying this definition and the seven "C's" of communication to school media center public relations programs is theoretically easy, but identifying the degree of effectiveness of public relations and communication has not been an area that most school media specialists have felt competent and/or comfortable in handling, possibly because of the lack of accurate measuring devices.

This uneasiness about the accurate measurement of public relations effectiveness has not been a unique problem for school media specialists. Considerable attention to this area has been shown by various groups and professions, and a number of suggestions on how best to measure public relations and communication effectiveness have been published. However, the efforts of one group, the International Communication Association, have been the most promising to date in offering concrete suggestions and appear to have the highest potential for adaptability, in part, to school media center situations.

ICA communication audit project

In 1971, the International Communication Association (ICA) began the development of a measurement system for assessing communication effectiveness in organizations. This measurement system is based upon five specific tools: a questionnaire survey of 118 items and 10 demographic characteristics of all organizational members; interviews with randomly and/or purposively selected members of the organization; computer analysis of the emerging communication networks; identification of typical successful or unsuccessful incidences of communication within the organization and the computer analysis of this information; and communication diaries of all organizational members.[3]

After considerable testing and revision, the ICA audit materials are now considered relatively standardized. One of the long-term objectives of this project is to consolidate this standardized information from various organizations into a computerized data base that will ultimately provide information regarding organizational communication.

This undertaking, obviously, is a sophisticated research project involving data collecting beyond that which most school media specialists can practically consider. The time required (about six months per organization) and the cost of computer analysis makes the conduct of such an audit a cumbersome and unrealistic consideration for the majority of school media specialists.

Examination of other possible measuring devices that might more easily be used by school media specialists reveals a lack of precise determination of actual communication within organizations, libraries, and media centers. This is probably due, in part, to the basic premises of these measuring methodologies, which are often based primarily upon attitudes and Likert scales, sociometric analysis, and the like.[4] Therefore, in spite of its rather complex structure and detailed methodology, the ICA communication system appears to have the most promising potential for adaptation for practical use by school media specialists.

A decided advantage in using an adaptation of the ICA communication audit rests in the extent to which the system has been examined in the field of organizational communication. Sincoff and Goyer have pointed out that the communication audit of the ICA should be used with three cautions kept in mind:

1. Audit data should not be gathered for their own sake.
2. The audit is a diagnostic technique, not a "cure" for illness.
3. The Communication Audit is only one of many organizational needs-analysis approaches.[5]

Gerald M. Goldhaber, one of the "founding fathers" of the ICA Communication Audit, and Paul D. Krivonos have suggested some of its strengths and weaknesses:

Strengths:

1. The Audit provides attitudinal, perceptual, and behavioral data on information flow, message content, and communicator attitudes and perceptions.
2. The Audit is based upon a sound conceptual framework and was developed and pilot-tested over a five-year period in a variety of organizational settings.
3. The Audit is the only standardized system of organizational communication measurement available today. . . .
4. The Audit uses five instruments. . . .
5. Standardization of instruments and procedures allows norms to be established and longitudinal comparisons to be made among organizations and across time. . . .

Weaknesses:

1. The Audit procedure has some practical limits, mostly related to time commitments by the organization.
2. . . . some audit data is collected in a subjective manner dependent upon the cooperation of the audited personnel.
3. Although subjected to constant revision, the instruments need to be regularly monitored so that language is easily understood by organizational members.
4. The Audit system needs to become more clearly cost-effective to client organization. . . .
5. . . . most of the audit data is gathered in a static method limited to a very short period of time. . . .
6. . . . most of the audits have been conducted in educational, medical, or governmental service organizations.[6]

In adapting the audit for use in school media centers, the last weakness becomes, in a sense, a strength. An examination of a list of sixteen audits completed under the ICA project shows that, to date, commercial, profit-making organizations have not been studied in any depth and that those service agencies studied are in many respects comparable to school media centers. The sixteen organizations studied were: an Arizona utility; a

Canadian hospital; a Florida school system; a U.S. senator's office; a Pennsylvania manufacturing company; a public defender's office; a university personnel office; a university public relations division; a U.S. federal agency; a university academic department; a Wisconsin volunteer agency; a New York bank; a Colorado hospital; a federal police agency; an Albuquerque hospital; and a Kansas university.[7] Since five of the sixteen organizations successfully audited were educational in nature, it would seem that a project such as a communication audit could be carried out in a school media center.

A communication audit for school media centers

A communication audit for the use of school media specialists, structured on the ICA questionnaire for all organization members and organized on the current school media center standards,[8] was developed by the author with J. Michael Rothmacker. The questionnaire is in two parts—the first deals with the facilities, services, and materials, and the second deals with the sources and channels of information by both formal and informal means of communication. The questionnaire was devised for use and/or adaptation with the traditional groups within schools—students, teaching faculty, and administrative staff.[9]

It is my opinion that the most crucial group to be concerned with in measurement of school media center public relations is the student body, since the students are the primary reason for the existence of the entire educational organization. Although the teaching faculty and the administrative staff are prime movers in the educational process and, as such, need to be considered in the public relations program of a school media center, it is the students' understanding and use of the media center that indicates whether or not it is fulfilling its purpose.

In fact, it has been pointed out that the students can themselves be the means for indoctrinating their teachers regarding the school media center. As Betty Fast wrote, "Some of the recent publications on school media programs emphasize the idea of concentrating on teachers who in turn can influence their students to use media resources. The media specialist, however, must also recognize the importance of reaching the *teacher* through the *students*."[10] Using children to reach adults is not a new idea, of course, as examination of library literature shows. For example, in 1917 a librarian in Passaic, New Jersey, sent letters home with 10,000 school children to encourage family use of the public library.[11] Fast, however, suggests an even more subtle approach by this use of students to encourage teachers' use of audiovisual materials and other library resources. She goes on to say, "Reaching teachers through kids presupposes that students feel welcome in the media center and come in on their own."[12] This, then, is one of the most important arguments for trying to determine the effectiveness of a school media center public relations program. It is *student* use and understanding of the school media center that justifies the existence of school media centers. The students' use of school media centers and the increased use of school media centers by teachers means a snowballing effect is possible and that precipitating such growth is desirable from the standpoint of the school media specialist.

School media specialists and the audit

Since the audit questionnaire for school media specialists is, at the time of this essay's composition, as yet an untested device for measuring public relations, the author held structured interviews with six media specialists in five different school settings in Tennessee. (The form used is shown in figure 1.) The purpose of the interviews was to determine the practicality of the audit form and the interest and willingness of practicing school media specialists to actually use the audit form to determine public relations effectiveness in their particular schools. All the schools are located in two major metropolitan areas. Three are public and two are independent.

The school media specialists interviewed ranged in age from 25 to 41 years. All had been school media specialists for less than 5 years. All held, or were working on, a master's degree in library science. All were female and white.

In all cases, the media specialists were enthusiastic about the concept of the audit as a measurement device, and four of the media specialists expressed interest in doing an audit in the near future. In the school where an audit will probably not be done, the two media specialists involved felt that poor relations with the faculty would be a major deterrent to having a successful audit.

A description of each school and the responses of the school media specialist for each school follows. A wide variety in the school environments and in the students in the schools was involved. For the purposes of this investigation, only elementary school media centers were examined.

School "A"

School "A" is located in a suburban area and has 750 students in grades K–6. The school is housed in a new physical facility which, in the opinion of the media specialists, has already been outgrown. The media specialist described the school and its community:

Name of Interviewee _____

Where currently employed _____

Years as Elementary School Librarian _____

Age of Interviewee _____

Public or Independent Public School _____

No. of Students in School _____

Brief description of nature of the school:

1. Do you see the communication audit as a useful mechanism for finding out about your public relations effectiveness?
2. Are any particular sections of the audit form of more interest to you than others?
3. Is there any information not included in the audit form that would be useful to you?
4. If you were to do a communication audit, would it be an entire school audit or some selected section thereof?
5. To what use will you put your findings if you do an audit?
6. Will you do an audit in the near future?
7. What do you think the reaction of your school administration will be if you do decide to do an audit?
   The faculty?
   The students?
8. Please feel free to make any additional comments on the back of this sheet.

Fig. 1 Interview Sheet

The community has had public education since the late 1800s. At least twice the community had to band together to save its school. In the early 1950's and in 1971 the county Board of Education announced the closing of "A" school. The rural community fought to keep the school. After the 1971 decision there was moderate growth, and in 1973 a new fast-growing subdivision was established in the school district. With this subdivision the complexion of the community began changing. From 1973 to 1976 this change was gradual as was the growth in the school enrollment. However, since 1976 the school enrollment has doubled and already has surpassed the 1980 projected enrollment. What was once a quiet rural community where students and teachers rode their horses to school has become a fast-growing suburb.

The media specialist of School "A" was particularly interested in the section of the audit dealing with the services of the school media center and is planning to do an initial audit with faculty because of her concern for finding out why a large group of teachers are nonusers of the media center. Whether or not these teachers will respond to the audit questionnaire is unknown. The media specialist describes the school principal as supportive and the students as enthusiastic users but predicts that a large portion of the teachers "would answer the audit grudgingly, a small portion will gladly participate, and a small portion will not return the forms. (These few never return any type of survey I do.)"

School "B"

School "B" has changed in a number of ways since its establishment in 1922. Now an elementary school of 450 students, it is part of a larger educational complex along with a middle and a high school. Because of its location near a naval air station, the school population is very transient. The media specialist stated:

> A new educational facility was opened in 1975–76 which includes an additional wing built onto the existing intermediate building. This wing contains 12 classrooms in clusters of three, a gymnasium, cafeteria, office, and library. The recent history of the school has been marked by unprecedented changes in organization, such as grades accommodated and the racial composition of faculty and student body. The faculty consists of 23 teachers, including a speech therapist, reading lab teacher, and three special education teachers. . . . Probably the most significant changes have occurred as a result of the redistricting of our school boundaries in 1975–76. As a result of this, our student body is now 60% white and accommodates grades K–6. Instead of serving a tenant farming community, we now serve a mobile military community.

The media specialist at School "B" anticipated that the administration, teachers, and students would all react positively to the audit. She was more interested in those sections dealing with facilities, services, and materials, and anticipated an audit's being particularly useful for assessing the collection of the media center. The media specialist plans to do a school-wide audit, starting with parents at a P.T.A. meeting.

School "C"

The third public school, School "C," is located within the city limits of a large metropolitan area with a predominantly black population. A small school of 320 students in grades K, 4–6, all classes are scheduled to visit the library during the course of a week. The school media specialist said about her school:

> The school draws from two neighborhoods for its students. One is predominantly white and the other predominantly black. The white students are bused in and comprise approximately 2% of the student body. The remainder of the students are from the streets around the school. It is a Tile I school, which means there are enough children in the school who receive free lunch to qualify the school for federal aid. The parents own homes and those who don't rent homes. Most of the parents of the students have had some high school education and 40% of them have graduated from high school . . . about 1% have advanced degrees. Most of the parents are employed. The neighborhood is transient, with about 20% moving every year.

The media specialist at School "C" was most interested in the materials and services sections of the audit form, and she could see using the results of the audit to improve services and selection procedures, as well as to encourage more use of the media center. Uncertain as to whether or not she would do an audit in the near future, this interviewee anticipated that reaction from the administration of her school, should she do one, would be generally favorable. Faculty reaction was anticipated as being apathetic and the students as being somewhat interested, but primarily feeling, "If I have to answer this, let's do it in a hurry."

School "D"

School "D" is an independent school of 450 students including both elementary and secondary grades. Two media specialists work at this school, one serving the elementary grades and the other the secondary. The individual who now serves at the secondary level was originally employed for the elementary grades. Both media specialists were interviewed in relation to their reactions about the communication audit form as it would pertain to the elementary grades only. The school was described as one that:

> . . . enjoys a tradition of excellence which dates back to its inception at the end of the nineteenth century. When the present building was erected in 1925, the school was known

as the ———— School. A spacious area on the second floor was planned for library facilities. The library has remained in its original quarters, two reading rooms and an office space with the addition of minimal storage space across the hall. A group of parents negotiated the purchase of the property (in 1976) and the school has continued as an accredited independent private school. . . . The positive factors that have affected the growth of the school have also benefitted the library program. The school serves a concerned, educationally motivated clientele. Many of the parents are in positions that enable them to donate time and services to the school, as well as make cash donations. The library receives donations of materials and has access to parent volunteer help.

This was the school in which a negative reaction to the audit was received. The two media specialists were not opposed to the concept and were interested in possibly doing one with older children. They felt that it would be difficult to use the instrument in its present format with young students and also expressed some concern for faculty negativism. They were more interested in Part II of the audit, which deals with sources and channels of communication, and saw it as a legitimate device for accountability and reporting purposes.

School "E"

School "E," also an independent school, was founded and the facility built at the time of busing orders. It is located with other independent schools in a predominantly middle-class suburb of a large metropolitan area. The media specialist stated:

The ———— School is a co-educational day school starting with a program for the four-year-old children through grade six. The school, while sponsored and guided by the First Presbyterian Church, is not sectarian. Denominational emphasis is absent, but instead the school seeks to establish a Christian environment. Music, French, Art and Bible are part of the curriculum.

The media specialist at School "E" was most interested in the services portion of the audit and would use results to make changes that might benefit the school. She would not consider doing an audit until a later time (because of her newness in her position) and anticipated complete cooperation from anyone involved should she undertake the audit. As the media specialists of School "D" suggested, she felt the audit would work best with the older students.

Summary of school media specialists' reactions

Although interviews were held with only six media specialists in five different school environments, certain trends seem to emerge that might be useful for school media specialists considering an audit based on this particular questionnaire form or other questionnaires. Two strong reactions can be seen that need to be investigated further in preliminary interviews and actually tested with the audit form itself:

1. Modification, revision, or a totally different format may be needed for younger children (probably ten years old and younger).
2. Anticipated apathy and negativism were laid at the feet of the teaching faculty by the majority of the media specialists interviewed.

Additional consideration may need to be given to the actual school communities and to other variables, such as the media specialists' training and attitudes, possible enforced student involvement in the media center, and teaching faculty's knowledge and awareness of basic concepts and philosophies regarding school media centers. Student attitudes about the media center need to be explored further since, as Marilyn Miller noted in her doctoral research, the personality of the librarian can be the most important influence on the perceptions of accessibility.[13] This last factor might well be tied to general communication theory and related, in turn, to communication and public relations effectiveness between school media specialists and students.

Conclusion

It is apparent as a result of this limited study that there is further need for examination of standardized forms and devices by which school media specialists can measure their communication and public relations effectiveness. There may well be opportunities for additional by-products of information in this particularized search for *what* individuals know about school media centers, *how* they found out about it, and whether or not that information was *important* to them. This information, such as attitudes about the media center and the media specialist, interest in the services of the media center, and even status games between teaching faculty and media specialists, should suggest further avenues for thought and investigation.

An area that might continue to provide opportunities for additional work by school media specialists is the relationship between students and their teachers, with the media specialist acting as an unobtrusive change agent. As Fast suggested, "When teachers and students share in the orientation to the media program, both groups gain from the experience. By observing young people use media, adults can more readily understand that media is 'first nature' to students. Students will realize that learning does not stop upon graduation from school."[14] Fast reiterates this final thought elsewhere: "While it is true that libraries have always inspired a few students to become lifelong independent learners, we cannot be content with an occasional random success today. The future will require almost everyone to possess this talent for self-directed learning."[15] This entire sequence involving the student's gaining motivation for lifelong learning, and the roles of the teacher and media specialist in this process, provides more possibilities for further consideration in relation to the assessment of public relations effectiveness in school media centers.

The role of a school media specialist within the larger educational environment provides a unique and important opportunity for concrete and positive action in playing a crucial part in formulating student attitudes and habits. In order to take an active, positive role, media specialists need to take action and investigate further dimensions for their own roles and those of others. By assuming a role of activism and working for change, school media specialists may well prove to be one of the most influential and positive influences in bringing lifelong learning motivation and increased understanding of societal change in tomorrow's world to children.

REFERENCES

1. Scott M. Cutliff and Allen H. Center, *Effective Public Relations.* 4th ed. (Englewood Cliffs, N.J.: Prentice-Hall, 1971), p. 2.

2. Ibid., pp. 260–61.

3. Gerald M. Goldhaber, et al., *ICA Communication Audit Survey Instruments: 1977 Organizational Norms,* pp. 2–3. (ERIC: ED–140–375, 1977)

4. Examples of recent such studies in the library field include: Marilyn Lee Miller, "Student Access to School Media Center Resources as Viewed by High School Seniors in Southwestern Michigan Schools Accredited by the North Central Association of Colleges and Schools" (Ph.D. diss., University of Michigan, 1976); Clifford Elmer Lange, "Communication Behavior and Interpersonal Coorientation Between Public Library Directors and Their Board Members' (Ph.D. diss., University of Wisconsin, 1972); and Cosette Nell Kies, "Unofficial Relations, Personal Reliance, Informal Influence, Communication, and the Library Staff: A Sociometric Investigation of Three Medium-Sized Public Libraries" (D.L.S. diss., Columbia University, 1977).

5. Michael Z. Sincoff and Robert Goyer, "Communication Audit Critique: The Researcher's Perspective," *Journal of Business Communication* 15 (Fall 1977): 58–59.

6. Gerald M. Goldhaber and Paul D. Krivonas, "The ICA Communication Audit: Process, Status, Critique," *Journal of Business Communication* 15 (Fall 1977): 51–54.

7. Goldhaber, *ICA Communication Audit,* p. 32.

8. American Association of School Librarians, ALA and Association for Educational Communications and Technology, *Media Programs: District and School* (Chicago: ALA, 1975).

9. Cosette N. Kies, *Projecting a Positive Image through Public Relations.* (Chicago: ALA, 1978).

10. Betty Fast, "Mediacentric: Polish Up Your Backhand," *Wilson Library Bulletin* 51 (March 1977): 572.

11. Elizabeth White, "Reaching the Parents Thru the Children—An Experiment in Publicity," *The Library Journal* 42 (July 1917): 522–23.

12. Fast, "Mediacentric: Polish," p. 573.

13. Miller, "Student Access."

14. Elizabeth T. Fast, "Blueprint for Action," in *Media Center Facilities Design,* ed. Jane Anne Hannigan and Glenn E. Estes (Chicago: ALA, 1978), p. 29.

15. Betty Fast, "Mediacentric: On Learning How to Learn," *Wilson Library Bulletin* 51 (December 1976): 311.

APPENDIX:
COMMUNICATION AUDIT FOR SCHOOL MEDIA CENTERS

Introduction

Following is a suggested communication audit survey questionnaire form. It is closely based upon the school media standards. It can be simplified and modified according to individual situations and/or personal preferences. It is possible to use only certain portions rather than the entire survey.

Before using the communication audit form, the school media specialist needs to determine his or her objectives for doing the audit. Based upon these identified objectives, the number of individuals to be asked to fill out the form can be determined. The categories of individuals to be involved can also be determined at this time. It may be that a total audit of an entire school is desirable, or merely a sample representing all groups. Single grades might be used or only media center users. It is also conceivable that individuals in the outside community, such as parents, might be involved in the audit.

This communication audit survey form was prepared with the assistance of J. Michael Rothacker, Associate Professor, School of Library Science, George Peabody College for Teachers.

Since the main purpose of the communication audit is to measure how well informed individuals are about certain materials and services and their satisfaction in learning about these materials and services, it is important to conduct the survey during a specific time period. Later audits should be taken to identify changes that will indicate the possible success or failure of the image projection program.

Tabulation of the results will, in most cases, be done by hand, since samples will often be small and can easily be displayed in frequency distribution. Computer use is possible, but it will require additional refinement of the instrument for adaptability to specific computer and/or scanning equipment. Not only is computer use possible but in certain instances highly advisable, particularly where the sample size is large and the audit more thorough. In this case, where criterion variables would be available, effective use could be made of the computer to produce cross tabulations, correlation coefficients, etc.

The importance of the audit lies not with individual, specific scores on each item, but rather with the overall trends indicated from specific groups of individuals. A fairly clear picture of attitudes about the media center and its information program should be obtainable as a result of a communication audit, and this should provide an extremely valuable basis for the setting up, implementing, and maintaining a positive image projection program.

Procedures

The media specialist must first determine exactly what information is being sought by the communication audit. In other words, what are the objectives of the audit? The following questionnaire was based upon the present standards and is only one possible communication audit form for media centers. Each media specialist will probably make modifications according to the preformulated objectives, identified respondents, and information desired.

The audit on the following pages is divided into five sections:

Part I. Kinds of Information
    Section A. Facilities
    Section B. Services
    Section C. Materials
Part II. Sources and Channels of Communication
    Section A. Formal Communication
    Section B. Informal Communication

Within each section are categorizations of information about which it might be useful to know the information level. These categories can be combined, eliminated, or enlarged according to the individual media specialist's predetermined needs. It is possible, of course, to take only those portions of the audit of immediate concern and eliminate information of lesser, or even extraneous, concern at the time of the audit.

The respondents for the audit may be selected on the basis of a number of criteria, such as finding reactions of teachers to the facility or a class of high nonusers regarding services. The respondents, like the survey form itself, need not be an inviolate, precisely balanced ratio of certain audiences. The categorization of the respondents is like the information sought, in that their incorporation in the audit serves a predetermined purpose. An example might be to ask all users of nonprint media in a single class about their level of information regarding materials in the media center. This would be a way to find out how successful the media specialist has been in letting a group of users know about the availability of materials.

Administration of the audit can be undertaken in various ways. Classroom teachers might cooperate in verbally presenting simple audits to the younger students. When written responses are being solicited, with both the older students and adults, full and careful explanations should be made about the purpose of the audit.

Individuals filling in the audit form should be asked to circle their responses on the five point Likert scales for each item according to two general categories:

1. How satisfied were you with the information received?
2. How important was the information to you?

It will need to be stressed that the items to be rated are in respect to the *information* about the items and not regarding the items' worth or value to the respondent. In using the audit form with younger children, the audit should be reworded so that each item is phrased as a specific, direct question, such as "Do you know there is a media center?" and "Is it important for you to know there is a media center?" It should be explained to respondents that the information level sought regards primarily information received passively. That is, the audit is more interested in identifying levels of information the respondents know because they heard it, saw it, or read about it somewhere, rather than information actively sought out by the respondent.

Media specialists will probably want to try a pilot audit with only a few people after settling on the information sought. In that way it will be possible to practice making clear verbal explanations and to find out if people understand how to fill in the form with a minimum of trouble.

INSTRUCTIONS

FACILITIES

For each item on the following pages, circle your level of response according to *two* questions:

1. How satisfied were you with the information received?
2. How important was the information to you?

You are being asked about the information you have seen, heard, or read regarding the media center, its services and materials. You are not being asked to judge the item itself, but what you know about it and how important knowing it is to you. If you do not know about an item, your circled response should be "1," or "low." It may be for this same item that your not knowing was unimportant, so that you would circle "5," or "high" on the second scaled response. If you do not know what an item is, skip it, or ask the media specialist what it means.

QUESTIONNAIRE SURVEY

Part I. Kinds of Information

For each item listed below, circle your response to both categories on the right. "Low" means both low satisfaction and/or importance to the item.

Section A. FACILITIES	*How satisfied* were you with the *information* received?			*How important* was the *information* to you?		
	Low	Avg.	High	Low	Avg.	High
1. Existence of a media center	1 2 3 4 5			1 2 3 4 5		
2. Location of the media center	1 2 3 4 5			1 2 3 4 5		
3. Size of the media center	1 2 3 4 5			1 2 3 4 5		
4. Atmospheric feeling (i.e., congenial surroundings) of the media center	1 2 3 4 5			1 2 3 4 5		
5. Space for:						
a. Individual study and research	1 2 3 4 5			1 2 3 4 5		
b. Group study and research	1 2 3 4 5			1 2 3 4 5		
c. Self-instruction	1 2 3 4 5			1 2 3 4 5		
d. Program activities and classes	1 2 3 4 5			1 2 3 4 5		
e. Materials	1 2 3 4 5			1 2 3 4 5		
f. Production of materials, including:						
i. Those by media center	1 2 3 4 5			1 2 3 4 5		
ii. Those by students	1 2 3 4 5			1 2 3 4 5		
iii. Those by teachers	1 2 3 4 5			1 2 3 4 5		

	How satisfied were you with the information received?			How important was the information to you?		
	Low	Avg.	High	Low	Avg.	High
6. Adequate electrical outlets for use of audiovisual equipment	1	2	3 4 5	1	2	3 4 5
7. Adequate lighting	1	2	3 4 5	1	2	3 4 5
8. Adequate sound control	1	2	3 4 5	1	2	3 4 5
9. Comfortable temperature and humidity	1	2	3 4 5	1	2	3 4 5
10. Appropriate furniture	1	2	3 4 5	1	2	3 4 5
11. Adequate display areas	1	2	3 4 5	1	2	3 4 5

INSTRUCTIONS

SERVICES

For each item on the following pages, circle your level of response according to *two* questions:

1. How satisfied were you with the information received?
2. How important was the information to you?

You are being asked about the information you have seen, heard, or read regarding the media center, its services and materials. You are not being asked to judge the item itself, but what you know about it and how important knowing it is to you. If you do not know about an item, your circled response should be "1," or "low." It may be for this same item that your not knowing was unimportant, so that you would circle "5," or "high" on the second scaled response. If you do not know what an item is, skip it, or ask the media specialist what it means.

QUESTIONNAIRE SURVEY

Part I. Kinds of Information

For each item listed below, circle your response to both categories on the right. "Low" means both low satisfaction and/or importance to the item.

Section B. SERVICES	How satisfied were you with the information received?			How important was the information to you?		
	Low	Avg.	High	Low	Avg.	High
1. Making materials available for in-school use						
a. To students	1	2	3 4 5	1	2	3 4 5
b. To teachers	1	2	3 4 5	1	2	3 4 5

	How satisfied were you with the information received?					How important was the information to you?				
	Low	Avg.			High	Low	Avg.			High

	Low	Avg.			High	Low	Avg.			High
c. To administrative staff	1	2	3	4	5	1	2	3	4	5
d. To PTA and other school-oriented groups	1	2	3	4	5	1	2	3	4	5
e. To student organizations	1	2	3	4	5	1	2	3	4	5

2. Making materials available for out-of-school use (circulation)
   a. Print students

	Low	Avg.			High	Low	Avg.			High
i. To students	1	2	3	4	5	1	2	3	4	5
ii. To teachers	1	2	3	4	5	1	2	3	4	5
iii. To administrative staff	1	2	3	4	5	1	2	3	4	5
iv. To individual parents (families)	1	2	3	4	5	1	2	3	4	5
v. To PTA and other school-oriented groups	1	2	3	4	5	1	2	3	4	5
vi. To student organizations	1	2	3	4	5	1	2	3	4	5

   b. Nonprint materials

	Low	Avg.			High	Low	Avg.			High
i. To students	1	2	3	4	5	1	2	3	4	5
ii. To teachers	1	2	3	4	5	1	2	3	4	5
iii. To administrative staff	1	2	3	4	5	1	2	3	4	5
iv. To individual parents (families)	1	2	3	4	5	1	2	3	4	5
v. To PTA and other school-oriented groups	1	2	3	4	5	1	2	3	4	5
iv. To student organizations	1	2	3	4	5	1	2	3	4	5

3. Reference and information services

	Low	Avg.			High	Low	Avg.			High
a. To students	1	2	3	4	5	1	2	3	4	5
b. To teachers	1	2	3	4	5	1	2	3	4	5
c. To administrative staff	1	2	3	4	5	1	2	3	4	5
d. To individual parents (families)	1	2	3	4	5	1	2	3	4	5
e. To PTA and other school-oriented groups	1	2	3	4	5	1	2	3	4	5
f. To student organizations	1	2	3	4	5	1	2	3	4	5

	Low	Avg.			High	Low	Avg.			High
4. Instruction to students in the use of the media center and of library materials generally	1	2	3	4	5	1	2	3	4	5

5. Media center staff consulting on the use of print and non-print media in instructional program planning

	Low	Avg.			High	Low	Avg.			High
a. In general curriculum planning	1	2	3	4	5	1	2	3	4	5

(Cont.)

	How satisfied were you with the information received?			How important was the information to you?		
	Low	Avg.	High	Low	Avg.	High
b. In individual program and class/instructional unit planning with individual teachers or teams	1 2	3	4 5	1 2	3	4 5
6. Media services and materials available from school media center						
a. Author, title, and subject index approach to books in the media center	1 2	3	4 5	1 2	3	4 5
b. Title and subject index approach to periodicals in the media center	1 2	3	4 5	1 2	3	4 5
c. Title and subject index approach to nonprint materials in the media center	1 2	3	4 5	1 2	3	4 5
d. Storytelling and other group programs	1 2	3	4 5	1 2	3	4 5
e. Production of nonprint materials	1 2	3	4 5	1 2	3	4 5
f. Instruction in the production of nonprint materials	1 2	3	4 5	1 2	3	4 5
7. Media services and materials available beyond the school media center						
a. Author, title, and subject index approach to books in the media center	1 2	3	4 5	1 2	3	4 5
b. Title and subject index approach to periodicals in the media center	1 2	3	4 5	1 2	3	4 5
c. Title and subject index approach to nonprint materials in the media center	1 2	3	4 5	1 2	3	4 5
d. Print and nonprint materials available within the school or from other agencies (e.g., public and state libraries)	1 2	3	4 5	1 2	3	4 5
e. Media program planning consulting services	1 2	3	4 5	1 2	3	4 5
f. Availability of special services, e.g.:						
i. Puppet shows	1 2	3	4 5	1 2	3	4 5
ii. Theatrical productions	1 2	3	4 5	1 2	3	4 5

	How satisfied were you with the *information* received?			How important was the *information* to you?		
	Low	Avg.	High	Low	Avg.	High
iii. Materials production beyond the capabilities of the school media center	1 2	3	4 5	1 2	3	4 5
iv. Instruction to school media center staff and others in production of materials	1 2	3	4 5	1 2	3	4 5
v. Computer services	1 2	3	4 5	1 2	3	4 5
vi. Management consulting to media center staff	1 2	3	4 5	1 2	3	4 5

INSTRUCTIONS

MATERIALS

For each item on the following pages, circle your level of response to *two* questions:

1. How satisfied were you with the information received?
2. How important was the information to you?

You are being asked about the information you have seen, heard, or read regarding the media center, its services and materials. You are not being asked to judge the item itself, but what you know about it and how important knowing it is to you. If you do not know about an item, your circled response should be "1," or "low." It may be for this same item that your not knowing was unimportant, so that you would circle "5," or "high" on the second scaled response. If you do not know what an item is, skip it, or ask the media specialist what it means.

QUESTIONNAIRE SURVEY

Part I. Kinds of Information

For each item listed below, circle your response to both categories on the right. "Low" means both low satisfaction and/or importance to the item.

Section C. MATERIALS	How satisfied were you with the *information* received?			How important was the *information* to you?		
	Low	Avg.	High	Low	Avg.	High
1. Number of book titles	1 2	3	4 5	1 2	3	4 5
2. Variety of book titles	1 2	3	4 5	1 2	3	4 5

(Cont.)

	How satisfied were you with the information received?			How important was the information to you?		
	Low	Avg.	High	Low	Avg.	High
3. Number of periodical titles	1 2	3 4	5	1 2	3 4	5
4. Variety of periodical titles	1 2	3 4	5	1 2	3 4	5
5. Number of newspaper titles	1 2	3 4	5	1 2	3 4	5
6. Variety of newspaper titles	1 2	3 4	5	1 2	3 4	5
7. Number of pamphlet titles	1 2	3 4	5	1 2	3 4	5
8. Variety of pamphlet titles	1 2	3 4	5	1 2	3 4	5
9. Number of microform titles	1 2	3 4	5	1 2	3 4	5
10. Variety of microform titles	1 2	3 4	5	1 2	3 4	5
11. Number of microform readers and printers	1 2	3 4	5	1 2	3 4	5
12. Number of filmstrip titles	1 2	3 4	5	1 2	3 4	5
13. Variety of filmstrip titles	1 2	3 4	5	1 2	3 4	5
14. Number of silent filmstrip projectors	1 2	3 4	5	1 2	3 4	5
15. Number of sound filmstrip projectors	1 2	3 4	5	1 2	3 4	5
16. Number of slide titles	1 2	3 4	5	1 2	3 4	5
17. Variety of slide titles	1 2	3 4	5	1 2	3 4	5
18. Number of slide projectors	1 2	3 4	5	1 2	3 4	5
19. Number of slide viewers	1 2	3 4	5	1 2	3 4	5
20. Number of slide sorting trays	1 2	3 4	5	1 2	3 4	5
21. Number of transparency titles	1 2	3 4	5	1 2	3 4	5
22. Variety of transparency titles	1 2	3 4	5	1 2	3 4	5
23. Number of overhead projectors	1 2	3 4	5	1 2	3 4	5
24. Number of opaque projectors	1 2	3 4	5	1 2	3 4	5
25. Number of posters	1 2	3 4	5	1 2	3 4	5
26. Variety of posters	1 2	3 4	5	1 2	3 4	5
27. Number of art prints	1 2	3 4	5	1 2	3 4	5
28. Variety of art prints	1 2	3 4	5	1 2	3 4	5
29. Number of study prints	1 2	3 4	5	1 2	3 4	5
30. Variety of study prints	1 2	3 4	5	1 2	3 4	5
31. Number of maps	1 2	3 4	5	1 2	3 4	5
32. Variety of maps	1 2	3 4	5	1 2	3 4	5
33. Number of globes	1 2	3 4	5	1 2	3 4	5
34. Variety of globes	1 2	3 4	5	1 2	3 4	5
35. Number of 16mm sound film titles	1 2	3 4	5	1 2	3 4	5
36. Variety of 16mm sound film titles	1 2	3 4	5	1 2	3 4	5
37. Number of super 8mm sound film titles	1 2	3 4	5	1 2	3 4	5
38. Variety of super 8mm sound film titles	1 2	3 4	5	1 2	3 4	5
39. Number of 16mm sound film projectors	1 2	3 4	5	1 2	3 4	5

	How satisfied were you with the information received?			How important was the information to you?		
	Low	Avg.	High	Low	Avg.	High
40. Number of super 8mm sound film projectors	1 2 3	4	5	1 2 3	4	5
41. Number of videotape titles	1 2 3	4	5	1 2 3	4	5
42. Variety of videotape titles	1 2 3	4	5	1 2 3	4	5
43. Number of videotape (television) receivers	1 2 3	4	5	1 2 3	4	5
44. Number of audio tape recording titles	1 2 3	4	5	1 2 3	4	5
45. Variety of audio tape recording titles	1 2 3	4	5	1 2 3	4	5
46. Number of audio listening units	1 2 3	4	5	1 2 3	4	5
47. Number of audio cassette titles	1 2 3	4	5	1 2 3	4	5
48. Variety of audio cassette titles	1 2 3	4	5	1 2 3	4	5
49. Number of cassette listening units	1 2 3	4	5	1 2 3	4	5
50. Number of audio disc (record) titles	1 2 3	4	5	1 2 3	4	5
51. Variety of audio disc (record) titles	1 2 3	4	5	1 2 3	4	5
52. Number of stereo and monaural record players	1 2 3	4	5	1 2 3	4	5
53. Number of audio card titles	1 2 3	4	5	1 2 3	4	5
54. Variety of audio card titles	1 2 3	4	5	1 2 3	4	5
55. Number of audio card listening units	1 2 3	4	5	1 2 3	4	5
56. Number of AM radio receivers	1 2 3	4	5	1 2 3	4	5
57. Number of FM radio receivers	1 2 3	4	5	1 2 3	4	5
58. Number of games and toys	1 2 3	4	5	1 2 3	4	5
59. Variety of games and toys	1 2 3	4	5	1 2 3	4	5
60. Number of educational models	1 2 3	4	5	1 2 3	4	5
61. Variety of educational models	1 2 3	4	5	1 2 3	4	5
62. Number of sculptures	1 2 3	4	5	1 2 3	4	5
63. Variety of sculptures	1 2 3	4	5	1 2 3	4	5
64. Number of projection screens	1 2 3	4	5	1 2 3	4	5
65. Number of copying machines	1 2 3	4	5	1 2 3	4	5
66. Number of duplicating machines	1 2 3	4	5	1 2 3	4	5
67. Number of dry mount presses	1 2 3	4	5	1 2 3	4	5
68. Number of paper cutters	1 2 3	4	5	1 2 3	4	5
69. Number of transparency makers	1 2 3	4	5	1 2 3	4	5
70. Number of typewriters	1 2 3	4	5	1 2 3	4	5

(Cont.)

	How satisfied were you with the information received?			How important was the information to you?		
	Low	Avg.	High	Low	Avg.	High
71. Number of mechanical lettering devices	1 2 3 4 5			1 2 3 4 5		
72. Number of cameras	1 2 3 4 5			1 2 3 4 5		
73. Number of videotape production equipment units	1 2 3 4 5			1 2 3 4 5		
74. Number of audio tape production equipment units	1 2 3 4 5			1 2 3 4 5		

INSTRUCTIONS

SOURCES AND CHANNELS OF FORMAL COMMUNICATION

For each item on the following pages, circle your level of response according to *two* questions:

1. How satisfied were you with the information received?
2. How important was the information to you?

You are being asked about the way you learned about the media center, its services and materials. You are being asked *how* you heard about each item on the following pages, not how you rank the item itself. You are also being asked how important this particular way of finding out was to you. If you have not heard about something in the media center by the way being asked, you should circle "1," or "low."

QUESTIONNAIRE SURVEY

Part II. Sources and Channels of Communication

For each item listed below, circle your response to both categories on the right. "Low" means both low satisfaction and/or importance to the item.

Section A. FORMAL COMMUNICATION	How satisfied were you with the information received?			How important was the information to you?		
	Low	Avg.	High	Low	Avg.	High
1. Information received from school media specialist by: a. *Student,* by means of: i. Displays, posters, news releases	1 2 3 4 5			1 2 3 4 5		
ii. Media productions/ presentations	1 2 3 4 5			1 2 3 4 5		

	How satisfied were you with the information received?			How important was the information to you?		
	Low	Avg.	High	Low	Avg.	High
iii. Classroom visits	1 2	3 4	5	1 2	3 4	5
iv. Bibliographies	1 2	3 4	5	1 2	3 4	5
v. Media packages	1 2	3 4	5	1 2	3 4	5
b. *Teacher,* by means of:						
i. Memoranda, handbooks, information sheets	1 2	3 4	5	1 2	3 4	5
ii. Conferences	1 2	3 4	5	1 2	3 4	5
iii. Staff meetings	1 2	3 4	5	1 2	3 4	5
iv. News releases	1 2	3 4	5	1 2	3 4	5
v. Media productions/ presentations	1 2	3 4	5	1 2	3 4	5
vi. Bibliographies	1 2	3 4	5	1 2	3 4	5
vii. Annual reports	1 2	3 4	5	1 2	3 4	5
c. *Administrative staff,* by means of:						
i. Memoranda, handbooks, information sheets	1 2	3 4	5	1 2	3 4	5
ii. Conferences	1 2	3 4	5	1 2	3 4	5
iii. Staff meetings	1 2	3 4	5	1 2	3 4	5
iv. News releases	1 2	3 4	5	1 2	3 4	5
v. Media productions/ presentations	1 2	3 4	5	1 2	3 4	5
vi. Bibliographies	1 2	3 4	5	1 2	3 4	5
vii. Annual reports	1 2	3 4	5	1 2	3 4	5
d. *Media center staff,* by means of:						
i. Memoranda, handbooks, information sheets	1 2	3 4	5	1 2	3 4	5
ii. Conferences	1 2	3 4	5	1 2	3 4	5
iii. Staff meetings	1 2	3 4	5	1 2	3 4	5
iv. News releases	1 2	3 4	5	1 2	3 4	5
v. Annual reports	1 2	3 4	5	1 2	3 4	5
e. *Volunteers, parents, other* "concerned" citizens, by means of:						
i. News releases, radio and television coverage	1 2	3 4	5	1 2	3 4	5
ii. Media presentations	1 2	3 4	5	1 2	3 4	5
iii. Open house programs, public exhibits	1 2	3 4	5	1 2	3 4	5
iv. Budget justifications	1 2	3 4	5	1 2	3 4	5
v. Annual reports	1 2	3 4	5	1 2	3 4	5
f. *General public,* by means of:						
i. News releases, radio and television coverage	1 2	3 4	5	1 2	3 4	5
ii. Media presentations	1 2	3 4	5	1 2	3 4	5

(Cont.)

	How satisfied were you with the information received?			How important was the information to you?		
	Low	Avg.	High	Low	Avg.	High
iii. Open house programs, public exhibits	1 2	3	4 5	1 2	3	4 5
iv. Annual reports	1 2	3	4 5	1 2	3	4 5
2. Information received from school administration	1 2	3	4 5	1 2	3	4 5
3. Information received from school district administrator	1 2	3	4 5	1 2	3	4 5
4. Information received from school district media supervisor	1 2	3	4 5	1 2	3	4 5
5. Information received from the state department of education	1 2	3	4 5	1 2	3	4 5

INSTRUCTIONS

SOURCES AND CHANNELS OF INFORMAL COMMUNICATION

For each item on the following pages, circle your level of response according to *two* questions:

1. How satisfied were you with the information received?
2. How important was the information to you?

You are being asked about the way you learned about the media center, its services and materials. You are being asked *how* you heard about each item on the following pages, not how you rank the item itself. You are also being asked how important this particular way of finding out was to you. If you have not heard about something in the media center by the way being asked, you should circle "1," or "low."

QUESTIONNAIRE SURVEY

Part II. Sources and Channels of Communication

For each item listed below, circle your response to both categories on the right. "Low" means both low satisfaction and/or importance to the item.

Section B. INFORMAL COMMUNICATION	How satisfied were you with the information received?			How important was the information to you?		
	Low	Avg.	High	Low	Avg.	High
1. Information received from the school media specialist by: a. *Student*, by means of: i. One-to-one communication	1 2	3	4 5	1 2	3	4 5

	How satisfied were you with the information received?					How important was the information to you?				
	Low		Avg.		High	Low		Avg.		High	
	1	2	3	4	5	1	2	3	4	5	
ii. Group communication	1	2	3	4	5	1	2	3	4	5	
b. *Teacher*, by means of:											
i. One-to-one communication	1	2	3	4	5	1	2	3	4	5	
ii. Group communication	1	2	3	4	5	1	2	3	4	5	
c. *Administrative staff*, by means of:											
i. One-to-one communication	1	2	3	4	5	1	2	3	4	5	
ii. Group communication	1	2	3	4	5	1	2	3	4	5	
d. *Media center staff*, by means of:											
i. One-to-one communication	1	2	3	4	5	1	2	3	4	5	
ii. Group communication	1	2	3	4	5	1	2	3	4	5	
e. *Volunteers, parents, other "concerned" citizens,* by means of:											
i. One-to-one communication	1	2	3	4	5	1	2	3	4	5	
ii. Group communication	1	2	3	4	5	1	2	3	4	5	
f. *General public,* by means of:											
i. One-to-one communication	1	2	3	4	5	1	2	3	4	5	
ii. Group communication	1	2	3	4	5	1	2	3	4	5	
2. Information received from school administrators by means of:											
a. One-to-one communication	1	2	3	4	5	1	2	3	4	5	
b. Group communication	1	2	3	4	5	1	2	3	4	5	
3. Information received from school district administrators by means of:											
a. One-to-one communication	1	2	3	4	5	1	2	3	4	5	
b. Group communication	1	2	3	4	5	1	2	3	4	5	
4. Information received from school district media supervisor by means of:											
a. One-to-one communication	1	2	3	4	5	1	2	3	4	5	
b. Group communication	1	2	3	4	5	1	2	3	4	5	
5. Information received from the state department of education by means of:											
a. One-to-one communication	1	2	3	4	5	1	2	3	4	5	
b. Group communication	1	2	3	4	5	1	2	3	4	5	

THE
COMMUNITY

From
School Media Quarterly

by BETTY FAST

STANDARDS OF EXCELLENCE
IN HARD TIMES

The current budget crunch has caused legitimate questioning of the ways in which the AASL/AECT document *Media Programs: District and School* can be useful as educators prepare to defend media programs against the cost cutters.[1] Why are the two national professional organizations promulgating expensive and expanded programs at a time when holding the line is proving to be a difficult feat?

There are philosophical and practical responses to this question, and both kinds of answers are important. Although some people dismiss the concept of standards of excellence as unrealistic in the actual world, there is a need for a vision of the educational program as it should be, even though its achievement may seem impossible.

In his book *Excellence,* John W. Gardner develops a rationale for the importance of excellence in all aspects of our democratic society. His statement about standards is noteworthy here:

School Media Quarterly 4, 2 (Winter 1976): 121–25.

> Standards are contagious. They spread throughout an organization, a group, or a society. If an organization or group cherishes high standards, the behavior of those who enter it is inevitably influenced. Similarly, if slovenliness infects a society, it is not easy for any member of that society to remain uninfluenced in his own behavior.[2]

Standards are valuable as professional goals, but our new standards transcend the media professional because they present goals of excellence for the learner. The new media guidelines represent a well-developed idea for a method for achieving quality education which is truly individualized and learner-centered. The "purposeful integration of curriculum and media" described in the guidelines is a worthwhile objective which can strengthen our educational programs considerably.[3] We need standards to help us determine if our present course is a wise one; program goals provide a sense of direction even though we may be able to move only a short distance.

There is another philosophical reason for clearly defined standards of excellence. In his Pulitzer Prize winning book, *So Human an Animal,* biologist René Dubos discusses man's apparent ability to adjust to unfavorable conditions in our world and concludes that "Paradoxically, the most frightening aspect of human life is that man can become adapted to almost anything, even to conditions that will inevitably destroy the very values that have gained mankind its uniqueness."[4] Although Dubos is referring primarily to the pollution of the physical world, he also mourns the potential loss of freedom as expressed in "sensitive literature, intensely personal art or unorthodox science"[5] that may result from our adaptation to the regimented life caused by overcrowding of our urban areas.

For several decades critics have stresed the shortcomings of the schools. If the lack of meaningful reaction and the continuance of the status quo in spite of new program labels tells us anything, it may be a restatement of Dubos's proposition. School personnel, parents, taxpayers, even children—we have accepted the imperfect school model and adjusted to it although it does not promote the values we cherish and, in fact, may well be destroying some of these values. We need standards of excellence to help us remember the discrepancies between the programs we have and the programs we are aiming to build, to keep us from adapting to the level of mediocrity which most school districts have budgeted for their media programs.

The practical values of the standards can be determined by a careful reading of the document, and each media specialist and school district will focus on different aspects according to the needs of the individual media program. Although the guidelines set goals for excellent programs, they also outline methods for operating a program that will make the most of available resources, however meager those resources may be.

Permeating the document is an emphasis on the systems approach, which is today's counterpart of logical thinking and common sense more than it is an esoteric product of the technological age. Like a computer, the systems approach is only effective when valid data are used. As Arthur W. Combs warns us, "A systems approach is simply a device for making certain you accomplish your objectives. If your objectives are in error, a systems approach simply guarantees that your errors will be colossal."[6]

Throughout the guidelines local choice among broad alternatives is stressed. This is true in the relationship between the school and district program: "A school media program, while responsible administratively to the district program, has sufficient autonomy to develop appropriate responses to differing educational requirements of the school."[7] It is the underlying concept in the chapters on collections and facilities and appears in one form or another throughout the book. The flexibility which this offers to the school and district in using the guidelines is obvious: "the key to program development is flexibility based on purpose and effectiveness."[8]

In chapter 2 where the user-oriented emphasis of the document is advanced, it is interesting to note the activities or behaviors that can be observed in quality media programs. One of the major problems in "selling" the concept of school media programs has been our tendency in the past to focus on shallow objectives such as teaching students to identify author cards in the card catalog or to operate a filmstrip projector. How different are activities such as "employing a variety of media to find, evaluate, use, and generate information," or one from the affective domain, "enjoying the communication arts and gaining inspiration from them."[9] When our goals for the media program relate to the learner's specific objectives rather than the mere techniques of locating information, we will have taken the first step toward proving that budget cuts in the media program will reduce the learning in the school.

Although the chapter on personnel presents no real increases in recommended staff beyond the 1969 *Standards for School Media Programs*,[10] it does spell out in detail the responsibilities of each type of staff member and the competencies needed to perform the duties. If the scope of the program function is widely understood, the effect of cutting staff is clearly related to learning. The cost-effectiveness of differentiated staffing is a feature that should appeal to the board of education and the taxpayers.

The emphasis on planning offers a practical tool for the practitioner. "An analysis of user needs and interests provides a sound data base for decision-making relative to setting goals, modifying them, and devising program strategies."[11] Careful planning "avoids unwarranted expenditures of resources on short-lived demands."[12] Aside from facilities planning, school districts have been woefully lacking in educational planning; the 1975 standards provide the media specialist with guidelines for using this powerful procedure. If our program priorities are firmly anchored to the needs and interests of the users (both students and teachers), our programs will be more resistant to budget cuts. Planning techniques help us to make wise use of available people, media, and money resources. Moreover, planning is a way of thinking that lays the groundwork for sound action.

Programs that help teachers and students meet their priority teaching and learning objectives should withstand budget chopping as parents join the users in opposing such moves. We will know that our programs are meeting teacher needs when their professional associations and unions rise to defend the elimination of media specialist positions not only because they are fellow members but also because the teachers recognize that media staff is essential for effective classroom teaching. When teachers feel strongly about the benefits of media programs in the total curriculum, they will volunteer to take larger classes to insure the continuance of media staff in the building. If our media programs are important to teachers, they will become a top priority when contracts are negotiated.

Media Programs: District and School takes a firm stand on the media program as an integral part of the instructional budget rather than a support service. Most existing planning-programming-budgeting systems (PPBS) have not placed media programs in this position, and media specialists in districts that take their PPBS designations seriously may find their programs will suffer as budget cutting begins with those services labeled peripheral.

If the media program is considered merely a support service and not a part of the instructional budget, media cannot be used as one or more of the alternatives for achieving instructional objectives. The value of media programs in the individualization of instruction or in guiding students to become independent learners, which may be priority goals of the educational process, means that media must be available to use as a tradeoff in the PPBS process. The percentage figure for financial support of school media programs is not so formidable if it is viewed as instructional costs, cost-effective alternatives which assure better learning.

The section on production, one of the most innovative parts of the 1975 standards, with its accompanying table, addresses itself to production by all users and suggests ways for determining the most cost-effective level for various media production. In keeping with the philosophy of the interweaving of curriculum and media, the document describes the values of student media production in these words: "Student production occurs as a natural component of the educational experience and develops capabilities to translate elements of the environment into meaningful modes of communication. Creating materials in all formats sharpens the student's critical response to media, expands dialogue and the transmission of ideas, and fosters growth in precise and effective written and oral expression."[13] Student production programs which are geared to objectives such as these will be able to assert their merit and withstand budget cuts while more haphazard production programs—use of the camera because it's here and we have the film—will be eliminated.

A public information program following the guidelines should lead to the practical goal of increased understanding and support for the media program. This is a place where a long-term continuous program is required for satisfactory results; a frenzied last-minute publicity campaign after the budget cut has been announced will rarely succeed unless it builds on the solid base of an effective public information program.

As the document points out, "A well-planned program of public relations interprets the role of the media program and expands public expectations."[14] The changing character and responsibility of the school media program in recent years has mandated this type of public awareness program. If the community comprehends the important new role of media in education, the program should have less trouble enlisting public support.

Although the section on program evaluation requires input from the school district to make it meaningful for the local situation, the need for effective evaluation and the guiding principles are stated succinctly. Student involvement in evaluation adds a new dimension to the process and fits into the user-orientation of the document.

The network concept as illustrated in the "extended provisions" columns in the chapter on collections offers the only practical way of providing access to the resources required to meet user needs satisfactorily. Nevertheless, the document is not promoting the sharing of inadequate collections, as "no substitute can replace the individual school collection in guaranteeing a high degree of user satisfaction. . . ."[15] The report of the National Commission on Library and Information Science makes us realize that networks involving school media centers are not science fiction, and the guidelines cover the idea in several places.[16] Networking is part of the total concept of access espoused by the 1975 standards and also rates its own section in chapter 3. Taxpayers can recognize the cost-effectiveness of sharing resources and may be more willing to invest scarce dollars in school media collections if they realize the materials will be accessible to people outside the school.

The size of the total building collection does not exceed the figures cited in the 1969 *Standards for School Media Programs,* which have been adopted by many states, but the composition of the collection is a decision left to the individual school. "The development of the media collection is based on program goals and characteristics of the school and reflects needs, prior action, and resources."[17] This built-in flexibility should lead to a collection based on user needs and interests which will demonstrate its value through widespread use.

The series of questions in the chapter on facilities allows for local options rather than nationally prescribed dictates. Even though new school construction has decreased in these recessionary times, the planning guidelines in this section should prove invaluable as media specialists work on remodeling empty classroom space to enlarge existing media centers or create new ones. When money is tight, planning assumes a more important role for program efficiency.

If we knew the formula for excellence we might see more of it in our schools. No document ever devised—media standards, curriculum guide, teacher's handbook, or other—can assure excellence in a program even when unlimited funds are available. Excellence can only result when human beings who care work to help other human beings achieve their true potential. Guidelines and standards of excellence play a role, but the success or failure of the program depends on the people in it.

For verification of the value of media programs to learners, we will have to look beyond the Greenwiches, the Oak Parks, and the Montgomery Counties. Their fine media programs, nurtured by the wealth of suburbia, are only part of a well-financed total school program. It is virtually impossible to identify the contribution of the media program to student achievement in these districts, even if we discount the idea that the high socioeconomic level students would do well regardless of the educational offerings.

We must locate school systems where the media program has a disproportionate share of the per pupil expenditure, schools in which media use has become a viable alternative to other forms of education. In these schools we may be able to evaluate the effectiveness of media programs as a way of achieving learning objectives. We must be in the vanguard of cost-effectiveness studies. These findings should be highlighted nationally.

As court decisions force greater equalization of educational funding, the new standards can be used as a rationale and method for planning for greater media use in the school systems that were the "have nots" of our country. State and national leadership efforts will be required in this area to point out the value of media programs in the total educational program since many of these districts have only rudimentary media programs. We have suspected for a long time that it was not enough to have "islands of excellence in a sea of slovenly indifference to standards,"[18] that well-developed media programs in wealthy communities did not compensate for neglect of student learning through media in less affluent districts, that we cannot move forward in a democracy unless we incorporate some degree of equalization into our quest for quality.

In spite of the fact that many school budget decisions are political rather than educational in origin, the school media program that can demonstrate the ways it is helping students to learn more efficiently will survive budget slashes. *Media Programs: District and School* offers the practitioner a framework for local adaptation in planning and evaluating an effective media program. It also provides us with an instrument for determining the standards of excellence that can guide us in local program development.

REFERENCES

1. American Association of School Librarians and Association for Educational Communications and Technology, *Media Programs: District and School* (Chicago: American Library Assn.; and Washington, D.C.: Association for Educational Communications and Technology, 1975).

2. John W. Gardner, *Excellence; Can We Be Equal and Excellent Too?* (New York: Harper, 1961), p. 74.

3. *Media Programs: District and School,* p. 10.

4. René Dubos, *So Human an Animal* (New York: Scribner), p. 94.

5. Ibid., p. 155.

6. Arthur W. Combs, *Accountability for Humanism* (Washington, D.C.: Association for Supervision and Curriculum Development, 1973). Audiocassette.

7. *Media Programs: District and School,* p. 14.

8. Ibid., p. 106.

9. Ibid., p. 5.

10. *Standards for School Media Programs* (Chicago: American Library Assn.; and Washington, D.C.: National Education Association, 1969).

11. *Media Programs: District and School,* pp. 37–38.

12. Ibid., p. 38.

13. Ibid., p. 47.

14. Ibid., p. 56.

15. Ibid., p. 63.

16. National Commissions on Library and Information Science, *Toward a National Program for Library and Information Services: Goals for Action* (Washington, D.C.: U.S. Govt. Print. Off., 1975).

17. *Media Programs: District and School,* p. 69.

18. Gardner, *Excellence,* p. 133.

THE SCHOOL LIBRARY
MEDIA PROGRAM
AND THE COMMUNITY

by D. PHILIP BAKER

Although the count varies depending on those counting, only about 14 percent of our population use libraries—all types of libraries—with any regularity. A more optimistic view holds that this figure is too low and that at least one-third of the population are regular library users.[1] Other statistics, some more optimistic and some less, may be used in support of whatever debate is occurring about the state of library services in the United States in the late seventies. Access by our citizens to adequate library and information services, the need to establish comprehensive network systems that bring additional or first-time services to many more persons, and improved library media services in school, public, academic, and special libraries are insistent and prevailing national concerns. Furthermore, the financing and governance of these activities is an intrusive and sometimes troubling matter to the profession and the public.

A problem we all share as professional librarians is the lack of reliable statistical data established from an objective, credible information base that may be used with assurance to substantiate some of our most cherished ideas about the needs of people for library services and the methods by which these services are provided. With those figures we do have, we often play fast and loose, in diffuse efforts (based more on intuition than fact) to justify our work, our programs, our expectations, and our plans. Unreliable data, used with a shotgun approach, often in an emotional and defensive situation where we are seeking to *prove* our worth, may effect a momentary relief. But this leads inevitably to dangerous credibility gaps with those we must convince of our worth, and this is a dangerous game! The sky-is-falling technique used as a method to justify the maintenance of premier library and information services will not work anymore—if indeed it ever did.

The purpose of this paper, however, is not how to gather reliable statistical data and use them well. Nor is it how to use these data to coalesce grassroot citizen support for exemplary information programs. That these are urgent needs is patently obvious, but the absence of reliable statistics, or a failure to use effectively what we have, cannot be used as acceptable reasons for failure to perceive or sense what is needed or what must be done. Too often statistics are used as a *festung,* the secure bastian from which we sortie smugly to "prove" whatever needs proving. While this is doubtless an excessively cynical view of statistical use, it is nonetheless an attitude that too often prevails.

Indeed, the ability to know instinctively what must be done, to shift resources (people and materials) to accomplish the job, to develop new services and programs in response to new needs (and discard the unnecessary), to assert a wisdom based on common sense and sound judgments, and to improvise based upon practical know-how, have always been the hallmark of excellent library program leadership. To *know* what is needed, and to move with a sureness and purpose to do it, is a quality not found in enough library administrators. To wait upon accumulation of data that will prove the need for this or that program or service is a sure way to buy trouble or at best provide a "grade C" information program. This kind of administrative muddling is a passive reaction rather than a creative one, shaping and changing programs. The reverse of this attitude is expressed well by cultural anthropologist Margaret Mead, who believed, "Our future is not determined for us already. . . . We can determine it for ourselves—from the small details of social evolution, to the large details of cosmic evolution."[2] Such a statement may seem too cosmic for the workaday world we inhabit, filled with seemingly trivial concerns about budgets, supervision of staff, and accommodation to the whims of the boss, but it is a worthy challenge. The alternative to not believing so is to be steamrollered by a future where choices and alternatives are demolished. This is not an acceptable course.

Even without a cosmic sweep-sensor, it is apparent, based perhaps on equal parts intuition and a review of current events, that the future for school library media programs will mandate new programs and different services, many of which will be carried out in settings far removed from the classroom, the school library media center, even the school building. Historically, the absolute for the school library media center (a circumstance different from any other kind of library) was that its clients, the teachers and students, came to it in constantly increasing numbers—in a cycle always renewing itself. From the 1940s through the early years of this decade, this certainty was the preeminent shaper of most educational planning. Next year there would be *more*—more teachers and more students—always more! This certainty was a pervasive influence in school library media program planning.

These times brought an explosive growth in the number of school library media centers and a significant increase in the number of professionals and support staffs to run these programs. During this period came the historic transition of the school library program from that of passive provider of services on request to an educational program that found its ráison d'être in instructional leadership, technological innovation, and educational reform. While many individual school library media programs may fail to achieve these universal goals, they do provide the dominant philosophy for library media program planning in the contemporary school setting.

Starting in the late sixties a single event, the precipitous decline in the national birth rate, became the pervasive influence upon educational planning. Because the school library media program is bound inextricably to whatever happens to its parent institution, dramatic changes were forced upon it as well. The assured foundation upon which the whole educational establishment rested, the constantly expanding population base, disappeared. Coupled with a pernicious inflationary economy, a rebelliously contentious antitax public mood, and a general crisis in credibility about much of what was going on in the publicly supported educational system, these events compelled school library media programs to assume a defensive posture, something manifestly different from the soaring optimism generated by the roseate sixties. The stress has been enormous but, as always, those more able persons and innovative programs have not folded; rather they have used this time to plan for and provide new uses for the school library media program.

As 1980 and the final years of this century approach, the altered course for school library media programs is becoming apparent, and it is a future whose portents are not necessarily ominous nor threatening. In fact, many school library media programs have already moved to embrace this future, and their activities and programs presage a future characterized by new programs, creative uses of staff, and a renewed optimism about times that promise new vitality and purpose for school library media programs.

One certainty remains—that education will remain a fundamental preoccupation of this nation. But education, as we know it, will undergo dramatic, perhaps revolutionary, changes. Partly these changes represent accommodations that reflect the survival instincts of all institutions; bureaucracy does have a life—indeed it asserts a tenacious hold on that life. And partly they reflect a recognition that changing times do require new ways. For schools and library media programs meeting the educational needs of only the five- to eighteen-year-old, our traditional clients, is a notion being rapidly discarded. There are not enough of them to serve anymore—an expanded clientele must be found. The new user of school library media programs will range in age from two to life's termination. They represent such broad educational expectations as preschool learning, child day care, career and vocational counseling, continuing education, economic and consumer education, compensatory education, health and nutritional education, and a host of other expectations that will appear as the future becomes the present. Meeting these expectations will be the nucleus of renewal for the school library media program.

Separate from this seeking process, one that has us search voluntarily on our own for clients, is the arena of programs and services to be provided by government fiat. Here a prime example is PL 94-142, Education for All Handicapped Children Act, a federal law which when it is fully operable in 1980 mandates that a "free and appropriate publicly supported education be provided for all children from three to twenty-one." Here externally imposed forces assert themselves and create an expanded user group for school library media programs. In similar ways, the growing predisposition of the courts to mandate local and state educational policy, ranging from the equalization of educational opportunity through tax reform to decisions about racial balances in individual school buildings, has a special impact upon school library media programs. The significant trend in court decisions about education is not just that there be some equalization of educational opportunity through tax reform, as evidenced by the *Serrano* decision in California.[3] Potentially far more important is the mandate of recent court rulings that public school systems must provide equal *opportunities* for an appropriate education for all learners from three to twenty-one. PL 94-142 legitimizes this judicial attitude about due process through legislative action. And opportunity means something very different from just access to "good" education or the equalization of opportunities to get it. If schools are mandated by the government to provide compensatory education to a population ranging across a wide age span, our users could expand rapidly to the same unsupportable loads experienced by the schools in the 1950s. We have not yet come to this, but given the prevailing judicial and legislative penchant to make educational policy, one must at least consider this possibility.

Between these admitted extremes of imposed judicial and legislative will is something that may be appropriately termed legislative action with *intent* to create and promote new services or programs. The best example of this is, of course, the Title IV-B program established by the Elementary and Secondary Education Act of 1975. In spirit and intent, Title IV-B anticipated that guidance and library media programs should work together to create innovative programs of career information and vocational guidance to students. If local school districts have not acted thus, it is not the "fault" of the law. Rather, the fault lies with a turf and territory attitude which says "protect mine forever and change never!" It is a view of life discouragingly prevalent in much of education. Here, though, is an example of a federal law, sweetened by financial support, that envisions service roles for school library media programs to expanded client groups. Even the separation of funding for guidance sallaries into Title IV-D in the amended ESEA of 1978 need not prevent this cooperative program service.

Other examples are evident and already are having an important effect on promoting new library media program services. The Youth Employment and Training Program (YETP), a component of the Comprehensive Employment and Training Act (CETA) of 1973, provides an example of a lushly funded federal program that can have a special effect upon the school library media program. Some school districts have used their YETP funds to create a new kind of career/vocational/media program, serving students often alienated from the traditional school setting. These programs demand excellent information and information referral services for the participants that is an expansion of traditional library services. Their counseling component is sometimes located within the school library media center, a significant breakthrough in programs for new users. Another example, the Law Enforcement Administration Agency (LEAA), provides grants to school districts and cooperating community-based agencies such as Youth Service Bureaus of Police and Health Departments that provide abundant financial and staffing support for the development of effective educational media-based programs. The use of grant funds to purchase equipment, materials, and supplies, even additional staff support to operate library media programs are possible, but it takes imagination and energy to pursue the process of grantsmanship. Community Education Grants and Career Education Grants provide other incentives for school library media programs to serve entirely new groups of learners by using diverse program methods and procedures unknown even five years ago. Note too that, with the exception of ESEA Title IV-B and Career Education funds, the Department of Labor and the Department of Justice are the funding sources for these innovative school library media programs. Whoever would have believed that these two federal government departments, so far removed from the school library media center, would have such a direct impact upon the school library media program? Yet it is happening if we will only see it.

Added to this variety of government imposed or sponsored public-service programs are some better known to the profession. The growing importance of networking and the more sophisticated application of technology to storing and retrieving information require increased cooperation among public, academic, special, and school library media programs. This too is fostering new programs and services to diverse and different users.

These are some of the major trends and issues now at work that will promote (or force) the entry of school library media programs into new program areas. Specifically, how do these trends show themselves? And what may be predicted for their course in the remaining years of this century? As is often seen, they manifest themselves in combination of the imposed (legal/judicial) and the intuitive (exceptional vision that fosters the new way). They ebb and flow, merging with each other, at times changing course and direction, but moving always toward an inevitable conclusion.

For years the more articulate visionaries of the school library media profession have urged expanded services to include a clientele ranging from the preschooler to immediate post-high school graduate. Head Start programs have been served by school library media programs as a natural event, often because they were lodged within close proximity to the school library media center. In the case of the community college and some junior colleges, the high school library media center facility has often been shared jointly, to the benefit of both programs. So the tradition is already established that the school library media program should range somewhat afield in its search for new users. Federal funds and state social service monies provided by Title XX[4] provide a secure financial base for many social service programs, and schools have the right and the obligation to become involved with them. It is a predictable certainty that the number of working mothers will continue to grow and that they will demand a full range of instructional services, not just custodial babysitting, from day care centers. So, while we know that the actual number of infants under five years of age will decrease (until at least the mid-eighties), more *actual* numbers of children to be served by school library media programs will increase because of the growing number of women who work and want care for their children.

With declining school enrollments, it may also be predicted safely that some excess classroom space will be filled with preschool or Head Start programs. For certain, the school library media specialist must become more knowledgeable about how young learners learn! Reliance on manipulatives, realia, and material that can improve physical coordination is essential to these programs. And an understanding of how the brain picks up and assimilates learning will provide new teaching methods for the school library media specialist. Understanding *how* the youngster uses these materials to learn is important. That there must be intense physical involvement with these materials to stimulate learning, an understanding of reading readiness, and an acceptance of the relationship between cognitive and affective learning must become more than theoretical components of the library media program. To be an effective teacher, the school library media specialist must have not just the materials that promote learning, but a theoretical knowledge of how learning occurs and, above all, the ability to apply this to the specific learning situations.

At the other end of this continuum of life is the senior citizen. No matter how we define who a senior citizen is, we know that this group represents a large (in fact, our fastest growing) group of potential users. Community education grants funded by the Department of Health, Education and Welfare provide one example of how the senior citizen can use the school library media program. Through competitive grants to communities for the development of experimental schools that have a community-wide use, HEW is helping to create schools that serve more than the traditional K–12 learner. The needs-assessment, the process that establishes program goals and objectives, is the heart of all successful grant funding. Community education needs-assessments have established that older citizens do want access to the materials, equipment, and services that accommodate their unabated desire for learning and education. Materials already present in many school library media center collections about economics, nutrition, citizenship, world affairs, and other topical concerns can find extended life and increased utilization with this new user group. Here, too, the school library media specialist will have to work at achieving the necessary skills and attitudes to work successfully with these "new" learners, for they too have their own learning styles.

Essential to the concept of community education is that truly all the members of the community, a community that is defined before the program is put in place, are included within the program. Thus, not only the senior citizen and the preschooler but other important groups—bilingual, black, church, political, and others—must be included in the planning and preparation. New attitudes, new methods, and new programs will be expected from the schools as this growing community becomes involved with the school. We should anticipate, too, that these new users will also make increased demands upon district or regional media programs using the films, video services, equipment, and services traditionally associated with this organizational level.

Other government programs nudge school library media programs into areas they have heretofore avoided or skirted. A single example is sufficient. While CETA programs have often been justly criticized for wasteful boondoggling, they do contain within them a Youth Employment Training Program (YETP) described earlier. By law, a minimum of 22 percent of the money made available to an area CETA must be apportioned to the local education agencies, and joint cooperation is expected. The student to be reached by the programs created from these funds is most often alienated from school and society and frequently holds a one-way ticket for a ride to the welfare wastebin at the end of the line. This is not the student traditionally associated with the school library media program.

In some districts, YETP funds have been used to hire career and vocational counselors whose responsibility is to work with small groups of these youths, providing a learning environment that helps the learner master the basic skills of communication while preparing for entry into the job market.[5] It is a form of individualized support education that aims to break the dismal cycle of no skills, no job, no life. And it is based within the library media center.

Youth Employment Training programs mandate cooperation among CETA Youth Services Councils, local government agencies, boards of education, and other community-based organizations. Their expectation for success with this alienated learner is based upon the belief that information about the survival and job skills, and the right people to help get at and use this information, will provide a program that will involve the learner in developing his or her own self-sustaining pattern of upward bound mobility. It is good sense to consider lodging the information/counseling component of these programs within the school library media center. Where else in any school do we associate putting information, the people who need it, and the persons who can help the learner use it best, than the school library media center? The fact that many of these programs are comfortably lodged in secondary school library media centers is encouraging too, for historically these have been our most tradition-bound bulwarks, practicing business as usual and seeing a mission to serve only a narrow clientele of teachers and educationally motivated students.

Title IV-C, the innovative educational funding portion of ESEA, can be used effectively to foster creative library media program innovations. The Putnam City High School in Oklahoma City, Oklahoma, provides a stimulating example of such through the use of Title IV-C funds to provide a comprehensive career counseling program and the staff to provide students with the information and guidance they need to use this information well.

The years 1978 and 1979 are also years of potential dramatic impact upon the future development of community-wide services by school library media programs. In September of 1978, the final report of the School Library Task Force of the National Commission on Libraries and Information Science was accepted by the commission and released. It is a report that emphasizes throughout that the school library media program can no longer afford to exist in aloof isolation from the forces and expectations that shape the public's need for information and the demand for efficient and easy access to it. Promoting school library media participation within networks that stimulate the exchange and special use of information, materials, equipment, services, and people is not a one-way street where what's yours is mine and mine is mine. Networking, distilled to its essence, means that we "give as good as we get." This means that basic school library media program collections and staffing *must* be improved to meet their own expanded user expectations before they can be serious about entering a wider and richer service network. In program operation and in attitude this means a vastly different existence for the school library media program. It is a dramatic break with the past. Participation in networks will develop an attitude about services and a program that delivers these services not just to a narrow and well-established "captive" group of clients, but that must accommodate whole groups of persons dispersed over a wide geographic area. Their demands for materials, equipment, and services are bound to promote the development of a new kind of school library media program quite different from the parochial concerns of the school building that have dominated most of its history.

While it is premature to predict exactly what the final report of the White House Conference on Libraries and Information Science, to be held in October, 1979, will say or precisely what it will call for, it requires little imagination to anticipate that it will call for an even greater emphasis on networking and the sharing of materials and services by all types of libraries. The state governor's conferences that have preceded the White House Conference show us the way, for in one way or another they have all supported the premise that the wave of the future is for more cooperative linkages between all types of libraries and information agencies. While the development of a nationwide information network may yet be visionary for schools, it is not when we consider the tremendous potential for such a network. Medical research, financial forecasting, and MARC cataloging are networks already in place showing the way to a future not far distant. Here is a nationwide constituency and user group undreamed of before.

It is tempting to spin a gossamer web of futurism. While we deal with the here and now, a number of factors force us as a profession to face the future immediately. Combinations of federal and state grants, programs, mandates, and our own survival tactics encourage the school library media specialist to look beyond traditional centers of operation, to establish new programs for different users. Such considerations will provide media programs a more satisfying, indeed essential, continued existence. This seems the truest course for these programs as the final years of this century play out their time.

REFERENCES

1. Governor's Conference on Library and Information Services, State of Connecticut, Minutes of the Advisory Committee meeting, July 10, 1978. Hartford, Connecticut.

2. "Education for an Open Society," *Yearbook of the Association for Supervision and Curriculum Development*. Delmo Della-Dora and James E. House, eds. (Washington, D.C., 1974).

3. *Serrano v. Priest,* California, 1971.

4. PL 93–647, 1st Session, 93rd Congress. Title XX, Social Security Act, Social Services Amendments of 1974.

5. The Stamford Public Schools, Stamford, Connecticut have established Career Counseling Centers in the high school library media centers using Youth Employment and Training Program funds.

FIELD WORK—
CONCERN AND CELEBRATION

by KAY E. VANDERGRIFT

Many of the happiest moments in a school media specialist's professional preparation are those spent in field work. Betty Fast knew this and was very much concerned with the quality of field work experiences both for library students and for all those with whom they work in the schools.[1] Field work allows students to "put it all together" and to work directly with students and teachers in the real world of the school. It allows them to translate classroom abstractions and theoretical ideas into action and to practice newly developed skills in the actual operation of a school media center. For experienced media specialists and for library educators, field work as a part of the educational program for entering professionals reaffirms our faith and our conviction in the direct relationship between the practicing profession and the educational community, a relationship to which Betty Fast dedicated so much of her professional expertise. The planning of field work opportunities helps educators and practitioners to establish and maintain a joint vision and to set expectations of excellence for school media professionals. Moreover, field work experiences are important as a means of developing professional men and women capable of synthesizing all aspects of their professional education to make sound decisions in the immediacy of a variety of situations in the school. Such experiences also help beginning professionals develop a sense of confidence in their abilities to function effectively "on the job" and to sharpen those interpersonal communication skills that make this possible.

If field work can do all this for the student and for the profession, why isn't it more widely used in the education of school media specialists, in fact, in all areas of library education? One might observe that some form of practical experience as a part of library education has had a quiet controversy surrounding it since its origin at Dewey's School of Library Economy in 1887, through the Williamson report in 1923, to the cries for "relevancy" of the students of the 1960s.[2] This paper will not present a historical perspective on the topic, but will instead focus on both the advantages of and obstacles to various forms of field work in the education of school media specialists.

In discussing field work in library education, one might include at least four different kinds of experiences. The first of these is simple observation, either in a single school or at a variety of sites selected for specific purposes. Such observations are very important for the potential media specialist and should be required at the very beginning of the educational program so that student images of school media centers can be tested out against some aspects of reality. These observations may be a part of a beginning course in school librarianship or may be arranged individually for those preparing for school certification. Group observations, of course, have the advantage of allowing students to share their perceptions of what they have seen and providing a common referent for future discussion.

The second type of field work provides students with the opportunity to try out specific skills or plan particular programs in a school media center on a one-time-only basis. For instance, a member of a children's literature class might go into a nearby school to practice reading aloud or telling a story to children, or a student might test out a media presentation on modes of inquiry in social studies or new science reference tools.

The third, and most developed of the types of field work, is the practicum. This is the equivalent to student teaching in teacher education and provides students with the opportunity for practical application in a field setting as a part of the regular educational program.

Internship, the fourth type of field work, differs from the previous examples in that it is much larger in scope and duration and takes place near the end of an educational sequence more advanced than the one-year master's program. Interns, normally paid by the participating school districts, have the primary responsibility for the work done, although they may receive assistance from both field and university-based supervisors. In addition, interns participate in a seminar or other course work in conjunction with the field experience. Thus, internship in library education approximates internship in the medical profession.[3]

Although this writer believes that there is a place for all four levels of field work in the preparation of school media specialists, the remainder of this paper will focus on the practicum, because this is currently the most relevant in library education. It will examine the several facets of practicum experiences as well as the problems attending each in the expectation that increased information and communication will improve practice.

The major problem in planning practicum experiences for students in school media specialists' programs is that of time. It appears obvious that this type of field work should occur near the end of an educational sequence after the completion of all basic courses and perhaps concurrent with some advanced study in the area. However, in a one-year, thirty-six credit program, this is very difficult to accomplish. If a student is taking eighteen credits each semester, there is scarcely enough time left to be physically in attendance in a school media center, let alone to do all the planning and preparation necessary to make that time truly beneficial. If the student is involved in only five courses (fifteen credits) each semester with the final two courses or six credits in a summer session, the situation is not much improved. The logical time for the practicum in the library school students' program is during the summer session, but this is also when school media centers are closed or at least not running normal programs. Even during an early summer session (May-June) now used in many colleges and universities, school media centers are likely to close before the end of the summer session and spend the few weeks prior to that in "winding down" activities atypical of normal operations. Graduate institutions with a long holiday/semester break in January might try to arrange for students to work full time in a school media center for several weeks during this time. The problem here is that the schools are also closed for a portion of this time, and neither students nor university supervisors may be willing or able to give up their vacation time.

Ideally, a library school might block the courses required for school media certification, allowing a period of time near the end of the program when students would be relatively free of other requirements to concentrate on the practicum. Unfortunately, except in some single-purpose programs, student schedules are inexorably interwoven with other courses and programs in the school. Therefore, many students must arrange to participate in practicum experiences while simultaneously carrying a full schedule of graduate courses during the spring semester. Such timing is not only difficult for students, it complicates arrangements for many of the other facets of the practicum experience.

In planning any type of field work experiences, one of the first factors to be considered is the choice of the particular schools in which to place students. The selection of appropriate field sites, especially in urban environments, raises a number of questions for the library educator. Should we try to place students in an "ideal" setting or should we try to replicate, as closely as possible, the types of situations in which they will most likely find employment? Setting, in this instance, may refer either to physical facility or to the media center program, with the program being the priority item. Must the overall academic program of the school be a concern in making field placements if practicum students are to participate effectively in the total education of the students in that school? Of course, the school media specialist in the setting is almost always the key element in the selection of a field site, but how do we decide which professional with whom to place our students? Field supervisors must be persons with dedication, commitment, and real concern for the continuation of the profession. In addition, they must have respect for library school students as beginning professionals and a belief in the educational program of the college or university so that they can support it with and for the library students who work with them. Library educators must realize that good field supervision demands far more of school media specialists than it returns to them. In most instances it takes less time and effort for professionals to do something themselves than it does to explain the process, help others with their planning and then be on hand to supervise and evaluate the work. Only media specialists who really care about the profession and about other people are willing to participate in practicum programs, and they seldom get more than a brief letter of thanks for their efforts.

Another question to be considered in deciding upon field placements is whether or not there should be some attempt to match the personalities of students with those of media specialists and student needs with the needs of the schools. To some extent this is appropriate, but we are library educators, not psychologists, and do not always make the best judgments in these attempts. We may be tempted to place shy, hesitant students with quiet and gentle media specialists who would carefully nurture their growth when these students might be better served by working with more boisterous personalities who would demonstrate and encourage very different patterns of behavior. In general, it is difficult enough to try to match grade levels and special areas of interest or competency without attempting to account for personalities. Field supervisors are our partners in library education and are often more able than we to accommodate differing individuals into the many facets of their programs.

When the final decisions about placements are made, it is often the location and the physical proximity of the field sites to the library education institution that is the controlling factor. If students are taking other courses along with the practicum, they need to be placed where travel time is not a major consideration. The closer the field placements to the center of students' activities, the more time they are likely to spend there. And, in this instance, the amount of time is often directly related to the quality of the involvement. I would rather have a student assigned to an average school media center next to my university than to an exemplary media center forty-five minutes away. The student assigned to the first school can go there between classes and at other unscheduled times to follow a project or meet with a group of students and is able to get a better picture of the total media center program than the student who commutes to a field placement for the specified number of hours on the same day each week.

Once the placements are determined, a major concern becomes the planning of particular activities required of students there. Obviously such requirements must be planned cooperatively with individual students, school media specialists, and the college or university supervisor. However, there are some general questions to be considered. Should the limited time allocated to the practicum include a sampling of the whole range of media center activities, or should it be devoted to one or two in-depth projects? Should we attempt to correlate field activities with the content of other courses taken concurrently in the library school? Should there be some sort of "trade-off" system in which the students spend a portion of the time in the field placement doing what is basically a "service" to the school or media specialist in return for opportunities to initiate activities or projects that primarily meet their own educational needs? Should practicum students, in order to better understand the schooling process, be encouraged to work closely with one classroom teacher in planning, curriculum interpretation, and teaching design even if it takes time away from more general media center activities?

There have been many articles in the literature discussing specific practicum activities or requirements, but too often these larger questions that need to be discussed among library educators are ignored.[4] The first of these questions can only be answered in relation to the total educational program for school media specialists. In a program in which there has been no previous field work of any kind, students need to see and participate in a wide variety of media center activities. If they have, on the other hand, already observed in several school media centers and have participated in short-term projects in these schools, there may be justification for the practicum to concentrate on a more narrow range of activities. In either case, of course, the decision is made only with careful consideration of the needs of a particular student in a particular situation. The second question also can only be answered in respect to the total educational program. Except for the seminar attached to the practicum, it is unlikely that there would be an exact correspondence of students in any other library school class with those involved in the practicum. Therefore, it would be difficult to establish too much specific interdependence between another class and the practicum. Of course, one hopes that all of the people involved in the program of education for school media specialists know the program, each other, and the students so well that relationships among all aspects of the professional education are continually drawn.

The third question in this sequence is the one that gives all those responsible for practicum programs the most cause for concern. Unfortunately some school media specialists see the practicum primarily as an opportunity to acquire some free labor. Such obvious misuses of the practicum can be weeded out in the university supervisor's initial selection of field sites, but this does not completely eliminate the concern. Most school media specialists do, in fact, spend some portion of their time in clerical or other nonprofessional tasks, and the execution of some of these duties might be considered necessary for an understanding of the total responsibilities of the media specialist. Students exempted from such menial tasks may not be acquiring a realistic sense of the day-to-day professional responsibilities and may also become the object of resentment from colleagues in the media center. Extensive blocks of time spent working with classroom teachers may also be looked upon unfavorably by media center employees who do not see this as necessary for library students' comprehension of the teaching-learning process so that they may better serve the total educational program of the school.[5]

The seminar attached to the practicum provides students with opportunities to share and discuss field experiences and to relate these experiences to the intellectual content of other components of their educational program. The simple act of sharing ideas about the procedures and programs of the various school media centers in which they work enables students to expand their understandings of the relationships of media center methods to school populations, organizations, and curricula. For instance, discussions of how circulation procedures, the classification and storage of nonprint media, and overdue fines are handled in different media centers may, under the direction of a skilled professor, be extremely useful in relating theory to practice. The seminar may also be used to supplement course content and relate that content more specifically to school media centers than can be done in general library school courses. The reference interview, for example, may be very different in an elementary school than it is in a college or public library, and the cataloging of multimedia kits, games, and toys takes on greater significance there than can be afforded in a general cataloging class. In addition, the seminar may include information or skills that cannot be included at all in the basic sequence of course work, often in response to particular incidents encountered in the field. Students working with child filmmakers may need a workshop on animation techniques or those working with curriculum committees may need to evaluate some of the latest social science materials. Of course, this seminar cannot be all things to all students but, with careful planning, at least a portion of it can be devoted to the immediate needs of those in the practicum. At times these needs might best be met in one of the field placements by the school media specialist, either alone or in tandem with the college or university supervisor. This alternative requires careful planning and close cooperation with colleagues in the field, but it is one that should be considered more frequently.

It is also the media specialists in the field who frequently assume primary responsibility for the supervision of practicum participants. They are the ones who regularly observe students in their interaction with others in the school and are ordinarily more able than a faculty supervisor who visits only infrequently and for short periods of time to assist with and evaluate the work. In order to do this most effectively, however, there must be a great deal of communication between the university and field supervisors. The school media specialists supervising practicum students must be fully aware of the expectation of library educators, both in general and in regard to specific students. The library educator must, on the other hand, be willing to negotiate those expectations in discussion with field supervisors.

Combs, in a recent article, suggested that the field work component of teacher education programs be turned over totally to the classroom teachers who supervise student teachers because of the cost to colleges.[6] Watts responded that "separating field experience from the instructional aspect of teacher education would result in a fragmented program" and that the "reduction of teacher education to an apprenticeship program would be a grave mistake."[7] Library educators should pay close attention to our colleagues in teacher education who have had more experience with field work and practica. This is not to say that they have all the answers, as is revealed in the controversy above, but they are more experienced than most of us in asking the right questions.

What we must do is figure out more effective ways for the supervision of educators and practitioners to complement each other for the benefit of the students with whom both of us work. Often the field supervisor sees a student from a different perspective than has been revealed in the graduate classroom. A student who has done extremely well in the classroom assignments may not be able to cope with the immediacy and unpredictability of life in a school media center. Or the student who fades into the background in a classroom may come to life working with children. Only regular communication and an open dialogue between field- and university-based supervisors will help such students achieve their full potential as young professionals.

Even when there is a regular verbal exchange, school media specialists supervising practicum students are ordinarily expected to submit written evaluations to the library school. Evaluation forms may include such things as ratings of attitude, appearance, initiative, and checklists of activities engaged in, as well as evaluative comments about the performance of specific teaching and media center tasks. Such forms are most valuable if they are completed in consultation with students in an evaluative conference. University supervisors may also record their observations of students in this way, and such documents will probably form a major portion of the overall evaluation for the practicum. Other factors that might be considered in the final evaluation are students' log-books, in which they record their field activities with questions about and/or reactions to them, student self-evaluations, conferences, products or materials produced and performance in the required seminar. It is a good idea for both school media specialists and the faculty supervisors to write their final evaluations in the form of recommendations that might be placed in students' placement files if requested. In most instances, students who have participated in a practicum will expect to get a recommendation from the professionals who supervise them, and it is easier, and often more accurate, if they are done at this time.

The final factor to be considered in examining practica experiences in library education is that of cost. There is no doubt that most types of field work are very costly, both in terms of time and money. The faculty member who arranges such experiences spends a great deal of time determining which schools are appropriate, placing particular students in each of these schools, negotiating requirements, observing students in action, and conferring with both students and field supervisors. All this is in addition to the regular meeting of the seminar. Visits to field sites may also be costly in actual transportation costs, especially when the number of students is high or the best field placements are not close to the college or university.

The practicum is a time and energy drain on school media specialists as well. Their instruction, supervision, and conferring with library school students is added to all their normal responsibilities in the school. Students also find their experiences in a practicum very demanding. Normally they are spending a great deal of time in preparation for and the actual performance of their first professional duties at the same time that they are writing papers and studying for examinations for other graduate classes. Commuting costs to a school media center not in the immediate vicinity of the library school may also add an additional financial burden at a time when they have little money to spare.

A possible solution to some of these problems might be to cluster students in a few schools close to the university. This is not only a savings to students and faculty supervisors, but it may be of greater value to field supervisors as well. When there are three to five students assigned to the same school, the media specialist can instruct them, as a group, in some aspects of the work of the media center; then they can support and assist each other in the completion of these tasks. Also, they can spend less time as individuals in technical services, circulation, or "housekeeping" jobs while in total providing greater service to the school media specialist. Although increased numbers of students do require more supervision time, media specialists who have worked with several students at a time often feel that the benefits outweigh the disadvantages and that the colleagueship among students relieves them of many minor student demands. In this situation, the library educator's time and energy can also be concentrated in one or two schools so that his or her expertise can be of real assistance to the media specialists there. This closer connection between educators and practitioners can only improve the educational program for school media specialists.

At least one additional problem needs to be considered in planning field experiences for library school students. Too often we overlook the special problems of the part-time students in such programs. A significant number of such students in school media specialists' programs are probably already holding preprofessional jobs in school media centers and completing their professional education in late afternoon or evening classes. Near the end of the sequence of coursework for certification, these students are often asked, in effect, to give up a job in a school media center so that they can participate in a practicum that will qualify them to hold the kind of position they have just given up. This is especially true of media specialists in private schools in which state certification is not required. The library school students, in this instance, are almost always those in charge of the school media centers and therefore have no certified professionals to supervise their work. It would be difficult to justify giving graduate credit for a required practicum in a position for which the student is being paid as a regular employee anyway. On the other hand, asking a student who has worked for many years in a school media center to give up paid employment, especially with the job market as it now is, and to pay university tuition for doing in another school basically what that person has been doing in his or her own media center seems absurd. There are no simple solutions to this problem, but surely we owe our part-time students more consideration than we are now giving them in library education.

In spite of all the concerns of library educators in providing sound field work experiences for students, the practicum is still a cause for celebration in the education of school media specialists. It is at this point that students truly committed to work in schools celebrate the culmination of their educational programs in the joy of working directly with children and teachers. Fortunately, this is most often the case, but it is at this point also that some students who have done well in college classrooms find that they just cannot cope with the real world of the school media center. This is always sad, but it is better for a student to discover it at this time than after a contract has been signed and he or she is alone in a new and demanding position. Thus, the practicum is often the critical point in the assessment of the competency of students, requiring them to put to the test their basic understandings of the missions and the materials of the field and their own abilities to make a contribution to the profession. There are few moments in library education so rewarding as those in which we meet with a student who has just successfully completed the first major assignment in the field and who pronounces with sheer exuberance, "I can do it." Such celebrations of self and of our work as school media specialists make all the costs and all the concerns fade into obscurity.

REFERENCES

1. Betty Fast, Council on Library Resources Research Grant during 1972–73 to study the relationship of field work and library education programs in the education of the school media specialist.

2. For a thorough background in this issue read: Alice Virginia Witucke, *The Place of Library Experience in Library Education,* (Unpublished doctoral diss., School of Library Service, Columbia University, 1974); recent statistics on field work in library education may be found in: Mildred C. Tietjen, "Playing the Field, or . . . Practice Makes Perfect," *Wilson Library Bulletin* 52, 1 (September 1977): 61–63.

3. For more detail in internships for school library professionals see: John O. Hempstead, "Internship and Practical Application in Educating School Library Personnel," *Journal of Education for Librarianship* 12 (Fall 1971): 116–32.

4. Several articles might prove useful in an examination of activities: Shirley B. Feenstra, "Fieldwork in an Elementary Resource Center," *California School Libraries* 46 (Summer 1975): 28–32; Patricia F. Beilke, "Field Experiences for Media Specialists," in William E. Hug, ed., *Strategies for Change in Information Programs* (New York: R. R. Bowker Co., 1974), pp. 209–15; Robert Case and Anna Mary Lowery, *Curriculum Alternatives: Experiments in School Library Media Education,* School Library Manpower Project. (Chicago: ALA, 1974).

5. Kay E. Vandergrift, *The Teaching Role of the School Media Specialist* (Chicago: ALA, 1978).

6. Arthur W. Combs, "Teacher Education: The Person in the Process," *Educational Leadership* 35, 7 (April 1968): 558–61.

7. Doyle Watts, "The Humanistic Approach to Teacher Education: A Giant Step Backwards?" *Educational Leadership* 36, 2 (November 1978): 87–90.

THE SCHOOL LIBRARY
MEDIA SPECIALIST AND
PROFESSIONAL ASSOCIATIONS

by PATRICIA B. POND

If, as Alice Fite, executive secretary of the American Association of School Librarians (AASL), suggests, "Membership in a national association brings understanding and meaning to the task of equating the word profession with librarianship,"[1] then school library media specialists have a long way to go to achieve professionalism. Only a small proportion of the estimated 74,000 certified school library media specialists in the United States choose to join the national professional association in librarianship, ALA. At the end of the ALA membership renewal period in 1978, for example, the 3,479 personal members of AASL constituted only 13 percent of the personal membership of ALA. The actual percentage of school librarian membership in ALA is somewhat higher, since a third or more ALA members typically do not join a division, but hardly as high as the estimated 45 percent of all the librarians in the United States who are school librarians.[2] The cost of joining ALA and a division, such as AASL, probably accounts in part for the low percentage of school librarian membership in AASL. When the ALA dues structure was changed in 1977 to require payment of dues for each division chosen, by contrast with the earlier practice of providing in basic ALA dues for membership in two divisions, AASL membership dropped substantially. It has not yet returned to the 1976 level.

School library media specialists do not, it would seem, find the case for belonging to a national professional association quite as compelling as either Alice Fite or Howard Hitchens, executive director of the Association of Educational Communications and Technology (AECT), suggest they should in a recent discussion of dilemmas facing school library media specialists. Fite emphasizes the value of professional association membership to the individual school library media specialist:

> Membership in a national association can provide the library/media specialist with the necessary tools for guidance in the successful personal management of a chosen career. Membership in a national association can provide the direction for establishing the criteria necessary for establishment of quality media programs.[3]

Hitchens, on the other hand, stresses the importance of professional associations in general:

> Professional associations are the agencies in the American culture which coalesce professional concerns, promote growth and progress within the research base on which the professional field rests, provide opportunities for individual professionals to enlarge their grasp of the field, and provide opportunities for individual professionals to contribute to progress in the professional field.[4]

Even if convinced of the value of membership, the school library media specialist is faced with a dilemma when it comes to choosing which professional association to join. Trained as a librarian, but working in a school environment, a school librarian, unlike a librarian working in a traditional setting such as a public library or a nontraditional setting such as an industrial organization's special library, finds that the educational system demands that a specialist be an educator first and a specialist second. Librarians are not, of course, the only individuals in education faced with having to join more than one association to cover the range of issues and interests facing a professional specialization. Nearly every educator has the same problem, whether an English teacher or a kindergarten teacher, whether a school counselor or a school principal.[5] It is largely a matter of choice which association or associations a school library media specialist joins, not a matter of coercion. Although it has been suggested that school librarians do not join ALA, for example, because they are required to join local, state, or national education associations, this has not been substantiated in a recent survey by Miller and Downen of AASL membership: only 15 percent of the respondents reported that membership was required in any of the three levels of teachers' associations.[6]

School library media specialists and education associations

School library media specialists are obliged to consider the advantages of joining national education organizations. Membership in the National Education Association (NEA) or the American Federation of Teachers (AFT) achieves unity and bargaining strength and can contribute to the achievement of such goals as securing federal funding for school library media programs, which these associations can help accomplish because they represent the larger education community as a whole. The Miller-Downen survey indicates that AASL members *do* recognize the importance of joining education associations. NEA membership was claimed by 55 percent of the respondents, district education association membership by 57 percent, and state education association membership by 59 percent. School library media specialists also turn to special interest associations in education. According to Miller-Downen, 25 percent of AASL members *do* belong to the national professional media association, AECT. This study does not examine AASL memberships in such groups as the Association for Childhood Education International (ACEI) or the National Council of Teachers of English (NCTE), both organizations with which AASL has maintained joint committees over a long period of time.[7]

Education associations like NEA and NCTE have a long history of supporting school library interests. In 1896, through the efforts of Melvil Dewey and John Cotton Dana (then ALA president), NEA formed a Library Department, which promoted library service to schools until 1924 when NEA reorganized its department structure. In 1960, department status for school library interests in NEA was reestablished with AASL initially recognized as a department in NEA and then, following revision of membership requirements for personal members of NEA-affiliates, as a NEA associated organization. By the 1970s, NEA had become more of a teachers' association than an umbrella organization for various education interest groups. In 1975, when NEA membership was required of all members of NEA-affiliated organizations, AASL's as well as AECT's and other special interest associations', affiliations with NEA ceased. In 1975 another organization, established in 1896 to promote cooperation between NEA and ALA, the ALA Committee on Cooperation with NEA which later became the Joint Committee of NEA and ALA, also ceased to exist. Until the ALA School Libraries Section, the predecessor AASL, was established in 1914, the NEA Library Department was the major national organization promoting school library interests. It was through a joint committee of the NEA Department of Secondary Education and the North Central Association, chaired by C. C. Certain, that the famous Certain standards, the first national standards for school libraries, were developed.[8]

Many school librarians are aware of the collaborative efforts of ALA and NCTE, which, through various joint committees (frequently including NEA), led to ALA publication of basic book collection lists for elementary grades, junior high schools, and senior high schools (the last dating to 1922), as well as to NCTE publication of reading lists for students such as *Adventuring with Books, Your Reading,* and *Books for You* (the last dating to 1923). What school librarians may not be aware of, however, is that NCTE, like NEA, once included an organization dedicated to promoting the interest of school libraries. An NCTE Library Section was established in 1913, just two years after NCTE was founded following withdrawal of English teachers from NEA in a protest over college entrance requirements in English. The NCTE Library Section, which promoted high school reading and development of high school libraries in conjunction with NCTE's primary interest during its early years in high school English, existed only until 1919, but school librarians have continued to work cooperatively with NCTE ever since.

Probably the special interest organization in education most familiar to school library media specialists is the media association, AECT, formerly the NEA Department of Audiovisual Instruction (DAVI), established in 1923. DAVI and AASL did not share common interests until the concept of school libraries as instructional materials centers for both print *and* nonprint materials began to gain acceptance in the 1950s. This concept was incorporated in AASL's 1960 statement of school library standards, prepared with the help of representatives from twenty-three national associations, including DAVI.[9] By the late 1960s, aided by substantial funding under the Elementary and Secondary Education Act of 1965, nonprint materials and the necessary equipment to utilize them had become widely available in school libraries across the nation. In 1969, new standards recognizing the value of media and the role of the school library media specialist in the instructional program were issued jointly by AASL and DAVI.[10] AASL and DAVI, under its new name AECT, began almost immediately preparing a revision of those standards published in 1975.[11] Spurred by the successful experience of producing joint standards, various suggestions have been made during the past fifteen years for formalizing relationships between AASL and AECT, including possible merger, but no action has been taken to date. Early in 1979, AASL appointed an ad hoc committee to investigate liaison relationships with AECT, but in the meantime, with no joint standards work underway, the only mechanism now existing for liaison between AASL and AECT is an informal agreement making it possible for the president of each association to attend the board meetings of the other.

It has been suggested earlier that the educational system demands that school library media specialists be educators first (certified teachers) and specialists second (librarians). The contribution of educational associations to the development of school library media programs has tended to follow this prioritization. The school library interest groups in NEA and NCTE, for example, were established by librarians, and throughout their brief history most of their leadership and membership consisted of librarians. The only long-established organization specifically for school librarians in existence today, AASL, is based in a library association, ALA. By far the largest number of publications in the field of school librarianship have been issued under the ALA imprint, not under the imprints of NEA, NCTE, AECT, or, for that matter, of such library publishers as H. W. Wilson or R. R. Bowker. Based on past history, it would seem that ALA has more to offer school library professionals than do education associations. But just what does ALA offer today?

School library media specialists and the American Library Association

Robert Wedgeworth, ALA executive director, states the case for ALA membership for the school media specialist in these terms:

> Why choose ALA? Because ALA does more for you to help you carry out your primary job—educating young people.
>
> The American Library Association offers you clout. We offer you the cooperation and support of other professionals and the public interested in delivering quality library service. This coalition has been and will continue to be a powerful force working for funding support, legislation, collection development, and program organization.[12]

Wedgeworth reviews specific ALA projects and programs of importance to the school library media specialist, such as protection of professional interests when positions are threatened by school budget cutbacks; assistance in establishing the National Commission on Libraries and Information Science (NCLIS) and the 1979 White House Conference; influence in rewriting the five-year extension of the Elementary and Secondary Education Act (ESEA) to provide consolidation of support for school library resources and instructional equipment in Title IV-B, with a separate section IV-D created to accommodate support for guidance and testing programs, originally in the library section; promulgation of standards for school media programs; publication of monographs on every aspect of the school library media center operation and journals such as *Booklist* and the AASL's *School Media Quarterly* and defense of intellectual freedom through the ALA Office on Intellectual Freedom, an especially important concern since 89 percent of all censorship cases reported to that office concern schools.

Wedgeworth suggests that ALA could do much more in the future if more school library media specialists joined it. Joining, however, is not enough. What is needed is active participation by school library media specialists in the governance and work not only of their own ALA division, AASL, but of other ALA divisions, committees, and governing bodies.

What categories of school library media specialists currently belong to AASL, and to what extent do they participate in the governance and activities of ALA? The percentage of respondents to the Miller-Downen survey of 1976 AASL members closely matched identified positions of AASL members listed in the *ALA Membership Directory*. Slightly over half, 57 percent, were building-level specialists. District supervisors and specialists represented 17 percent of the respondents; retired professionals, state-level consultants and college and public librarians, 15 percent; and faculty in library or media higher education programs, 17 percent.[13] The educational level of the AASL respondents to Miller-Downen was considerably higher, however, than estimates in the 1976 Cooper study, which was based on analysis of published library statistics. Cooper estimated that approximately 20 percent of the school librarians in the United States held master's degrees from ALA-accredited library education programs and that 15 percent held master's degrees in fields other than library science. By contrast, 72 percent of the respondents to the Miller-Downen survey held ALA-accredited master's degrees and 29 percent held, or also held, master's degrees in education or educational technology.[14] The Miller-Downen data suggest that AASL has been relatively ineffective in attracting recent graduates of library science, education, or educational technology programs: only 5 percent of the respondents were first-year members of AASL, and fewer than 1 percent were in their first year in the school library media field. The survey also suggests that AASL consists largely of long-term members: 56 percent of respondents had been members of AASL for six or more years, 34 percent for 11 years or more.[15]

The Miller-Downen survey data indicated that about 25 percent of AASL members also belonged to the Young Adult Services Division (YASD) and the Children's Services Division [now the Association for Library Service to Children (ALSC)] of ALA, but no data were provided on choice of other ALA divisions.[16] A survey that I conducted of persons joining AASL during a heavy membership period, February and March, 1978, the last two months of the 1977/78 membership year, also shows YASD and ALSC as the most typical ALA division choices of AASL members, but the percentage of AASL memberships in either division is considerably smaller than the 25 percent reported in Miller-Downen. Of the 275 persons who joined AASL in the period studied, 15 also joined YASD, 8 ALSC, 4 the Resources and Technical Services Division (RTSD), 3 the Library and Information Technology Association (LITA), and 1 the Library Administration and Management Association (LAMA). This survey also reveals that AASL members are much less likely than the average ALA member to join more than one ALA division. The March 31, 1978, summary of ALA membership indicated that 33.9 percent of ALA members chose no division, 38.2 percent one division, 20.2 percent two divisions, and 7.7 percent three or more divisions.[17] Because the data available to me identified only members who chose AASL as a division, it was not possible to determine the number of school library media specialists who joined ALA but not AASL. It was possible, however, to determine that of the persons joining AASL during the two-month period, February-March 1978, 90.2 percent chose *only* AASL, and only 5.9 percent joined one other division, with the number joining two or more divisions smaller than 1 percent.

AASL has for the last several years ranked either third or fourth in total membership among the twelve ALA divisions in existence before 1979. The March 31, 1978, summary of ALA membership, for example, showed that among a total of 37,142 ALA division members, the Association of College and Research Libraries (ACRL) ranked first with 6,926 members, RTSD second with 4,590, the Reference and Adult Services Division (RASD) third with 4,206, and AASL fourth with 4,150.[18]

Because of its relatively large membership and the dues income derived from it, AASL is able to support an executive secretary and a full-time professional assistant. As a result, AASL can provide more direct services to members and more program planning and development than is possible in smaller ALA divisions. In spite of its rank among ALA divisions, however, AASL lacks visibility in the association. This is due in part to the insularity of its members who do not, typically, join other ALA divisions, except the traditionally youth-serving divisions, YASD and ALSC, and are thus not eligible to serve on division committees. Without significant AASL membership and visibility in ALA divisions, school library media specialists are cutting themselves off from one of the most effective means of influencing those decisions that are vital to the future development of school library media programs.

Within AASL, membership participation in decision making and governance is provided through an affiliate assembly and a board of directors. The affiliate assembly is a new organization consisting of the representatives and delegates of state and regional school library media organizations affiliated with AASL. The specific purpose of the assembly, which meets during the ALA annual conference, "is to provide a channel for communication for reporting concerns of the affiliate organizations and their membership and for reporting the actions of the American Association of School Librarians to the affiliates."[19] In 1978/79, there were 46 affiliate organizations in the assembly, and at the 1979 ALA Midwinter Meeting three affiliate organization representatives elected from the assembly became members of the AASL Executive Board. That board previously had included only division officers, supervisors section chairperson, and seven regional directors, serving staggered terms and elected at-large by AASL membership.[20]

Prior to the reorganization of the ALA governing body, Council, in the early 1970's, it consisted of councilors-at-large nominated by the ALA Nominating Committee and elected by ALA membership; division councilors nominated by the divisions and elected by ALA membership through a method that assured representation of councilors in proportion to division membership in ALA; and chapter councilors elected or appointed by state library associations. Since its reorganization, Council consists of 100 councilors-at-large, 50 chapter councilors, and 12 members of the ALA Executive Board. Some division representation on Council was reestablished through provision in 1978 for nomination and election by each division of one division councilor.

In an attempt to influence election of AASL members to Council and thus provide additional input from the division to this ALA governing body, AASL recently instituted the practice of endorsing AASL member candidates for councilor-at-large positions. While there are currently twenty or more AASL members among the councilors-at-large and chapter councilors, AASL currently lacks a representative on the central management board of ALA, the Executive Board. Following Betty Fast's death in 1977, her replacement on the Board for the remainder of her term did not come from the school library media field, nor did Rebecca Bingham's replacement upon expiration of her term on the Executive Board in 1978. With Rebecca Bingham as its 1979/80 president, however, AASL does have a leader with substantial Council as well as Executive Board experience and with considerable knowledge of ALA politics and governance—a plus for the association. It remains to be seen if the provision for an AASL Division Councilor who sits on both the Council and the AASL Executive Board will provide an effective means for increasing AASL's visibility and power in ALA decision making and governance.

In addition to increasing AASL visibility and power in ALA through AASL membership participation and representation in AASL, its affiliated organizations, and through AASL representation on the ALA Council and Executive Board, AASL could also utilize ALA's "clout," as Robert Wedgeworth suggests in his paper, through cooperation with and support of other professionals interested in delivering quality library service. If more school library media specialists joined AASL, and if AASL members also joined other divisions, it would be possible for AASL to form coalitions with other ALA divisions on issues and programs of importance to the achievement of excellence in school library media programs. AASL could also build upon past and present liaisons with other professional associations. One is dismayed to find, however, that only half of the AASL members responding to the Miller-Downen survey ranked relationships with national organizations as important.[21]

What are some areas in which AASL could develop coalitions and liaisons? One is supervision and management. AASL has, for many years, had a Supervisors Section, the chairperson of which is a member of the AASL Executive Board. The purpose of the section, "to provide a means for discussion of and action on the problems relating to all phases of school library supervision," is achieved primarily through programs the section sponsors annually at the ALA conference.[22] Some members of the supervisors section are also members of ALA's Library Administration and Management Association. Although AASL has cooperated in the past with various sections of LAMA, particularly the Buildings and Equipment Section, in sponsoring programs at the ALA conference, it has usually been difficult to find enough AASL members who are also LAMA members to appoint to LAMA committees. Among LAMA discussion groups and sections that would seem to provide a promising base for AASL coalitions are the Women Administrators Discussion Group and the following sections, with examples of committees in parentheses: Buildings and Equipment (School Library/Media Facilities Committee), Library Organization and Management, Personnel Administration, Public Relations, and Statistics (Statistics for Nonprint Media Committee and Statistics for School Library Media Centers Committee). Many building-level school library media specialists as well as district and state supervisors have long been members of the formerly NEA-affiliated Association for Supervision and Curriculum Development (ASCD). This organization is also one that could continue to provide a base for AASL activities since it includes curriculum development as well as management among its priorities.

Audiovisual materials have been a vital part of school library collections since the mid-1950s when AASL adopted an official policy statement on school libraries as instructional materials centers. For AECT, audiovisual materials have been an express concern since its origin in 1923 as the NEA Department of Visual Instruction. At its 1976 convention, AECT organized a task force, Project: Media Base, which took as its primary objective the identification of a computer-based system—or set of systems—to function as the national network for bibliographic control of information concerning audiovisual resources. Project: Media Base later became a joint effort of AECT and the National Commission on Libraries and Information Science. The final report of the project has just recently been published.[23] In ALA today, concern for audiovisual materials is reflected in the Joint Advisory Committee on Nonbook Materials, with representatives from ALA, AECT, the Association for Media and Technology in Education of Canada, and the Canadian Library Association, and in the following ALA divisions, sections and committees, many of which offer opportunities for AASL coalitions:

Association of College and Research Libraries (ACRL):
   Nonprint Media Publications Editorial Board
   Audiovisual Committee
Association for Library Service to Children (ALSC):
   Liaison with Mass Media Committee
   Film Evaluation Committee
   Filmstrip Evaluation Committee
   Print and Poster Evaluation Committee
   Recording Evaluation Committee
   Toys, Games, and Realia Evaluation Committee
Association of Specialized and Cooperative Library Agencies (ASCLA):
   Audiovisual Committee
Library Administration and Management Association (LAMA):
   Statistics Section—Statistics for Nonprint Media Committee
Library and Information Technology Association (LITA):
   Audiovisual Section
   Video and Cable Communications Section
Public Library Association (PLA):
   Audiovisual Committee
   Alternative Education Programs Section—Visual Literacy and
      Audiovisual Communications Task Force
Reference and Adult Services Division (RASD):
   Adult Library Materials—Audio-Visual Cassettes Committee
Resources and Technical Services Division (RTSD):
   Audiovisual Committee
Young Adult Services Division (YASD):
   Audio-Visual Producers and Distributors Liaison Committee
   AV Presentations Committee
   Media Selection and Usage Committee
   Selected Films for YA Committee
   Television Committee

One of the most recent priority concerns of AASL is the place of the school library media program in networking. In January, 1977, the National Commission on Libraries and Information Science, with the recommendations and assistance of AASL, appointed a Task Force on the Role of the School Library Media Program in the National Network. The task force was asked to look at the current framework of networking in the United States and the potential role of school library media specialists and the school library media program. NCLIS accepted the task force report in September, 1978, at which time its staff began to prepare a plan for the NCLIS role in implementation of the task force recommendations. In the published report Alphonse F. Trezza, NCLIS executive director, stressed that implementation of its recommendations was dependent upon closely coordinated efforts among national and state agencies and organizations such as AASL, AECT, the American Association of School Administrators, state education agencies, and school library media professionals at the building and district level.[24] Subsequently, NCLIS and AASL have sponsored presentations on the task force recommendations at the national conferences of the American Association of School Administrators and AECT, and NCLIS and AASL representatives have met with several national agencies and associations. Included among them were the National Association of Elementary School Principals; the Council of Chief State School Officers; the National Association of State Educational Media Professionals; AECT, especially through Project: Media Base, ALA's Association of Specialized and Cooperative Library Agencies; and the School Media Branch of the Office of Libraries and Learning Resources of the U.S. Office of Education.

In ALA a number of divisions are concerned with issues related to networking. Two AASL committees are currently involved in implementing the Task Force recommendations: the Networking and Interconnection of Learning Resources Committee, a study and liaison committee, and the Resources Development Committee, which has written a funding proposal for a project designed to train school library media specialists in skills needed for linking the primary clients of school library media programs—students, teachers, school specialists, and school administrators—to information resources available through resource sharing, interlibrary loan, and networking. The Association of Specialized and Cooperative Library Agencies has not only an Interlibrary Cooperation Discussion Group "to provide a forum for discussion of interests in interlibrary cooperation and statewide development of library service, emphasizing the interdependence of all libraries,"[25] but also a Multitype Library Cooperation Section (MLCS) with seven active committees. Other ALA divisions with committees on interlibrary loan or interlibrary cooperation include the Public Library Association, the Reference and Adult Services Division, and the Resources and Technical Services Division.

These three concerns—supervision, audiovisual materials, and networking—are only examples of ways in which AASL, working in cooperation with other ALA divisions and with related professional associations, could build issue-oriented coalitions that have the potential for increasing AASL power and visibility in ALA, serving the professional needs of individual school library media specialists, and assuring excellence in school library media programs. As a former AASL president, Bernard Franckowiak, noted in a recent *American Libraries* issue focusing on school libraries:

> To accomplish things we cannot do alone, we form groups. School library media specialists must use the mechanisms provided by local, regional, state and national associations to communicate and institutionalize good programs, and they must do so in cooperation with people from all types of libraries. . . . The library profession must stop talking only to itself about its problems and get to those who can help in the change process.[26]

REFERENCES

1. Alice Fite, "Networking: An Old Word Goes Back to School," *American Libraries* 9 (November 1978): 603.

2. Memorandum from Ernest Martin, Associate Executive Director, ALA Administrative Services, to ALA Headquarters Staff re: Membership Statistics as of 3/31/78; Michael D. Cooper, "What the Statistics Say," *American Libraries* 7 (June 1976): 327.

3. Alice Fite, "People, Programs, and Publications," *Illinois Libraries* 60 (September 1978): 588.

4. Howard Hitchens, "One Foot in Each," *Illinois Libraries* 60 (September 1978): 588.

5. Hitchens, p. 588; Eleanor A. Ahlers, "Professional Affiliations," *Bulletin of the National Association of Secondary School Principals* 50 (January 1966): 71–74; Dawn Heller and Ann Montgomery, "A Dilemma for All," *Illinois Libraries* 60 (September 1978): 590–91.

6. Marilyn L. Miller and Thomas W. Downen, "A Look at AASL Membership: 1977," *School Media Quarterly* 7 (Fall 1978): 41.

7. Miller and Downen, p. 41.

8. Patricia Pond, "Development of a National Professional School Library Association: American Association of School Librarians," *School Media Quarterly* 5 (Fall 1976): 12–18. Information on AASL, NEA, NCTE, and DAVI in the *School Media Quarterly* article and this paper is extracted from Ph.D. dissertation-in-progress at the Graduate Library School, University of Chicago: Patricia Brown Pond, "The American Association of School Librarians: The Origins and Development of a National Professional Association for School Librarians, 1896–1951."

9. American Association of School Librarians, *Standards for School Library Programs* (Chicago: ALA, 1960): pp. 11–12.

10. American Association of School Librarians and the Department of Audiovisual Instruction of the National Education Association, *Standards for*

School Media Programs (Chicago: ALA; Washington, D.C.: National Education Association, 1969).

11. American Association of School Librarians and Association for Educational Communications and Technology, *Media Programs: District and School* (Chicago: ALA; Washington, D.C.: Association for Educational Communications and Technology, 1975).

12. Robert Wedgeworth, "ALA and the School Media Specialist," *Illinois Libraries* 60 (September 1978): 588.

13. Miller and Downen, p. 40.

14. Miller and Downen, p. 41; Cooper, p. 328.

15. Miller and Downen, pp. 40–41.

16. Miller and Downen, p. 41.

17. Memorandum, p. 5.

18. Memorandum, p. 2.

19. *ALA Handbook of Organization 1978/79* (Chicago: ALA, 1978), p. 16.

20. *ALA Handbook of Organization 1978/79*, pp. 16–17.

21. Miller and Downen, p. 44.

22. *ALA Handbook of Organization 1978/79*, p. 16.

23. David H. Jonassen, "National AV Data Base: A Deficient Knowledge Base," *Bulletin of the American Society for Information Science* 5 (February 1979): 17–18.

24. Task Force on the Role of the School Library Media Program in the National Program, *The Role of the School Library Media Program in Networking* (Washington, D.C.: National Commission on Libraries and Information Science, 1979), pp. i–iii.

25. *ALA Handbook of Organization 1978/79*, p. 34.

26. Bernard Franckowiak, "They Can't Keep a Good Profession Down— Or Can They?" *American Libraries* 9 (November 1978): 601.

SCHOOLS—THE ON-LINE
MEDIA CONNECTION

by PHYLLIS LAND

Library networking can be thought of as the ultimate information connection in this country—it makes available the information resources to users by organizing all types of libraries into a bibliographic system and yet allows library services to be provided at the lowest possible level so long as it is cost effective. While a nationwide library network is not a reality, much energy is being directed to this end.

The National Commission on Libraries and Information Science, recognizing that the elementary and secondary schools of this country are a vital link in the nationwide information connection, convened in January of 1977 a task force to address the role of the school library media program in networking. The task force report, *The Role of the School Library Media Program in Networking,* issued in December, 1978, finds that the school library media program is capable of making valuable contributions to a library network. Listed among the specific contributions were the substantial collections of audiovisual materials now available in schools and the fact that school library media specialists are skilled in effective use of all types of media in meeting individual needs and interests of the user. The significance of schools to networking programs is obvious to those in school systems, but such a contribution often must be demonstrated to their larger library community. Schools are a part of networking plans in relatively few states and are a part of the law in even fewer.

Based on the belief that audiovisual resources in schools have a unique contribution to make to library networking, a plan was developed by Indiana library personnel in 1977 to utilize schools as the most expeditious connection in the cooperative development of a machine-readable audiovisual media data base. The purpose of this paper is to examine the need for such a project, to discuss the approach and implementation of this project, and to anticipate the outcomes.

School representatives of the statewide library network, Indiana Cooperative Library Services Authority (INCOLSA), identified the bibliographic control of audiovisual materials as a priority to be addressed in the network's plan of service. They reported that, in comparison to books, audiovisual materials are difficult to handle physically and bibliographically, that cataloging from commercial sources varies with the vendor and is sometimes not usable, and that estimates by school media professionals indicate that it costs three to five times as much to process an audiovisual item as it does to process book material.

An ad hoc committee of INCOLSA was assigned the task of examining the caliber of cataloging provided by school systems in Indiana and to determine how close the cataloging came to national standards. The committee members rapidly became convinced that no common standards were being followed but at the same time most systems were recording the major elements prescribed by national standards. The elements were arranged haphazardly and often do-it-yourself methods had been devised. It was concluded, however, that with training all would be able to bring local media cataloging up to national standards.

The committee also examined the OCLC, Inc., system and found that it handles audiovisual media, provides a variety of access points to bibliographic records, and delivers output products including catalog cards, accession lists, and magnetic tape records. The committee agreed that access to the system is beyond the means of the majority of school media programs. It was also noted that present on-line systems do not have the capability to allow every school system to have its own computer terminal even if budget and staff constraints were not considerations.

Large scale processing at the INCOLSA processing center did not seem to be the answer for several reasons. For one thing, it would be costly for the central agency to buy specialized equipment to use for previewing the various media formats. For another, shipment and handling is expensive, making the central service cost more. And, finally, the large scale centralized service does not involve the school library media professional in building a cooperative data base.

Having the needs-assessment data, it was determined that a demonstration of cooperative development of a machine-readable audiovisual data base for schools be undertaken. Barbara Evans Markuson, executive director of INCOLSA, and Phyllis Land, director of the Division of Instructional Media, Indiana Department of Public Instruction, teamed to write a proposal for funding the demonstration. The proposal, subsequently funded with a grant from the Library Research and Demonstration Program, U.S. Office of Education, is designed to develop a technique for a decentralized network audiovisual cataloging cooperative.

The working hypothesis of the demonstration project is that the cost of providing bibliographic control of audiovisual media can be significantly reduced through cooperative sharing of human, machine, and network data base resources. Specific objectives of the demonstration testing this hypothesis are to (1) operate a project that will lead to a continuing service of providing audiovisual bibliographic data for schools; (2) improve cost-effectiveness of cataloging by delivering products and services through cooperation; (3) upgrade quality of audiovisual media bibliographic control to national standards for cataloging and machine-readable format: (4) train school library media cataloging staff in understanding and use of national standards for media cataloging; (5) provide practical evaluation of the utility of national standards for audiovisual materials and to suggest modification as needed to agencies that have responsibility for national standards; (6) identify user-oriented products that could be automatically produced from a cooperative machine-readable audiovisual media data base; and (7) encourage the integration of school media centers into the state and national network.

Department of Public Instruction staff acquainted all potential participants with the demonstration project and invited representatives to a planning workshop. At the workshop the participants assisted in refining procedures for the decentralized cooperative system. INCOLSA staff explained how profiles would be created to accommodate the needs of each school district. It was established that the profile would allow for juvenile or adult subject headings, depending on the school's need, and that items to reflect funding sources, such as "ESEA IV-B," could appear on the cards.

It was established that some school districts would have to abandon local practices in order to make the cooperative work. It was suggested that now may be the time to replace elaborate color-coded cards with the written designators "filmstrip," "sound filmstrip," "motion picture," etc. This is particularly true with the emergence of new media formats such as videodisc.

The school personnel represented districts that had no previous association with INCOLSA, districts that were using the INCOLSA processing center for book materials, and two school systems—Vigo County School Corporation and School City of Gary—already had OCLC, Inc., terminals in the district processing centers. Since the beginning of the project, Lafayette School Corporation and Crown Point School Corporation have requested and have received their own terminals. INCOLSA is able to pay for the terminals and the cost of telecommunications with funding provided by the state. Local agencies purchase or lease printers for making labels, pay for cataloging on the "first time use" method used by OCLC, Inc., and pay the cost of catalog cards. Those districts already up on OCLC who participate in the audiovisual project will be reimbursed for the first-time-use costs of all audiovisual items.

Eleven school districts, representing 333 school buildings, are involved in the demonstration. In addition to the four having terminals, Carmel-Clay Schools, Evansville-Vanderburgh School Corporation, Indianapolis Public Schools, Monroe County Community School Corporation, Portage Township Schools, Richmond Community School Corporation, and South Bend Community School Corporation elected to participate. Requirements for participation include: (1) a commitment to cataloging to a national standard; (2) professional staff capable of doing high quality cataloging; (3) a commitment to permit staff to attend three days of training; and (4) an agreement to pay the cost of catalog cards produced by OCLC (presently 3.4 cents per card).

Training kits, prepared by INCOLSA, included copies of *Anglo-American Cataloging Rules, Revised Chapter XII,* specific examples and illustrations of the rules, and material relating to machine-readable encoding for audiovisual media. The kits were supplied at formal group sessions.

Other training modes used in the project are individual on-site training and written or oral feedback on errors. The objectives dealing with upgrading cataloging skills was measured with test items following training sessions even before the standards were applied to local cataloging.

Participating school districts follow the procedures that were cooperatively developed by INCOLSA staff and local staffs. For each audiovisual item that needs cataloging, the local school district will request a search of the OCLC data base. This request can be sent to INCOLSA processing center on a project request form, on a local order form, on a publisher or producer's blurb, or by a telephone. After the OCLC data base is searched, a printout is made of each relevant record and forwarded to the participant. Local catalogers can review the printout for conformity to the item in hand, for addition of any missing data required by national standards, and to add any needed local data such as call number, additional subject headings, etc. Upon receipt of the worksheets at INCOLSA, the catalog cards are ordered via OCLC terminal. Cards are mailed directly to the local agency in the filing order specified for schools. The participating school also receives automatically produced sets of labels produced on the printer in the processing center.

When no record is found, the participant is advised and asked to do original cataloging on the worksheets. The data on the worksheets is put into the data base by INCOLSA staff. Any local access requirements are noted on the worksheets so that input and card production can be accomplished in one keyboard session.

As each participant produces catalog records new to the system, a data base is being built that will lower the overall need to do original local cataloging in Indiana schools and for OCLC participants in other states as well. Initially records are found for a small proportion of what is being purchased, but, over time, the proportion grows so that processing for audiovisual materials becomes faster and less expensive.

The demonstration, at writing, is not developed to the degree the other benefits can be measured, but expectations are high. It is the contention of project staff that the cataloging skill level of building library media professionals will be upgraded as the district media staffs participate. It is anticipated that user services will improve as some building level professionals are relieved of cataloging duties. In Indianapolis, for instance, when the second person was added to the library media staff at a high school building, it was for the purpose of cataloging. This practice had been allowed through the years.

Through the shared audiovisual cataloging in the demonstration, the present data base should be expanded by more than ten thousand new items. It is likely that these bibliographic records can be utilized in the development of a fiche catalog of audiovisual resources that can be disseminated.

While primary benefits will be accrued by the participants in the demonstration, the benefits to other networks within the United States and to other school districts and libraries within Indiana must not go unnoticed. In addition to their using the expanded data base, school systems and other libraries are able to use the training materials and will be able to improve bibliographic control through use of techniques devised in the demonstration. The problem of audiovisual bibliographic control is not generic to school media centers as illustrated by data from a 1973 survey of all types of Indiana libraries.

Provision of services to aid in processing and use of audiovisual media was ranked fifth out of fifteen proposed cooperative bibliographic services. Indiana is utilizing schools to address this need. In Indiana decisions are made by all members—the smallest participating school system has the same one vote as the largest university or public library.

The strength of a library network lies in the cooperative spirit of its members and, thus, the high quality member contributions. In this instance, it is eleven Indiana school districts that have the opportunity to contribute as they provide high quality bibliographic records for the audiovisual resources they acquire while they benefit by sharing. They serve as the on-line audiovisual media connection for library users throughout the country . . . and the schools like it!

THE FUTURE

From
Wilson Library Bulletin

by BETTY FAST

THE MEDIA SPECIALIST AS AN AGENT FOR CHANGE

No one ever accused the traditional school library of revolutionary tendencies; its serene and studious atmosphere epitomized a passive role in the educational scene. Its function was to support the curriculum of the school in a subservient handmaiden fashion. The leadership that a few outstanding librarians managed to demonstrate in their schools came despite and not because of their positions.

While the librarian was building a book collection and offering reading guidance to students at one end of the school, the audiovisual specialist was tending ailing machines and offering teachers how-to-do-it instructions at the other. Occasionally, an audiovisual educator like Carlton W. H. Erickson envisioned the AV director as a change-agent in the school; in actuality only a few people were even able to change their after-teaching media duties into a full-time job.

Moaning librarians and AV tinkerers

While librarians bemoaned the advent of newer forms of media and

Wilson Library Bulletin 49, 9 (May 1975): 636–37.

spent their time scanning the horizon for readers, and AV tinkerers scouted the terrain and announced an imminent takeover by librarians as the major hazard to avoid, true media specialists began to put the strengths of their two fields together and found they had the capacity to become "shakers and movers." The new breed of media specialist, functioning on the school level, quietly assumed the position of curriculum coordinator in the school.

Who would suspect that a merger of the fields might result in a combination whose sum is far greater than its two parts? Although Frances Henne led a small band of prescient educators toward the unified media concept, even today most people do not realize the potential of the fusion. It is a force whose time is yet to come.

One reason for the time lag in recognizing the potential of the media specialist has been the do-it-yourself aspect of the situation. Since library and education schools have moved with less than deliberate speed in the direction of integrated programs to educate media specialists, the major impetus has come from perceptive professionals in the field who grasped the unified philosophy and found their own means to acquire the necessary skills and knowledge.

In individual schools some talented media specialists have interwoven curriculum and media to encourage learning. Occasionally these new media-curriculum specialists are classroom teachers, especially English teachers, who understand that media is the language of today's youth and have become effective media teachers. Fortunately, there is a growing number of educators who believe that curriculum and media cannot be considered as entities.

Changing learning patterns

Media programs are vital in education because of the great changes in the learning patterns of youngsters, caused largely by their exposure to television and other mass media. If schools are to move from a classroom and teacher-dominated routine—already declared outmoded by the students—to a learner-oriented environment, the media program must emerge as a key component, an integral part of the learning process. Media must play an active, not a passive, role in the school experience, since the success of the educational program depends in large part on the way learners use resources to find, evaluate, and apply information.

The media specialist—with the ability to make connections between the people, ideas, and media that are the essence of learning—has become a key member of the educational team. In fact the logical conclusion of this learning interplay is an educational program in which media and curriculum, media and learning, and media specialists and teachers have become identical. There is no such thing as a separate media program or a physical entity called the media center apart from the rest of the school. Since the media program's goal is the improvement of instruction, it is possible that the media program might self-destruct when it becomes totally integrated into the learning process.

Although such integration is in the future, for the present the innovative media specialist is in a unique position to have an impact on the entire school. Example is still a successful way to cause change, and the example of the media center is easily observed. Unlike a teacher, whose classroom door is closed and who works with only a small segment of the student population, the media specialist can touch every student's life. The media center should present a model for media use with a variety of learning opportunities (including media production) replacing the class instructional or study hall mode. In a good media center program, the time saved by utilization of self-instructional materials could be used to help students develop an appreciation of media and to encourage its improved use in the classroom.

Innovative changes can originate in the media program and cause fundamental alterations in the life of the school. The media specialist, working with one part of the curriculum or one group of teachers at a time, can bring about changes in the style of teaching in the classroom. Often it will be necessary to set up some of the new learning methods in the media center with classroom-related subject matter. Then teachers can send their students there to use materials individually or in groups until the teacher feels confident and enthusiastic enough to incorporate them into the classroom situation. In some schools taped teaching, individualized reading programs, use of simulation games, and learning center techniques have been initiated by the media specialist and then have moved into the classroom.

How to export innovation

Instead of building larger and larger centers to accommodate most of the media use in the school, media specialists should consider farming out the activities, the equipment, and even the carrels into the classrooms.

There is no reason why the individual use of media cannot become part of the regular classroom life. The ultimate goal of media programs, including student production, should be to integrate it into the school's learning program. As each activity moves out of the media specialist's domain, the specialist is freed for another innovation which will also be exported when it proves its worth in the curriculum.

At the same time that the media specialist is working as a master teacher using resources in innovative ways in the media center, s/he must also wage a campaign for active involvement in curriculum planning. Although it is vital to have media specialists function as part of the team that designs curriculum guides at the district and/or school level, it is equally important to have this input on the firing line where the student meets the curriculum. By its use in cooperative lesson planning, the media specialist's expertise can help teachers clarify objectives and select the mix of media and method which can be used most effectively. As the media specialist becomes indispensable to the improvement of learning through demonstrations of innovative practice and curriculum planning, it will become easier to justify additions to the staff and to the collection.

How can this concept of the media specialist as a change-agent become a reality rather than a rarity? The vision must precede the realization: Media specialists must have this self-image before it can become a reality. The new national guidelines for media programs, *Media Programs: District and School,* describe this person functioning at the center of the learning program. The combined roles of curriculum consultant and innovator should attract educators with leadership qualities to the field. What is needed are flexible people with a receptivity to change and the courage to overcome institutional inertia: media specialists who are eager to work with people as well as with media. Educational training programs must assume an influential position as well as offer the background necessary to help media specialists to meet their destiny. This presupposes an understanding and commitment that many programs have been slow to recognize.

The new improved media specialist

The name of the game is important, for a label helps to create the mental set. Changing names to media center, media specialist, and media program is crucial if the new program is to dramatize how it differs from the traditional library. Although imposing a name change does not create an instant media orientation without an attitude change in the media center staff, the school library that clings to the traditional label and attempts to operate a change-oriented media program must cope with a residue of stereotyped associations that impede its progress. The quickest way to change the image is to change the label; by calling the program something different, we make people aware of a change to a new improved entity.

Written philosophies of education to the contrary notwithstanding, the idea of a truly learner-centered school program is revolutionary in the real world of the public schools. Why can't the media specialist and the media program lead the way toward this fundamental change in education?

"DEAR BETTY, . . ."

by MORTON SCHINDEL

In August, 1972, I received a letter from Betty that moved me greatly. She started out by saying she was writing "a sort of love letter."

With this prelude, she went on to say how very much Weston Woods has meant to her and her colleagues in the library profession and to children. She wrote: "Through you I have come to understand that the real value of media is the humanness behind it; when this is lacking, there is no impact. When it is present . . . there is no end to the effect on human beings."

I acknowledged Betty's letter, but never really *answered* it. It was just not possible at the time. But now that six years have passed and things are beginning to sort themselves, I think it's time I did answer Betty.

Weston Woods
Weston, Connecticut
December, 1978

Dear Betty,

This is my long past due reply to your letter. Please forgive my tardiness but it has taken these years for the real meaning of your words to take hold.

When you wrote about the real value of media being the humanness behind it, you shared with me your insight into the relationship of the various people connected with children's literature. The publisher, the producer, the librarian together form the pipeline for the mass dissemination of ideas and feelings from a relatively few rare and talented people to masses of children. Betty, you realized how interdependent we are and how interactive we need to be to do the best possible job. And I realize that our interaction with you and others in the library profession has played a major role in shaping Weston Woods and me, personally. I can recall the specific contributions librarians have made over the years to our conceptual development.

The first librarian to have a profound influence on my work was Maria Cemino, the head of the central children's room in the New York Public Library. I asked her to show me some books with pictures that were regarded as "good" books for children. As she turned the pages, I saw for the first time *Make Way for Ducklings, Millions of Cats, Madeline, Hercules, Little Toot,* and *Andy and the Lion*—books that became the foundation of Weston Woods. Something in the way she spoke about *Millions of Cats*—her awe and reverence and love and devotion—impressed me. But the books' apparently simple black-and-white drawings depressed me. It had never occurred to me that I would be called upon to make a film out of material like that, but it was the beginning of a voyage of discovery. I took books home and read them to my children. Their fresh, uninhibited senses perceived and showed me things that I had missed. Their expressions mirrored the feelings in Maria Cimino's talks to me about these books. As I listened with one ear to the expert librarian and with the other to my children, something gradually began to seep through the long hardened emotional scar tissue in the middle that was me. I had met my first librarian, and she had conquered.

I soon learned that *Millions of Cats,* first published in 1928 by Coward-McCann, was more than just a book—it was a cliché for a whole genre of picture books. When people asked me what kinds of books I was hoping to adapt, those who knew anything at all about the field only needed to hear "books like *Millions of Cats*" to know just what I was talking about. Hence, it was important for me to acquire the film rights to *this* book.

At Coward-McCann, I first met Alice Torrey, the children's book editor. She told me that the rights had been asked for many times before but had never been granted. No children's book publisher had ever had a satisfactory experience with a film producer. When rights had been acquired for a modest one-time payment, the film producer walked off with all the subsidiary rights, including filmstrips, recordings, etc. The book publisher had no recourse. No wonder Coward-McCann was jaundiced.

When I explained that I had in mind to use the original pictures and text from the book, Alice was intrigued. I got an appointment with Tim Coward, then president of the company. Almost apologetic for taking my time, he explained that the rights to *Millions of Cats* were no longer theirs to sell, but instead, it was his feeling, belonged to children.

His message made a deep impression on me, one that I have often had occasion to reflect upon and repeat. The rest is history. I agreed to make the film in consultation with Alice Torrey and to destroy it if at any stage during production Alice felt that it would impinge on the rights of children. By now more than 2,000 prints of the film are in circulation.

The first film that I worked on was *Andy and the Lion*. Coincidentally, I had acquired rights to do a live-action film of this book some years earlier. I had been looking for something more stimulating than another fifth-grade science project to film for schools. But to be acceptable in schools educational films had to have "content." *Andy's* preamble said that it was "a tale of kindness remembered, or the power of gratitude." I deceived myself into thinking that was "content" by school standards. The project never got off the ground.

Now, aware that the charm of the book was in the illustrations, I came back to *Andy and the Lion*. Also, having made up my mind that I would be an antidote to Disney, I determined that my films would be a direct reflection of the books themselves, using the pictures and text just as they appeared. I cut out the pages of *Andy* and pinned them on the wall. Through trial and error, in six months' time I had devised a new system in which the camera was stationary and the picture moved. Trying to refine what is now called the iconographic technique, I made most of the shots in *Andy* at least ten times. Splicing them together, I had made my first work print.

With great trepidation I called Maria Cimino, who arranged for me to show my work to key members of the staff at the New York Public Library. Frances Landers Spain was then coordinator of work for children. Augusta Baker was one of the principal librarians of her staff, in charge of the storytelling activities throughout the library system. Both would influence the development of my films.

Andy was much more than just a book to these librarians. James Daugherty had dedicated it "to Lady Astor and Lord Lenox, the library lions who have so long sat in front of the New York Public Library and with such complacent good nature and forbearance looked down on the Manhattan parade." And this was to be possibly the first film based on a children's picture book that had ever been shown in the library. I remember that we sat in a small conference room with a projector brought in for the occasion. The reel I strung up must have had 150 splices in it, and, of course, no sound had yet been recorded. That showing was another landmark. The librarians not only complimented the film's fidelity to the book, which was just what I most wanted to hear, but what was even more important, they asked how I had gotten Jimmy Daugherty to make so many new illustrations for my film. The fact was that everything in the film had been in the book. A detail like youngsters hanging on a pole watching a parade gave me a scene to cut away to, and it gave the needed extension to the parade scene that the film required. I had shown the librarians something they had not seen before, a dimension beyond the book itself.

A discussion of storytelling followed my showing of *Andy*. I had always hired narrators for my pedagogical films, and the difference between a narrator and a storyteller had never crossed my mind. Augusta Baker offered to help me develop the storytelling technique. For me, at that time, she was just another librarian. Litte did I know that I was being offered the help of one of the outstanding people in her profession.

Starting, naively, with narrators I had used before, I came into the library with recorded tapes of *Millions of Cats, Andy* and some other books. But something was wrong. Before my recording had run for more than a few minutes, I knew I had to go back and try again. I made many such trips over a period of three months. These were all trained voices, people who knew instinctively how to emphasize each syllable and word in reading the news or advertising a product. But they were beyond taking a simple book, making it their own if they cared enough about it to do so, and then giving it back to the audience with the perception and affection that they had developed for it. It is no wonder that Augusta's comments told me more about what was wrong with the storytelling she heard than what would be right. After all, how does one elucidate beyond words like "love for a story"? And I could not hope to progress from narrator to storyteller until I, myself, understood what this meant.

When would-be storytellers came for an audition, I ushered them into a room in which I had set out about ten books. They could select any they liked and study them in anticipation of doing a reading in front of the microphone. One day a man came in, looked at the books, lit up like a torch and said, "Gee! These are just the books I've been reading for years to my kids; we love them." That was Owen Jordan. He read *Millions of Cats* and *Make Way for Ducklings,* capturing the rhythms and nuances of fast and slow, light and dark, and displaying obvious knowledge of the stories and affection for characters and their situations. I knew I had a storyteller, and Augusta Baker concurred.

Following my showing of the work print for *Andy,* word got around about what I was doing. Anne Izard, who was the coordinator of children's services at the Westchester County Library System, invited me to make a presentation at a meeting of the New York Library Association in Lake Placid in the fall of 1954. My world was expanding. From exposure to one librarian I had gone on to relate to a handful. Now I was going to be confronted by the membership of an association.

Andy would not be ready in time for showing as a finished film. It would be a work print—just pictures, accompanied by storytelling over a microphone and the sound system from the projector. A recorded storytelling was one thing, a live performance something else. I needed someone special. My search for a storyteller led to Beman Lord, who agreed to be the voice of Andy.

The film was well received among the 300 librarians who attended the showing. In my talk afterwards, I begged the audience to admit me to their ranks. Betty, I wanted to be an insider, a part of what they were doing. And, instead of just relating to some people in the library profession, I felt an affinity to the whole profession.

Through 1954 and 1955, I brought seven films to completion. But without finishing those in the works I started another and yet another. This going back and doing things over and over again probably made all the difference and has characterized our way of doing things ever since. Just as I lacked the taste and judgment to select books on their merits at the outset and depended on the recommendation of others, I also lacked the assurance that the way I adapted a story was the ultimate and the best. I learned that when you are closely involved with the creative effort, you don't see certain facets of the work. Authors, illustrators, and people in the library profession served as my editors, helping me shape my work into acceptable productions.

Partly by accident, partly by design, my films turned out to be a cut above those being made for educational purposes in the 1950s. I was aiming for a television market. Hence, the artistic qualities of my films assumed a different importance than they might have if I were making "mere educational films." For example, no one went to the trouble of writing and recording original music for films intended for schools and libraries. Stock music was selected from recording libraries. Still, my films were rejected by television people as being nice films but essentially for schools. And prospects for distribution to schools appeared to be no better. Dick and Jane were the characters that reading teachers were accustomed to lean on, not *Hercules* or *Mike Mulligan*.

At a loss to know where to turn, I rented the screening room at the Museum of Modern Art in New York and invited people from the children's book world to a showing of my films. In attendance were about

300 teachers, librarians, authors, illustrators, publishers, reviewers and people from organizations concerned with children. After the screening I talked with people in the audience. A number of them said that they thought they could use the films effectively. I encouraged them to borrow prints and report back to me how they made out. This way, I was able to find people from each of these spheres of influence who could bridge from my work to a prospective audience.

I commissioned one person from each area to write a utilization guide telling how my iconographic films, based on children's books, could be used. These guides, plus the general announcement, became the basis for my first promotional piece. Again, people from the library profession had come to my rescue. I fed them films to use experimentally in their programs; they fed back to me information about the films and the reassurance I needed.

Unable to find a distributor for television or schools to handle my films on a satisfactory basis, I decided to pick a name, set up a company, and distribute the films myself. My first mailing, featuring seven prints, went out to a list of 5,000 people in schools, libraries, and colleges. I soon received a number of requests for preview prints, which I sent out with a note saying they could be retained for purchase or returned with no obligation. To my surprise, nothing was being returned. So with great trepidation, I started calling the people who had requested the previews—mainly large public libraries. They were all retaining the prints for purchase. Weston Woods was in business!

It turned out that about 60 public libraries had started circulating film collections. Materials for children were notably absent. There hadn't been anything produced that librarians felt was proper to introduce into their collections. My films filled this gap perfectly. We started out with about 40 customers. We sold 700 prints—about a hundred of each title—in the first year. My emotional affinity to the library profession had long since been established; now my economic dependence began to surface.

Once Weston Woods films got into distribution, an active correspondence developed between children's librarians and myself. They wrote evaluations of the films I produced. Then, once Weston Woods got into circulating collections, I started getting suggestions from librarians, titles of books that they especially liked and wanted to see filmed. I remember getting some suggestions from you, Betty.

The other request that started to show up became the basis for an expanded product line for Weston Woods. Librarians using films in their story hours had been accustomed to telling the stories themselves while showing youngsters pictures from the books. They liked using the projected pictures because now all of the youngsters could see all the details even when there was a large group. Inquiries trickled in asking whether the soundtrack might be turned off and the text read to the children.

My answer was no—the pictures move along at an inexorable pace and should be subordinated to the live storyteller, rather than the other way around. But I had the solution—the ideal medium for telling stories to projected pictures from picture books—filmstrips. We proceeded to make eight filmstrips, each based on one of our motion picture titles. To keep the text intact, we printed it in a separate booklet with the now-familiar cuing picture corresponding to each section. Librarians were immediately responsive. But people in audiovisual departments rejected the format. They were concerned that the text booklet would easily be lost in the process of circulation and requested that we make versions with the text, even though it would mean paring it down, on the filmstrip frames. We resisted the audiovisual people and deferred to our friends in children's libraries. Their support reinforced our still wavering conviction that our productions must be faithful to the original work.

I have noted how our first productions—motion pictures—gave rise to a demand for filmstrips and recordings and how we put these two media together as sound filmstrips. Because of the lower price and greater ease of handling, our market for filmstrips soon outstripped that for motion pictures, and by the early sixties our production followed suit.

The first titles that came to our attention as likely filmstrip productions included Caldecott Medal winners. The Caldecott Medal had great meaning, but only to a select few—mainly children's librarians in public libraries, authors, illustrators, and their publishers.

It occurred to me that using the Caldecott Medal on our filmstrip releases would help to identify Weston Woods with quality and responsibility in children's literature. When I started to study the books, however, I observed that the book for which an illustrator had received the award was not necessarily his or her best. Hence, I felt that adding a book to our list only because it had won the Caldecott Medal would be a compromise. So instead I assembled a list of titles by illustrators who had won the Caldecott Medal, not necessarily the award-winning books themselves.

Weston Woods had been in business only a few years. We had made a point of making ourselves known to the American Library Association, but we were relative newcomers and an unknown quantity in children's publishing. It is understandable, then, that Mildred Batchelder, executive secretary of the Children's Services Division, examined my request to use the Caldecott Medal in connection with books by medal winners with due caution. She referred my request to the executive committee of CSD, who reported back favorably.

In 1962—the fourth year after Weston Woods began releasing film-strips—we announced a series of eight filmstrips based on Caldecott Medal-winning books. Each box had fixed to it the same gold medal that publishers purchased from the ALA to stick onto their book jackets. The association with the medal and the assurance that librarians derived from the series' eight titles built a new fire under established Weston Woods activity. Librarians, authors, illustrators, and publishers all sat up and took notice. And so did I.

Betty, I began to realize that we were now inextricably involved with the most revered of children's publishing and children's librarianship. I had read Paul Hazard's *Books, Children and Men* and virtually committed to memory his passages about the world republic of childhood. I realized that the books we had been entrusted to adapt were the substance that created the world community of which Hazard spoke. I also realized that our rights to these books were exclusive. Now, not only did we have the rights to books, but we had the right to display an emblem that impelled librarians to their order forms. We had been accorded a privilege to be respected and enhanced, not flaunted or exploited. Now it was my turn to give something back.

Seeing that we had almost inadvertently stumbled into the mainstream of the literary heritage of youngsters, I looked around to see what else constituted this heritage. Most obvious were the books of Randolph Caldecott himself. In the process of discovering Caldecott, I discovered other picture books that predated *Millions of Cats* by a generation or more: *The Tale of Peter Rabbit* and the other works of Beatrix Potter and Leslie Brooke's *Johnny Crow's Garden*. In the following year, we would strengthen Weston Woods' roots by grafting them to the roots of children's literature itself as these titles showed up on our filmstrip list.

My personal relationship and dialogue with Mildred Batchelder continued through the years. In the fall of 1965, she telephoned me from a meeting of the board of directors of the Children's Services Division in Chicago. She wondered if I had any program ideas for their division during the next ALA conference—they were considering art in children's books as a theme. In the ensuing months I talked with people like Bob McCloskey and Jimmy Daugherty and Ezra Jack Keats about this. I also had occasion to be in touch with Joanna Foster Daugherty at the time. She had been executive secretary of the Children's Book Council, but was moving out to become an independent promotion counselor for a number of children's book publishers. As I talked with these people, some ideas started to crystallize. I started to see a program that one of these people described as "a living newspaper." It would be authors reading from their books and illustrators showing slides and commenting about their work—all in a well-paced, dramatic presentation that would have some artistry in itself. The idea grew and became more exciting as we talked.

The following month, during the midwinter ALA conference, Mildred called again, this time asking me to *put on* the convention program. Ordinarily, she said, about 800 of the influential children's librarians in America attended. I knew this was an opportunity I could not turn down. On the other hand, it was one that I could not afford to accept unless I could put on a good program. Mildred said there would be no strings attached and that she would act as liaison with the board, which would retain ultimate control of program content.

Betty, the night of the program in St. Louis sticks in my mind as though it were yesterday. A huge sea of chairs filled the ballroom. We had arranged for a large screen and good projection. I prayed that our 56-minute program would go off without blowing a bulb or breaking a splice. Everything worked perfectly, and the program got a standing ovation.

People who saw the film in St. Louis wanted to share it with their teachers and librarians and supervisors and parents back home. We put the film into distribution, and nearly 2,000 copies are still in circulation. Almost no one leaves library school without seeing *The Lively Art of Picture Books*. It was cited in the twenty-fifth anniversary edition of *The Horn Book* as one of the significant milestones in children's literature.

A short time later we felt the impact of the Elementary Secondary Education Act. It hit like a bombshell! We were a half-dozen people, mainly part-time, working up in the woods, not tuned in to what was happening even in nearby Westport, Connecticut, let alone Washington, D.C. So when, almost overnight, the small handful of daily mail became a pile of envelopes a foot high, we didn't know what to think. The fact was that legislation enacted with the fiscal year beginning in July of 1965 did not release money until around March of 1966. This money had to be expended by the end of June. Schools did not have the time to preview materials. They had to buy on the reputation of the supplier. Our business quadrupled overnight.

ESEA funding gave tremendous impetus to the opening of school libraries with greater expenditure allowances for materials. Librarians started moving away from the children's rooms in public libraries to key positions in school libraries, and new people who had been trained for work with children gravitated toward schools as well. Audiovisual directors became more hardware-oriented, assuming primary responsibility for equipment within school systems. School librarians became the software people, responsible for audiovisual materials as well as books. This new role has expanded ever since.

Not long after this, Betty, came our first meeting. The ALA was meeting in New York City, and because of our close proximity, we offered to open our doors to out-of-town librarians as a pre- or post-convention tour. You were part of the committee that organized the tour of more than 700 librarians to visit our facility in the woods of Connecticut. Your kind and gracious helping hand was just the first of your many contributions to Weston Woods.

We've fortunately had many other occasions to meet and consult. Your school in Groton was one of the first in which I actually saw our materials "at work" with children. We were taking stories that appealed to us, internalizing them and giving them back to youngsters in the best way that we knew how, the audiovisual media. But we were covering new ground. So the reassurance of seeing a classroom full of youngsters enjoying our films was a rare and treasured experience.

And it was through you that we came to understand the appeal our films and filmstrips had for teachers as well as youngsters. Teachers did not need to know the literature or be storytellers to enjoy our materials and use them effectively; all they had to do was use them. With no special preparation they would learn the stories and through them build a relationship with youngsters. The youngsters reflected their enjoyment back onto the teachers.

But two generations of teachers working with youngsters in schools had not been exposed to this contemporary genre of children's literature as they were growing up or training for their jobs. More traditional educators suggested that our materials would be more useful to teachers if we would prepare utilization guides indicating how best to use each production. You, Betty, were one of the people who had strong reservations about this. Literature, you said, was for enjoyment, for enlightenment, for enrichment; a good book could appeal to a wide range of children, each perhaps having a very different interest.

From a meeting of educators that I convened in 1969, you helped me to conclude *not* to create utilization guides for our films and filmstrips, at least not in the traditional sense. Instead we would become active participants, perhaps even major contributors, to the job of training teachers and librarians through all of the means available to us in print as well as the audiovisual media. Some of the specific forms this took were: production of our "Signature Collection," films about authors and illustrators intended to enrich librarians' and teachers' understanding of the background of children's literature; publishing and reprinting of articles and then offering them in quantity free of charge to teachers of teachers and librarians; institution of tours and workshops at Weston Woods accommodating up to 1,500 people per year; offer of all adaptations of children's books in the Weston Woods catalogue free of charge for use in courses and workshops for demonstration purposes.

These have been magic moments for me, marvelous years. I'm constantly aware and appreciative of the heritage and dedication of the people from the library profession and of their hand in molding Weston Woods' destiny. Our productions—like picture books—would never get to children without the adults who care enough to open and share them.

When I first read stories like *Millions of Cats* and *Make Way for Ducklings* to my own youngsters many years ago, I had been completely desensitized to the arts. Never an avid reader, I certainly had never read aloud. Each word had the same value to me; nuances in pictures completely escaped me.

The response of my children contrasted sharply. They commented excitedly, pointed out tiny details with the glee of discovery. They wanted to dress up like children's book characters at Halloween time. What to me was dead was very alive to them. Listening to them, beginning to share, then feeling more comfortable about responding on their level, brought us closer together.

I know that teachers value our films and filmstrips today for reasons paralleling my own. Not all are storytellers and not all have developed a real appreciation for children's literature, but ever since Dick and Jane expired and schools turned to good literature for enrichment and motivation, teachers have looked for ways to share it. When they do so with a film or filmstrip, an emotional response comes back from the youngsters; it involves the teachers not only with the youngsters, but also with the books.

Herein lies the humanity you spoke of in your letter—the real value of this or any medium—the *sharing* with youngsters of a book or film or filmstrip. The humanness that the author has poured into the book is absorbed and carried along by the publisher or producer, librarian and teacher and on to the child. If anyone falters along the way, it doesn't work. That's why the affinity among these people is so strong, that's why they become so involved, that's why this bond must be preserved.

As for the future, Betty, you recognized a long time ago that the future lies in audiovisual materials and that librarians will be in the forefront monitoring every step of the way. But some have expressed fears that we are moving children away from books. You and I agreed that through films and filmstrips we can help children to discover the treasures that are stories by showing them something special they have not seen before. But, more importantly, if we do it right, we can use these materials to motivate youngsters to read the books for themselves. So instead of moving children away from books, we can work at stimulating their interest and motivating them back to books.

Now it's time to move forward and shepherd the literature for children into the next age—that of telecommunications. It's a dynamic, far-reaching era, one where the risks may be greater. It will be even more necessary to preserve the standards you helped to set and the humanness you recognized as the key.

My thanks to you, Betty, for all your guidance, and with much love.

Sincerely,
Mort

CONTINUING EDUCATION— GENERAL CONSIDERATIONS, WITH APPLICATION TO SCHOOL LIBRARIANS

by BERNARD S. SCHLESSINGER AND PATRICIA JENSEN

The literature of continuing education in librarianship has seen an enormous growth in the past ten years, due to the impact of the work of Elizabeth W. Stone.[1] Stone's work has not only guided the thinking of the profession, but has led to publications as diverse as those from the Continuing Library Education Network and Exchange (CLENE) as well as Barbara Conroy's *Library Staff Development and Continuing Education.* Two major themes are found in the recent journal literature on the subject: general support for continuing education and the presentation of models for continuing education.

The area of continuing education for school librarians, however, is sparsely covered in the recent literature. An extensive study by Elizabeth W. Stone summarized in *School Libraries* (1969) attributes this lack of interest to the fact that "the activities concerning involvement (for professional growth) that the school librarians ranked highest were: working for increased accessibility of books and libraries, participation in library associations, reading professional literature in library science, reading in a subject specialization, promotion of new materials and equipment."

That same issue contained, coincidentally, a questionnaire[2] designed by Betty Fast asking supervisors in school libraries about their perceptions of continuing education for themselves. No publication was found of the data derived. Furthermore, the literature of the past two years reveals no articles that specifically deal with continuing education for school librarians.

The need for continuing education

It has been suggested that there is general support for continuing education efforts by the profession, that a number of models have been suggested for continuing education in specific areas of librarianship and, finally, that there is a general lack of attention to this area by and for school librarians.

It might be helpful to discuss the needs for continuing education by librarians in general. These needs can be divided into two categories: the needs of the partaker in the program (hereafter referred to by the traditional word "student") and the needs of the institution offering the program (hereafter referred to by the traditional word "school"). The use of the traditional words is noted because it is important to recognize in all continuing education planning that neither the student nor the school is operating in the traditional roles. Perhaps the lack of recognition of this fact has been responsible for the failure of more continuing education efforts than any other single factor.

The student comes to continuing education activities for three basic reasons:

1. A need for further education or training

   In librarianship, this need divides into several populations, which accounts for some of the difficulty in structuring programs. On a very fundamental level, one finds the person who has worked in libraries without benefit of any degree credentials for a number of years and wishes to affirm the procedures he or she has developed or been taught, to listen to an exposition of the principles behind the procedures, and to investigate other procedures in the library. A second type is the individual with some training at the technician level, possibly an educational credential below the bachelor's level and some additional experience, who has the same three desires as the first person, but probably not in the same mix; that is, the desire to learn principles would probably be stronger in this trained individual. Still higher in the library staff hierarchy is the third person who possesses a bachelor's degree credential (with or without some library science courses) and has worked in libraries. She or he, usually still unsure as to whether to enter into formal study toward the professional degree (or in the process of such formal study), has much the same needs as the first two types.

At the professional level, no matter what the degree status, there are two types of students. The one, recently trained, is anxious to pick up knowledge and competencies in areas that he or she had no time for during the academic training. The second, well into a career, is concerned about newer knowledge and competencies that were either not included in the curriculum during his or her education, or have been recognized as necessities with the growth of responsibilities of the job.

One might view the above as a distinction between those who are without professional credentials, who are using continuing education primarily to strengthen and expand knowledge, and those educated at the professional level who are pursuing continuing education not only to expand and strengthen knowledge but also to update credentials.

2. A need for socialization

Librarianship is often a solitary profession. For large numbers of libraries, there is only one person in the library, and contacts with the patrons are superficial and shortlived. Larger libraries may provide more contacts, both with other library staff members and patrons, but the pressures of "getting the job done" prevent any more than a brief and business-like encounter.

The value of the social opportunities afforded by continuing education activities should not be overlooked. There is an accumulation of dissatisfaction with librarianship as a career, partly due to this lack of socialization, that may be related to the fact that some of our best people leave our ranks. Continuing education opportunities help provide a partial solution here.

3. Needs (intangible) that may be recognized or may be fringe benefits rather than real needs

   a. The contact with other librarians provides an opportunity to discuss "nitty gritty" and to discover if there are better ways or or other ways to accomplish day-by-day tasks effectively.

   b. Increasingly, librarians do not stay in the career path within librarianship that served as an entry point. Many move to related professions in which the skills of librarianship are especially useful. These changes, in the view of the authors, are healthy for the profession. They are aided by precisely the content of many continuing education opportunities available today.

   c. Many librarians find that their next job comes from contacts made in pursuing continuing education. The same contacts may provide a work opportunity on committees or in professional associations that is challenging and fulfilling, while, at the same time, providing additional avenues for continuing education.

d. The self-actualization achieved in continuing education is a final positive effect for students. If librarians are to project the type of lively, questing, active image that is desirable, the growth and stimulation available in continuing education will be an integral part of developing that image.

The school also provides continuing education opportunities for a variety of other reasons:

1. Such programs provide evidence of the commitment of the school to the profession. No matter what the nature of the school, the involvement in continuing education is a real mark of commitment to the upgrading of the profession and to maintenance of its collective health.

2. The relationship between the school and its alumni is strengthened. Like the person who saves another individual's life, the institution that trains an individual should accept responsibility for that individual's future professional health. Part of that responsibility must be the provision of adequate maintenance and expansion capabilities for those basic skills imparted in the curriculum.

3. In the exposure to the professional community, the school builds up a degree of credibility that will be useful as a support mechanism in both good and bad times.

4. With the acceptance as a legitimate force for excellence by its professional community, the school also builds up credibility within its own academic community. All of us yearn for the respect and support that is embodied in 3 and 4.

5. The involvement of faculty in continuing education enhances both faculty development and student perspective. Especially in interaction with graduates now at the higher levels of responsibility in the profession and seeking continuing education stimulation, the faculty member must bring to bear all the skills of group work learned in classroom teaching, as well as current knowledge of the profession's status, to avoid damaging the reputations earned earlier. Furthermore, the faculty member benefits from direct confrontation with the problems and perplexities of current library practice.

6. Finally, although many participants in a continuing education experience may not be directly involved as alumni of the library education program, the participation develops a vested interest in the school and its success. If previously an alumnus, that commitment is renewed. Such support should not be taken lightly.

These six points apply in general terms to all librarians. Some points, however, are most important for school librarians. On the student level, school libraries have every level of trained and partially-trained personnel. Not only do these people need strengthening and expansion of skills and competencies, but in many cases such experiences are mandated.

School librarians are more isolated from their peers than any other type of librarian. They also are serving the young, a population that emphasizes that isolation from the adult world. Because of their isolation and the skills/competencies requirements, the intangible needs spelled out are vital to the health of school librarianship.

On the school level, much has been made of the failure of library schools and professional organizations to relate to the school librarian. A commitment to include the school librarian in continuing education programs would be useful in combatting that feeling.

School librarians are large in number. In instances where numbers count, their support would be welcome.

After meeting faculty in a successful continuing education program, misunderstandings about scope of service, school needs, etc., might be clarified, increasing the likelihood of more effective practicums and better success in job placement.

Program sponsors

Unlike academic programs, continuing education opportunities can be sponsored by a wide variety of institutions and agencies. Among these are library schools and other academic units of colleges and universities, state library agencies, state education agencies, professional library organizations, other professional organizations, libraries, information centers, and even individuals with special expertise. Because most school librarians see continuing education as a means of maintaining certification, they have, for the most part, involved themselves in those programs that carry with them academic credit that is acceptable toward mandated updating required by state supervisory organizations. Unfortunately, credit programs are not designed with the particular goals a school librarian has in mind. The net result is that most school librarians, while satisfying the certification agency, do not accomplish the intended goals of school media specialist.

School librarians would be well advised to look more carefully at the many continuing education opportunities available that are not credit-bearing. Not only can these provide updating and expansion of present skills and competencies, but they further allow for contact with practitioners in other areas of librarianship that could better satisfy the other needs which have been identified.

Record keeping

For professionals in any occupational group, education (and advancement) are synonymous with credentials. Librarianship is no exception, and school librarianship, with its certification regulations, is even more insistent on some record of educational effort.

Continuing education opportunities that offer academic credit are appealing to the librarian, since they provide a permanent record that can be called up at any time that it is required. As noted earlier, however, the structure of such academic credit opportunities is not always fitted to the generally stated goals of continuing education for school librarians.

The development of the new credential, the Continuing Education Unit (CEU), granted for "10 contact hours of participation in an organized continuing education experience under responsible sponsorship, capable direction and qualified instruction" provides another possibility for recognized credit. One such approach may be found in the draft of a CEU program for Rhode Island librarians by the Rhode Island Library Association's Continuing Education Committee, which states:

> For recognition of a program for CEU credit, a description should be submitted to a sub-committee of the Rhode Island Library Association Continuing Education Committee. The sub-committee is to be appointed by the chairperson of the Continuing Education Committee and will consist of six members: at least one library educator, one representative from the administration of the Division of University Extension of the University of Rhode Island, one library administrator, one staff librarian, and one paraprofessional library worker.

The draft further establishes record-keeping responsibility at the Division of University Extension.

In addition to academic institutions and their continuing education facilities accounting for traditional or CEU credits, there are many other organizations that should be considered as potential record keepers, as well as approval agencies for offerings. These include:

State Library Agencies. With their responsibilities to many types of libraries, their control of state funds, and their obligation to promote effective staffing, this would seem to be a legitimate role.

Professional Library Organizations. At the national level, library organizations have accepted this role to varying degrees, ranging from the comprehensive offerings, record-keeping and certification efforts of the Medical Library Association to the supportive (but not active) role of the American Library Association. State organizations have been equally inconsistent with efforts ranging from the example of the Rhode Island

Library Association noted earlier, to states without any plan of development. In this connection, CLENE should be included as a potential agency for both recognition and record keeping.

State Education Agencies. These would seem to be a logical base for recognition and record keeping of school librarians' continuing education efforts, especially in light of certification requirements.

Whoever assumes the role of agency for recognition and record keeping, the goals of continuing education, and the rationale for acceptance of programs as well as the mechanism for such acceptance and recording, should be carefully and thoroughly considered before embarking on any system.

Philosophical and practical considerations in continuing education programming

Two philosophical considerations are paramount in continuing education discussions: the question of mandating participation and the desirability of greater structure for the apparatus surrounding continuing education involvements.

Proponents of mandated participation argue that, human nature being what it is, librarians will only pursue continuing education if they are forced to. Opponents argue, again using human nature as the focus of their argument, that forced participation ensures an enormous loss of effectiveness of any program. School librarians are often used as examples by both proponents and opponents of this argument.

The authors are of the opinion that mandating would certainly be an important force for excellence (and should be encouraged) if, at the same time, the participant is involved actively in evaluation of programs with the understanding that negative reactions will result in the termination of the program involved. On a statistical basis alone, the mandated involvement of all librarians in continuing education would result in improved service to the patrons as skills and competencies are updated and expanded.

The arguments for greater structure for continuing education programs seem weak when considering the need for flexibility in such efforts. Regular library education programs are heavily structured and do not permit much choice. Admissions requirements are tight, and they exclude many. In continuing education programming, librarianship has an option that permits students without "all" the qualifications to partake of library education. This is a welcome option, especially in light of the increasing number of persons in librarianship without the first professional degree. Continuing education should remain "barrier-free" to allow for maximum participation by the "handicapped."

While the philosophical considerations of continuing education are important, even more vital to the success of any such programming are practical considerations that were the focus of discussion in the planning of a continuing education program at the University of Rhode Island's Graduate Library School in the 1977–78 academic year. Conversations and interviews with the participants defined several significant concerns which might be of interest to those involved in continuing education planning.

1. Duration of the Experience

Most librarians view continuing education as a drop-in/drop-out involvement. This necessitates restricting the length of offerings to between one and five days. The longer the offering, the less likely its acceptance by large numbers of librarians. School librarians, in particular, have difficulty attending longer sessions, since absence from a one-person library (and the majority of school libraries fall in that category) requires closing of the facility, with resultant interruption of service to students.

2. Timing

Because of the necessity for staffing libraries during open hours and the reductions in staff necessitated by budget cuts in the seventies, continuing education is most easily accomplished in evening or weekend hours. Evenings permit only relatively short sessions, while weekends offer opportunities for more intensive, continuous programming. The Rhode Island scheduling concentrated on one-day (Saturday) offerings and multiday offerings that incorporated Saturday and/or Sunday. In the case of multiday offerings, the incorporation of weekend days was an effective selling point for librarians with management (especially special librarians who could point to their contribution of personal time matching that given by the employer). School librarians should, of course, be attracted by continuing education offered at weekday and weekend hours when school is not in session.

In addition to the day of the week, the season of the year is important, especially in the case of school librarians. The Rhode Island programming was placed primarily in the summer block to encourage involvement at times of generally lower library activity and during vacation-granted periods. With no formally scheduled work activities in summer, school librarians should find this an ideal time for continuing education involvement.

3. Cost

Many librarians, otherwise very interested in continuing education, are discouraged by the high costs attached to such activity. Costs of $100–$150 per day place continuing education in the realm of luxury rather than the necessity it should be. This is increasingly true for librarians in the public sector, where employers resist financial support. The Rhode Island program concentrated on an upper level figure of $30–$40 per day including costs of food and on-campus lodging. Although such a figure restricts the nature of the offering, it increases enormously the likelihood of acceptance.

4. Structure and Environment

That continuing education participants are different from those interested in standard educational offerings has been noted. This has important consequences for structure and environment. The program must be intensive and content-filled while avoiding the impression of a pressure situation. Interest should be maintained at high level throughout to avoid losing the student who is there because he or she has chosen to be, rather than because of pressure as a credentialing measure.

The environment, although educational, should be designed to permit students to interact without making this the primary focus. Provision of comfort features such as coffee and social breaks during the day and variance of pace during the program are critical to success.

5. Faculty and Teaching Techniques

Academic programs require highly-credentialed instructors who are valuable in continuing education programs as well. But in librarianship there also exist a large number of practitioners without the Ph.D., but with excellent teaching skills and with an excitement derived from sharing their expertise and from the novelty of being involved in a teaching role. These practitioners are especially useful in continuing education programming.

As for teaching techniques, to maintain the interest level it is best to avoid the pure lecture format. Seminar discussions, interactive dialog, hands-on practice, and media presentations should be employed extensively. A variety of teachers should also be used. The key to successful programs is perception on the part of participants that there is a dynamic action moving toward the accomplishment of the overall learning goals.

6. Content

Most studies have asked librarians to indicate their continuing education needs and have come up with basically similar lists. The landmark Stone study shows interest in "updating, management, human relations, automation, and nonprint media." Recently, a New York State survey notes "substantial interest in management and administration, new developments in media, and computer-based systems."[3] An extensive recent survey of New England libraries, broken down into responses by professionals and support staff, shows that professionals are interested in public relations, collection development, grants/proposals, materials selection, planning and budgeting, while support staff expressed heaviest interest in materials selection, public relations, cataloging, computer applications in cataloging, materials acquisition, reference tools, and supervisory skills.[4] The interests of school librarians, in the opinions of the authors, coincide with these general interests, with perhaps addition of children's literature and greater emphasis on media, management, and materials selection and acquisition.

Is continuing education wanted?

Although few would dispute the arguments that there is a need for updating and strengthening skills, the authors have noted some disenchantment with continuing education programs. One source of this irritation may be related to the lack of presence of the consumer at many of the programs; another, to the lack of income from such programs.[5]

Continuing education programming should not be approached as an income generating activity. Those involved in it for that purpose are bound to be disappointed, except in the long run when other fringe benefits are included as values. For schools, the hope is to break even in the process of fulfilling their obligation to the profession, and to work toward a healthier future. For students as well, it might be noted, significant income gains from continuing education involvement are only promises for the future. The University of Rhode Island offerings in 1977–78 were a source of great satisfaction to the Graduate Library School dean and faculty in that all the five offerings were attended by significant numbers of people, the participants almost without exception indicated benefits from the attendance, and the school and the community were both the better for the experience. The monetary profits from the efforts were almost negligible.

One source of concern in looking at the attendance at the five sessions related to the minimal success in attracting school librarians. Although the opportunities were structured with school librarians in mind, very few attended. Only 13 attendees (of 131) were from the school librarian ranks, 8 of these at a single Saturday offering of a media workshop. Even if the Annual Gathering statistics are included (this having been conceived and billed as a continuing education activity), only 11 more school librarians are added to the total (135 attended the Saturday Annual Gathering).

Conclusion

It is clear from a review of the literature, from personal experience, and from the results of the University of Rhode Island program that, in the future:

1. Continuing programs will be needed.
2. Continuing education programming should not be the responsibility of any single agency.
3. A record-keeping apparatus should be made available.
4. Programs should be carefully structured to provide maximum access and attractiveness for librarians.
5. School librarians should be encouraged to more actively join in continuing education activities, as being vital to their future professional health and that of the profession in which they are included.

REFERENCES

1. Elizabeth W. Stone, *Continuing Library Education as Viewed in Relation to Other Continuing Professional Education Movement* (Washington, D.C.: ASIS, 1974).
2. Betty Fast, "Questionnaire about Continuing Education for School-Library Media Supervisors," *School Libraries* 18 (Summer 1969): 53.
3. *Library Journal/School Library Journal Hotline,* April 17, 1978, p. 4.
4. "What New England Librarians Want to Know," *NELB LINK* 3 (March/April, 1978).
5. *Library Journal* 103 (April 15, 1978): 810.

A STUDY IN CONTRADICTIONS— THE EDUCATION OF SCHOOL MEDIA SPECIALISTS

by JANE ANNE HANNIGAN

It might be said that the education of the school media specialist is, and should be, more closely aligned to the education of the teacher than to the education of the librarian. It is also true that teacher education traditionally has examined its educational programs with more frequency and intensity than has library education.[1] Thus, the uneasiness among colleagues in library education with the study of and the prospective changes in the education of school media specialists may be explained. This very unresponsiveness of the larger institution of which we are a part acts as a deterrent and often prevents our moving with an intensity and commitment parallel to that of teacher educators in the examination and evaluation of the educational programs of our profession.

As school media specialists, we have always been willing, although often under constraints and caveats we did not ourselves impose, to invest time, energy, and money in programs and projects for the improvement of the profession. For example, an examination of the 1960s and 1970s demonstrates this concern through such multileveled programs as the Knapp School Manpower Project, the many institutes funded under the National Defense Education Act, and the more recent responses by institutions to competency-based state certification laws. Each of these was a sincere attempt to meet our responsibilities as school media professionals, but too often the programs themselves were more a repackaging or a rephrasing of what already existed, rather than a true reformulation and revision. Too much energy was expended conforming old and tried ideas to new modes or new definitions without really altering the basic structure of the programs. Some of these projects and institutes were far better than others, and I have no doubt that the people involved in each of them gained a great deal as individuals. However, as a profession, we did not move forward significantly. In response to these projects, school media educators, rather than focusing on those new ideas that might have been developed into innovative and exciting programs, too often avoided the more challenging aspects in a search for those elements with which we could justify our own programs. Thus, a closer scrutiny reveals that the relationship between what we have learned through such activities and what we have subsequently done in library education is very disparate.

This disparity is quite evident in library schools' responses to the laws concerning competency-based teacher certification. The competency-based movement, which has forced us into the mode of examining our priorities and determining various levels of expectation for practice, should provide us with an exciting opportunity to move forward in library education. However, when attempting to design a proposal to meet the requirements of the law, one immediately faces the dichotomy between the ideal and the reality of existing institutions. For instance, although many would agree that an adequate program cannot be completed in one year, lowering enrollments and the financial crunch evoke a response of timidity toward the consideration of a two-year program. Often, new programs are constricted by the unwillingness of our colleagues in library schools to share the necessary study and evaluation. We spend far more of our time talking to our counterparts in other institutions who teach in the school media area than to other members of the faculty of which we are a part. It seems to me we are second class citizens in some schools because we have let ourselves be classed as such. Perhaps what is needed is a more aggressive demonstration of the intellectual vigor of our work and of the pride we take in it.

On the one hand, competency-based teacher education requires a forum for dialogue among peers, while alternatively, the constraints of both format and language in preparing such proposals defeats involvement. Over and over, I have noted that change in language, format, and strategy often frightens people who are otherwise quite sane. There is no question that the use of objectives and the implications of a competency-based style are frightening. I firmly believe that, in some instances, it is basic laziness on the part of faculty who do not want to deal with such processes, but also it is reflective of a sloppy methodology in teaching as well as an unaccountable behavior toward students. For those faculty who have always cared about teaching, the need to come to grips with the underlying principles of such requirements creates an active and dynamic interchange that produces the best possible design for the education of students. The problem is that higher education has not, as a rule, valued teaching. It functions under the erroneous premise that content is vastly more significant than either teaching strategy or teaching competence. Thus, there is an inevitable depletion of our intellectual and emotional resources as we seek to convince our colleagues of the value of teaching.

One of the long-standing patterns in library education is the requirement of a strong background of liberal arts from applicants. Although this is desirable it has, in effect, prevented those applicants who made an early career decision and entered baccalaureate programs with either a library science or an education major from doing graduate work in the field. This is one more example of library educators' not valuing education programs and, given the identified requirements of the profession for the school media specialist, is truly absurd.[2] I believe that inherent in this stated requirement is an elitism that may have roots in a lack of pride in our profession of librarianship.

Another example of our lack of professional pride might be the school media field's consistent paranoia with regard to educational technology. We often have adopted a new approach simply because of fear, not a true belief in what we are adopting. This causes undue harm in our programs. The "bandwagon" approach is a version of weak educational planning. In the process of such change, the means become the end. It seems to me that we must examine the various recommendations made and place our emphasis in such a way as to be assured that what is a priority is of true value.

One of the strange incongruities of our profession is that on the one hand we support the American Library Association's Committee on Accreditation and on the other we adopt school media standards and certification models. The interrelationships between the two are primitive at best. The school media field perceives a specific role for its practitioners, and yet COA does not measure in precise terms how successful a school is in describing and evaluating the requirements for the education of school media specialists. It would be significant if the newly established Library Education Committee of AASL were to begin a strong communication network with COA, attempting to convey the sense of our professional judgment. It may be that COA should require a statement in the self-study documents that details to a visiting team and to the committee just how that institution meets the requirements for certification of school media specialists which it authorizes in its program. (The school under review should also be asked to provide this for any other specialized certification.)

It seems important to examine three major aspects in the education of the school media specialist: (1) the education or schooling compound; (2) the librarianship component; and (3) the school media component. In planning any program the library educator is faced with making a determination of "how much is enough?" in deciding the degree of competence necessary in each of these areas. In education, for example, how much must the prospective candidate for our professional positions know about child and adolescent development, curriculum change, or even general educational theory and practice? We have attempted to answer this by either requiring courses in schools of education or adding "bits" of information to our already oversaturated programs of study. Vandergrift is undoubtedly correct when she states that such piecemeal preparation is inferior to that provided by an undergraduate major in education.[3]

The next aspect is that of librarianship. Those courses in our programs in cataloging, reference, general administration, information science, and so forth, are often taught from the aspect of either academic/research-based institutions or large public libraries. It is not that I would recommend we alter this radically—but that we at least begin to pursue a dialogue with our colleagues on what is the expectation of the level of cataloging or reference performance in the school. Often the answer might lie in making sure that the student has the opportunity to translate the theoretical to the practical; that is to say, students should be evaluated on whether they can take the principles of search strategy or subject analysis and make the necessary application to the environment of elementary or secondary school.

The third aspect is that of the school media courses. I will explore this area in four parts: (1) courses dealing with the acquisition of information and critical skills about materials; (2) courses that might be labeled service-oriented; (3) administrative courses; and (4) the field work requirement.

In looking at this first part (acquisition of information about materials), one sees almost no consistent pattern beyond a set of similarly titled courses. For example, we often approach children's literature in our teaching as if the memorizing of a "magical" list of titles would prepare the student for the job to be done in a school. Or we concentrate our courses on the sociological approach of issues and "isms" before the student even has the basic knowledge or understanding of the literature involved. Consciousness-raising is not, in my view, the primary responsibility of the library educator. Rather, it is of primary importance that we design our courses to enable the student to acquire the most highly developed set of critical competencies that will permit successful evaluation and selection of all types of materials in schools in the future. Courses in media are often designed to train students in the handling of equipment rather than in developing visual literacy and critical skills in multiformats. I do not believe that we are really relating what we teach in our courses to what we accept as competencies expected of the media specialist. If we examine statements in the American Association of School Librarians' *Behavioral Analysis Checklist, Media Programs: District and School,* and the *Certification Model,* we might have some difficulty in justifying much of what we do.

Courses in library services to special age groups in our programs suffer from reliance on what has always been the pattern in such courses. Emphasis is in the right direction—program activities for children and youth —but we are neither imaginative nor apparently capable of seeing the necessary distinctions between preparation for school and for public library work. Most such courses are often based on the public library model, not the model of the school media center. For example, we still teach primitive arts and crafts as gimmicks that take little cognizance of the vast changes in schools in these areas. Thus we are educating our students in poor or outdated techniques and methods. We need to devise surer means of placing our programmatic activities more in tune with the needs of the school.

Administrative courses make almost no distinction between elementary and secondary schools, although there is probably no school library media educator who would not acknowledge that there is a vast difference between these levels. We often teach our courses using the "cookbook concept," requiring that the student learn the so-called right way to solve any situation. We either teach as if the student were entering a multistaffed media center with a limitless budget or a situation similar to the log cabin school with almost no support or budget. The undue emphasis on management techniques is costly when it comes to functional performance in the school. Often the student is led to believe that applying a systems analysis or completing a PERT (Program Evaluation and Review Technique) chart are critical before a simple decision can be made in an everyday operational need. We have placed so much emphasis on management competency that I sometimes wonder if we are not losing sight of our true purpose. The basic administrative skills must be assured so that the practitioner can function as the outstanding change agent in the school. However, first and foremost, the goal statement must be "I am an educator who has the competencies of a manager among many additional skills."

Field work is the one opportunity the new member of the profession has to measure his or her personal performance against a set of criteria. It is most probable that librarianship should include a required field component for all of its students, but the costs would be staggering. What is tragic is the unwillingness to study this problem in a diagnostic way and provide new directions. For example, it seems to me that we might require a year of field practice after the completion of course work but before the degree is granted.

Betty Fast was primarily an outstanding practitioner, but there were many times in which she also assumed the role of educator.[4] During the many years in which I shared lengthy conversations with her, the topic was invariably linked to library education. There were several issues that formed the focus of our concern and persisted throughout our years of friendship. They were expressed by us as questions and I will share them with you, the reader, in the hope that such questions will evoke a response that may enlarge your view of the education of the school media specialist.

> How do we assure that, while developing the decision-making competency, we do not establish it as an end in itself?
>
> If the media specialist is to assume the role of a change agent in the school, what is the degree of participation in curriculum development that should be achieved?
>
> How do we relate the planning process as a competency to the reality of everyday functioning in a school media center?

How do we provide the necessary experience of the district level operation to the professional who will function in the building level?

Is the continuing education program of the school media specialist linked solely to supervision as the new career objective? How would this affect the programs in library schools?

How do we establish communication links among all the educational programs responsible for the preparation of the school media specialist?

How do we begin the process of evaluation of the educational program in order to foster a continuance of excellence in the profession?

Before any of these questions can be answered, there are certain basic concepts that must be addressed by those of us in library education who are responsible for the planning of educational programs. The first priority I would identify is the need for a clearly articulated statement of the theoretical foundation of school librarianship. I do not believe we have done this, although there have been several attempts over the years.[5] I think that some of our difficulty over definition and terminology may well be traced to our lack of a basic philosophy. Without such a philosophical underpinning we are easily trapped into accepting definition of our ráison d'être as "instructional design personnel" or "media managers." A second priority, which I consider critical, is the need for a serious study of our role as teachers.[6] We have historically proclaimed our responsibility in this area, but I do not believe we are educating the new members of our profession to accept this as a primary obligation. For me, the role of teacher is the treasured essence of our position in the school. There is no doubt in my mind that the first and second priorities are inextricably linked and it is in that linkage that the aesthetics of our profession emerge.

In order to respond effectively to the first and second priorities, we must recognize that there are several alternative models in the education of the school media specialist.[7] Betty Fast always expressed her deep concern for recognition of our constituency, and I would agree that we need to examine more fully the relationship of constituency to the kind of educational program we design. Alternatives do not necessarily presuppose a hierarchy of importance. In the education of the media specialist, the more we extend ourselves to design alternatives in our programs, the more likely we are to respond to the educational needs in the schools and, more importantly, to seize the vision and tread with sensitivity as we move forward to the next century.

REFERENCES

1. American Association of Colleges for Teacher Education, Report of the Bicentennial Commission on Education for the Profession of Teaching, *Educating a Profession* (Washington, D.C.: American Association of Colleges for Teacher Education, 1976). This is a fine example of the pattern of concern in the teaching profession.

2. There are a number of items that might prove useful to the reader in locating information on the requirements of the profession. Among them are the following: Certification of School Media Specialists Committee, American Association of School Librarians, *Certification Model for Professional School Media Personnel* (Chicago: ALA, 1976); American Association of School Librarians, American Library Association, and Association for Educational Communications and Technology, *Media Programs: District and School* (Chicago: ALA, 1975); Kay E. Vandergrift, "The Making of a School Librarian," *American Libraries* 9 (November 1978): 605–6.

3. Vandergrift, p. 606.

4. Betty Fast did teach for several years on the faculty at the University of Connecticut, and was also a member of several institutes in various universities. Her speeches and writing formed another direct aspect of her role as teacher.

5. Certainly a number of monographs and articles have attempted to include aspects of such a theoretical base; perhaps only the *1960 Standards for School Library Programs* of the American Association of School Libraries came close to formulating a statement.

6. In the new series issued by AASL the third title is on teaching. The AASL Publications Committee identified this as a key area of concern. See: Kay E. Vandergrift, *The Teaching Role of the School Media Specialist* (Chicago: ALA, 1979).

7. I would make clear that alternatives are used to describe a suggested variety within the same program. Although the Knapp Project did examine five different alternatives, I believe the profession has not reacted in either evaluative fashion or modeling pattern.

CREATING ACCREDITATION
AND LEGISLATIVE PROGRAMS
FOR SCHOOL LIBRARY
MEDIA CENTERS

by THOMAS HART

School library media programs are recent additions to the school scene. The first high school library was established at Erasmus High School in Brooklyn, New York, during the early 1900s. Legislative interest in improving school library media programs has also been a recent development. School library media specialists have depended primarily on three approaches to improve their programs. The major efforts have been focused on regional accrediting associations, state boards of education rules or legislative mandates, and national legislative efforts.

An analysis of each of these approaches is a first step to the exploration of emerging patterns that may be worth replicating on a national, regional, state, or local basis. Regional accrediting bodies have been successful in raising the expectation levels for boards of education, superintendents, and lay citizens; primarily, high school libraries have been affected. Examination of the evaluative criteria for library media programs established by the six regional accrediting associations reveals similarity at the high school levels and the middle and/or junior school levels and disparity in evaluative criteria at the elementary level. In fact, only two regional groups accredit elementary schools (North Central and Southern). These two groups have developed very different approaches to the accreditation process.

The Southern Association of Colleges and Secondary Schools provided for the affiliation of elementary schools in 1952 and for the accreditation of them in 1958. In fact, in 1963 the name of the association was changed to the Southern Association of Colleges and Schools to reflect the impact of this new area of accreditation. Elementary schools were accredited by the Committee on Elementary Education for the first time at the 1963 annual meeting of the association in Memphis, Tennessee. The first group included 98 elementary schools. The full impact of this accreditation process can only be understood when it is recognized that by 1977 more than 4,000 elementary schools were accredited by the Southern Association and another 2,500 schools were affiliated, not yet reaching the accreditation standards of the association. For example, the Birmingham,

Alabama, elementary schools were just recently accredited. One major problem that kept them from being accepted earlier was the lack of elementary library media centers and full-time professional media specialists. The Birmingham community wanted the prestige of accreditation, and with the leadership of a far-sighted superintendent, they passed a bond issue to insure the establishment of quality library media centers in each school, therefore qualifying them for accreditation by the Southern Association of Colleges and Schools.

The Southern Association has been successful in raising the standards and expectations of more than one-half of the public and private schools in the south, serving more than 3.5 million students. This success story has not been true in other regional accrediting bodies. As mentioned earlier, the only other regional association that has attempted to develop criteria for accrediting has been the North Central Association which, as recently as 1978, lowered their basic standard regarding a full-time library media specialist and now allows accreditation for elementary schools that share professionals among several schools.

Even with the admittedly low standards that all regional accrediting associations have established and the lack of any standards for elementary schools in four of the associations, they still have made an important impact on the development of uniform library media programs throughout the nation. As we examine that impact, there are several key points that are useful in guiding the profession to improve its participation in the accreditation process.

1. One of the key areas in the accreditation process is the program of the library media center. Whenever an accreditation visiting team makes its final report, the library media program is usually highlighted as an area for commendation or one of the most important areas with deficiencies that need to be corrected. The media program is one area that cuts across administrative and instructional lines serving the entire school.

The library media specialist should play a key role in developing the self-study report that must be submitted to an accrediting group before a team visit can be scheduled. Many school self-study committees are chaired by the library media specialist. This is a key indicator of the status of the library media program within the total school operation.

2. Another area for improving library media service is the decision of the various boards that establish the assessment criteria established for evaluating schools. They need to be moved to favor strong school library media programs. The library media profession can work at all levels to make sure that important criteria are kept above minimum requirements in order to strengthen library media programs.

3. Yet another area is that of the membership of decision-making panels of the regional accrediting associations. Local, district, and state representatives of the library media profession must be prepared to assess the position of each representative and strengthen this position if it favors strong library media programs. If the representative seems unwilling to take a strong position, then the local group should assess what measure to use in changing the stance of that representative. If there is no chance of changing the stance, then measures should be developed for replacing the representative with one holding a more favorable stance. Each library media program with professional staff must be exemplary, within budgetary and building constraints. Since most voting representatives are administrators, they will in most cases support strong evaluative criteria for these programs if they are aware of the elements of a good library media program.

Federal legislation

In addition to working to improve accreditation standards for library media programs, the profession has established a strong lobbying force in the U.S. capital. This effort resulted in some library media elements in the NDEA (National Defense Education Act) of 1958. This beginning reached its zenith when the ESEA (Elementary and Secondary Education Act) of 1965 doubled the budgets for resources in school library media centers in one year. The requirements for eligibility to receive these funds also resulted in the centralizing of elementary library media collections in more than half of the elementary schools in our country where previously only classroom collections existed. This act also resulted in hiring thousands of library media professional aids and technicians to manage these centralized collections.

Through the years there have been many cliff-hanger decisions regarding ESEA Title II, which provided monies for media center materials. Finally Title II was changed to Title IV-B and merged with guidance programs. This created an enmity between two elements of the school's program that should always work cooperatively for the good of the students, parents, and teachers of each school.

By regrouping the elements of ESEA in 1978, library media resources were separated from guidance program funding for the 1979 fiscal year. This only took place because of strong evidence and support from local school library media specialists. This important program has provided millions of dollars for library media resources since its inception in 1965.

There are several elements that have made federal legislative efforts effective. They include, first, the maintenance of a strong lobbying staff in Washington, D.C., initially through the leadership of the American Library Association and the American Association of School Librarians. Later this group was supported by the Association for Educational Communications and Technology and a coalition of other educational and professional groups. Second, the development of a trust situation between the profession and federal legislators is necessary. Whenever congressional leaders are asked about the library media profession, they are able to state frankly that they trust our lobbyists, and decisions contrary to our professional stance are difficult and are accomplished only after assessing all alternatives. Finally, the maintenance of open communication between the lobbying staff and their constituency through a legislative network and a regular newsletter should be supported. The *ALA Washington Newsletter* orchestrates grassroot support which then places pressure on the federal legislators who are in key positions.

State legislation

Even though federal legislative efforts are important, of more significance are state legislative efforts. The profession has made notable progress in influencing the decisions of regional accrediting associations and federal legislation, but statewide legislative efforts have been less successful over the years.

Florida is credited with having one of the first successful legislative efforts in the mid-fifties. The state school library association was able to influence the passage of state statutes that required the establishment of a centralized library in every school and a professional librarian for every 500 students. This program was never funded by the legislature, but local districts accepted the costs and indeed there is a centralized library in nearly every school and in most situations a full-time library media specialist—but in 1976 there was one library media specialist for every 685 students. Other states have also had notable success in working with legislators, including such as North Carolina, Pennsylvania, and Washington.

The development of successful legislative programs requires patience. Many states have started programs but have abandoned them because they were unable to obtain quick results. It is essential that all of the steps that follow be thoroughly developed and implemented.

A chairperson of the legislative program should be located in the capital. This strategic location is essential for obtaining information quickly and then disseminating it to those who can influence legislators. Statistics are a vital part of the legislative process, and they can be gathered more quickly through sources located in the capital. It may be necessary to join with other related groups to fund such an office.

A legislative network of key members of the professional association must be selected early in the program. The network should consist of a core committee of five to eight representing various levels of expertise with contacts in the legislature. The rest of the network should represent local and/or existing regional groupings within the state. Regional contacts should be selected for their contacts within the region. They will be responsible for passing information on to their constituents in the local districts of their area. These network people should be in communication with the chairperson.

Once the system has been developed, the legislative effort should turn to developing a bill or series of bills that build on each other. A beginning should be through a bill that defines or redefines the elements of a library media program within the parameters of the existing educational program.

The chairperson should develop contacts with politically influential groups to gain their support for library media bills. These groups include teacher unions, PTA, and the League of Women Voters, among others.

It is important to work with legislators in key positions to introduce or cosponsor library media bills. Key library media specialists should be identified and enlisted to persuade legislators to introduce and/or support the passage of the bills. These people, working for passage of the legislative bills, must understand the importance and impact of the bill's passage. Nothing is more damaging than to provide legislators and other community leaders with incorrect information.

Once the legislative network is established, it is important that regional contacts be trained and their responsibilities clearly delineated. The responsibilities of regional contacts include establishing local contacts in each district in the region; arranging activities such as workshops that will help local contacts and others to learn how to effectively promote support for the legislative program; coordinating legislative activities within the region in order to gain widest support for those activities; and disseminating pertinent information pertaining to legislative activities to local contacts and urging them to perform the action indicated to achieve legislative objectives.

Regional legislative workshops aimed at training regional leaders in developing the legislative networks within their areas should be planned. It is important that those leaders understand the importance of this workshop to themselves and their profession. Try to find a central location in the region for the workshop. Plan it for a day on which people can attend. In setting the time, keep in mind the distance people must travel.

The agenda of the workshop should be aimed toward (1) educating local contacts and others about legislative issues that are to be promoted so that these individuals will be thoroughly familiar with concepts for which they must gain legislative support; (2) helping workshop participants to develop strategies for accomplishing legislative goals; and (3) gaining specific commitments from local contacts about procedures they will follow and actions they will initiate when they go home in order to achieve legislative objectives.

Suggestions for specific areas to be included in the workshop are:

1. Importance of the bill to improved library media programs;
2. Background of the bill;
3. Explanation of each part of the bill;
4. Current status of the bill;
5. Strategies for gaining support for the bill; and
6. Plan of action through which local contacts can gain widespread support for professional legislative activities.

In a number of instances organizations such as the League of Women Voters can give much help in providing literature and speakers to deal with effective strategies for gaining support for legislation. In addition, members of the state legislative committee can serve as resource people to offer advice relating to the workshop.

Set up a means of reporting to keep individuals aware of relevant legislative activities taking place within their region so that efforts can be coordinated and actions by contacts and others can build and expand upon past legislative activities. It is imperative that the legislative chairperson also be immediately aware of activities within each region, so that efforts can be coordinated on a statewide basis.

Each legislator should be visited as soon as possible, preferably by a group of constituents containing a personal friend of the legislator.

On a local level, stress the need for contacts to enlist the active support of such groups as the PTA, teachers, administrators, the school board, and other influential groups and decision makers in the community.

Write articles regularly in state journals so the membership can be constantly apprised of legislative developments.

A priority should be given to hiring an advocate or lobbyist as soon as possible. Once bills are introduced it is important that someone be able to attend the various hearings and contact the right people to testify. The advocate should be knowledgeable about library media programs and also have contacts in the political process.

When the bills are passed by the legislature, it is important that recognition be given to key legislators.

Legislative activity must become a priority of our library media profession; it is essential for the development of equal access to library media resources.

REFERENCES

1. Elizabeth W. Stone, *Continuing Library Education as Viewed in Relation to Other Continuing Professional Education Movements* (Washington, D.C.: ASIS, 1974).

2. Betty Fast, "Questionnaire about Continuing Education for School-Library Media Supervisors," *School Libraries* 18 (Summer 1969): 53.

3. *Library Journal/School Library Journal Hotline,* April 17, 1978, p. 4.

4. "What New England Librarians Want to Know," *NELB LINK* 3, March/April, 1978.

5. *Library Journal,* 103 (April 15, 1978): 810.

POWER, SURVIVAL, AND BETTY FAST

by PEGGY SULLIVAN

Several months ago, when I served as a member of a committee planning a regional White House Conference for the Chicago area, I was invited to suggest a theme for the conference and, keeping in mind Carl Sandburg's poem about Chicago as the city of the big shoulders, I said: "I think we should call it the Big Shoulders Conference, and it should be about power. It should be about the power of libraries, the power of people, the power of knowledge." The theme was not the one chosen, but I like to think it is the one that Betty Fast would have understood and voted for.

It was about 15 years ago that I met Betty Fast, and I observed her life over that period of time. She had been an enthusiastic user of the library, but also a critic of libraries. She had become interested as a parent, in a way that many parents do, in the work of libraries and what they might mean for her boys. It must have been because of that that she became a trustee of her local public library. It seems inevitable now, but it certainly was not a customary pattern then, for her to have become a school librarian at a time when the need for school librarians was desperate and when many people were finding new satisfactions in that still-developing area of specialization. She was an ardent recruiter of others, and she found many, especially among the Navy wives in the Groton area, to influence. They responded by becoming school librarians who worked with her and who have since gone to many parts of the country and, I suppose, to other countries as well, spreading some of her enthusiasm and competence. It was natural that her drive led her to a position of supervisory responsibility and to action, first at the state level, and eventually and for a long period of time, in national professional associations. It may seem to point out the quirkiness of career development to note that at the time of her death, Betty was working on a doctoral degree that she had convinced herself she needed. She had gone from being a trustee and a maker of policy to being a student and researcher, but she had acquired the political power, which in Chicago we call "clout," that helped her to have the effect on library development that she clearly has had.

To my knowledge, it does not happen often that library education programs, or even continuing education workshops, concern themselves with instructing people in how and where, or even why, they should find out where the power that determines the fate of libraries really lies. But this is important. It is important to know that policies are not made by managers, nor even usually by the highest level administrator who is on the payroll. Policies are implemented by those people, but they are made elsewhere: by school boards, by boards of public library trustees, by faculty councils, by political appointees and elected officials, and others. Of course, that means that the power comes from the people in a country like ours, and that it is in keeping in touch with the people and encouraging them to speak up in the most forceful and useful ways possible that we are ensuring the use of power for the better development of libraries.

It seems to me interesting, as I think of it now, that this topic of power is one that Betty Fast and I did not ever discuss very much, but I am very sure our thoughts were much alike. She believed in knowing her community, and she knew it. Not everyone sees that so clearly, and not every librarian understands both how significant and how simple it is. Community surveys, questionnaires, and a dozen other trappings of getting to know the community do not take the place of being alert on shopping trips in the community, reading about it, asking intelligent questions at community organization meetings, which might be those of parent-teacher associations or local business groups. These are sensible ways, and ways accessible to almost all of us, to find where the power lies. It is important to work with the community in terms of its own goals, and to relate library needs and goals to them. The present concern of many community groups about illiteracy is a natural to lead to library support, but it is important to be aware of the terms that make it simple to see the connection. It is also important that community groups know how to use effectively the shortcomings as well as the strengths that they possess.

I do not know, nor clearly remember, the full story of Connecticut's success in having demonstration school libraries throughout the state. I do know, because I directed the Knapp School Libraries Project from 1963 until its completion in 1968, that Connecticut was the first state (and a significantly successful one) to capitalize on the idea of having demonstration school libraries of its own. Rheta Clark and Virginia Mathews were two of the strongest proponents of this idea, but Betty Fast was among them. They recognized that it was important for people in their state to see something close at hand that could be replicated, whether it was at the highest or most sophisticated level of school library development or not. They took an idea that was being implemented at the national level and they brought it home, but they brought it home not so that others could regret or resent the lack of development in the state, but so that they could benefit from what might occur if the state supported the idea to the extent that it was possible. All of that, it seems to me, showed a good grasp of what power can do. In turn, of course, this means that people who get the idea transmit some of that power on their own.

Beginning as she did with public libraries as a trustee, Betty Fast was fairly free of the ignorance of other kinds of libraries that is too often the characteristic of someone whose entire career has been devoted to one kind of library. She saw the relationship between public libraries and school libraries and, in a different way, the relationship between public libraries and schools. She understood what a state library agency could and should be. She attempted, whenever possible, to work within the patterns of each kind of library so that all would be used most effectively. That, too, is the result of knowing something about power.

In professional organizations, where Betty Fast had some of her greatest successes and probably some disappointments that some of us can surmise, Betty knew that there were many ingredients of power. One of them is loyalty. Although I did not always agree with her, I respected the fact that she felt that within the American Library Association her basic loyalty was to the American Association of School Librarians. Even when it was painful, both physically and psychologically, she honored her commitment to explain to the board of that association decisions in which she had participated in other parts of ALA, whether they were to the taste of that board or not. She considered that important in terms of loyalty. I also believe that in much of her drive for recognition within ALA, whether as a member of Council, as member and chairman of the prestigious and hard-working Committee on Program Evaluation and Support, and, at the time of her death, as successful candidate for the presidency of the Library Administration Division, she was keenly aware of herself as a representative of school librarians or, as she might have preferred, of school media personnel. Knowing that she had won the respect of a wider audience, she saw the importance of using that respect to acquire further recognition, not just for herself but for the others whom she represented and for the field of specialization that she knew best.

In a profession that seems to me to have more than its share of people who underrate themselves or have poor self-images, it is especially difficult to find people who are willing, indeed eager, to press for the program support they need and for the recognition of their beliefs when they are likely to be challenged on the basis that they are promoting themselves. Betty was honest enough to know that such charges were sometimes made about her, but she was determined enough to know that the important thing was to keep pushing for the programs. Although I know little about her recent years in the school system in Groton, I know that the characteristic of pushing for her program sometimes led her to appear to be promoting herself, but I believe that the long run proved that there was need for her to act as she did.

One of the ways in which power can be used effectively to improve programs and to acquire support for libraries is by an original overextension of resources. Others besides myself have said this better, but the gist of it is that it is important to say "yes," even when it may seem impossible to extend one's efforts any further. Then, at some more politically expedient time, one makes it necessary to implement that "yes." It is dealing from strength rather than weakness to say "We can do more for you, such as you have seen here," instead of having to say something like "I'm sorry I couldn't help you the other day, but now I would like support in order to. . . ." I think that was a difference that Betty understood and used to her fullest ability.

To speak of Betty Fast's fullest ability probably recalls to most people Betty when she was at her physical peak, before illness had weakened her, and before she had shown some of her frantic concern about time— probably because she knew that her own was limited in a way that few of us have opportunity to know about ourselves. Yet, for me, when I think of using talent and ability at its fullest, I think of Betty in the last months of her life, when she knew that she had to guard what vitality she had. She told me once that when she was still working at school she brought her work home and went to bed, working on it as best she could while resting. I think it was a slip of the tongue that caused her to reveal this, because she usually preferred to indicate that her schedule had not changed and that she was not "coddling" herself. But I struck fire from her one time in the last year or so of her life. I was in a meeting room after a meeting had broken up and Betty was chatting with someone else at a table. Someone proposed to me that an award should be given to an elderly librarian whom I considered somewhat less than deserving, and I said forcefully, "No, I won't write a recommendation. I don't think that survival is any reason to get an award." Betty looked over at me and said, "Oh, sometimes it *is*."

Betty was right, of course. Survival is a power of its own. Survival has many forms. It means surviving one's own death, not just in the sense of whatever life after death we may each envision and cherish, but surviving in the minds of others, whether they know it or not. For Betty, this power goes on as long as people whom she recruited to librarianship are serving effectively as librarians and recruiting others to share in their interests and abilities. A part of her survives in the prestige associated with COPES which she chaired especially well. And for those of us who survive her, a part of her survives as long as her memory brings memories and impressions that give us the power to accomplish more for the development of libraries, whether what we do is exactly what she would have envisioned or not.

A long time ago, I learned that the people who live in our memories and who have the greatest effect on us are not necessarily those who have had the greatest effect at a given point in time, but rather those whose hold on the future is such that we can imagine how they would have reacted at other times and in new situations. I feel fortunate to have had a number of friends who are in that category. I can picture Allie Beth Martin charging around at a 1979 White House Conference on Library and Information Service, although by then she will have been dead three years. And I can see Betty Fast, not necessarily agreeing, but thinking over that it might be good for an interested parent to consider school librarianship as a career, or participating in a Newbery-Caldecott Awards Committee meeting, as she so enjoyed doing when she was a member of that prestigious committee. Survival is power, as life is power, and libraries and survivors benefit when we have opportunity to have a grasp on the future through people who may not share it with us in person.

LIST OF
CONTRIBUTORS

D. Philip Baker, *Coordinator of Media Programs,*
 Stamford Public Schools, Stamford, Connecticut

Virginia M. Crowe, *Associate Professor, Chairman of the Library*
 Science Department, Edinboro State College, Edinboro, Pennsylvania

Evelyn H. Daniel, *Associate Professor,*
 School of Information Studies, Syracuse University, Syracuse, New York

Richard L. Darling, *Dean,*
 School of Library Service, Columbia University, New York, New York

Alice E. Fite, *Executive Secretary,*
 American Association of School Libraries, Chicago, Illinois

Thomas J. Galvin, *Dean,*
 School of Library and Information Science, University of Pittsburgh,
 Pittsburgh, Pennsylvania

Lillian N. Gerhardt, *Editor-in-Chief,*
 School Library Journal, New York, New York

Jane Anne Hannigan, *Professor,*
 School of Library Science, Columbia University, New York, New York

Thomas Hart, *Associate Professor,*
 School of Library Science, Florida State University, Tallahassee, Florida

CLARA O. JACKSON, *Associate Professor,*
School of Library Science, Kent State University, Kent, Ohio

PATRICIA JENSEN, *Associate Professor,*
University of Rhode Island, Kingston, Rhode Island

COSETTE N. KIES, *Assistant Professor,*
School of Library Science, George Peabody College,
Nashville, Tennessee

MARGARET MARY KIMMEL, *Associate Professor,*
School of Library and Information Science, University of Pittsburgh,
Pittsburgh, Pennsylvania

PHYLLIS LAND, *Director,*
Division of Instructional Media, Indiana Department of Public
Instruction, Indianapolis, Indiana

PATRICIA B. POND, *Associate Dean,*
School of Library and Information Science, University of Pittsburgh,
Pittsburgh, Pennsylvania

MORTON SCHINDEL, *Founder,*
Weston Woods, Weston, Connecticut

BERNARD S. SCHLESSINGER, *Dean,*
Graduate Library School, University of Rhode Island,
Kingston, Rhode Island

PEGGY A. SULLIVAN, *Assistant Commissioner for Extension Services,*
Chicago Public Library, Chicago, Illinois

KAY E. VANDERGRIFT, *Assistant Professor,*
School of Library Science, Columbia University, New York, New York

BRENDA H. WHITE, *Teaching Fellow,*
School of Library and Information Science, University of Pittsburgh,
Pittsburgh, Pennsylvania

BLANCHE WOOLLS, *Associate Professor,*
School of Library and Information Science, University of Pittsburgh,
Pittsburgh, Pennsylvania

BERNICE L. YESNER, *School Library Consultant,*
Woodbridge, Connecticut

Designed by Vladimir Reichl
Composed by FM Typesetting Company in Linotype Times Roman
    with Serif Gothic display
Printed on Warren's 50# 1854, a pH neutral stock
and bound by Braun-Brumfield, Inc.